GUIDEBOOK TO INTELLECTUAL PROPERTY

This is a unique book about Intellectual Property. It is aimed not only at law students studying the subject but also at interested users of IP – business people, inventors, scientists, designers and the like. It provides an outline of the basic legal principles which underpin and regulate the subject, educating the reader as to the shape of the law. However, critically, it also gives insight into how the system actually works. You cannot understand chess by merely learning the rules – you also have to know how the game is played: so too with Intellectual Property.

To achieve its object the authors deliberately avoid technicalities: keeping things simple, yet direct. There are no footnotes to distract. Although cases are, inevitably, referred to, they are explained in a pithy, accessible manner. The authors try wherever possible to be both serious and light-hearted at the same time.

All the major areas of IP – patents, trade marks, copyright and designs – are covered, along with briefer treatment of other rights and subjects such as breach of confidence, plant varieties and databases.

A novice reader should come away both with a clear outline of IP law and a feeling for how it works. Students will be able to put their more detailed study into perspective. Users will be able to understand better how IP affects them and their businesses.

Southampton
SOLENT
University

LIBRARY

for reference only

Guidebook to Intellectual Property

Sixth edition

Sir Robin Jacob
Daniel Alexander QC
and
Matthew Fisher

·H A R T·
PUBLISHING
OXFORD AND PORTLAND, OREGON
2013

Published in the United Kingdom by Hart Publishing Ltd
16C Worcester Place, Oxford, OX1 2JW
Telephone: +44 (0)1865 517530
Fax: +44 (0)1865 510710
E-mail: mail@hartpub.co.uk
Website: http://www.hartpub.co.uk

Published in North America (US and Canada) by
Hart Publishing
c/o International Specialized Book Services
920 NE 58th Avenue, Suite 300
Portland, OR 97213-3786
USA
Tel: +1 503 287 3093 or toll-free: (1) 800 944 6190
Fax: +1 503 280 8832
E-mail: orders@isbs.com
Website: http://www.isbs.com

British Library Cataloguing in Publication Data
Data Available

ISBN: 978-1-84946-325-6

Typeset by Hope Services, Abingdon
Printed and bound in Great Britain by
TJ International Ltd, Padstow, Cornwall

PREFACE TO THE SIXTH EDITION

The wheel has come full circle – time for a new edition of 'Blanco's little book'. Despite all the changes in IP law over the years, the heart of what that greatest of all IP lawyers, Thomas Blanco White, wrote in the three little pamphlets just after the War remains unchanged – for this book tries not so much to expound the detail of the law (which has changed a lot) but how it actually works. Whether the reader is a student or businessman or even a lawyer from outside this area of law, what we intend is what Blanco intended: that the essential nature of living IP law should be described. That is why there are no footnotes, few case references in the text and little attempt at any detailed exposition. What we want is the reader to come away with a good idea of how it all works in practice.

It is that which makes this book special and different – what Blanco achieved with his pamphlets. Some of the text, we are glad to say, remains his. And some of it is so relevant now that we wish economists and competition lawyers would not only read it but understand it. One of the authors (Robin Jacob) even read a passage from the 1947 pamphlet at the 2008 European Commission's presentation of its preliminary findings in its Pharma Inquiry. The Commission thought it had discovered new things about the patent system – what it called 'patent clusters'. But Blanco described them back in 1947 and you will find the same passage here in Chapter 5 (see 'Improvement Patents'). It was all there from Blanco all those years ago. No other work we know contains such a description – yet that is part of how the patent system works both now and at least since the modern era of patents started with the procedural reforms of the mid-nineteenth century. Perhaps it goes back to Boulton and Watt.

Actually, therefore, we regard ourselves as *custodians* of this book, rather than authors. Our job has been to *preserve* it by bringing up to date such detail as it contains but to avoid changing it. We hope we have succeeded.

Since our intended readership goes wider than students and includes non-IP lawyers, economists, businessmen and journalists for example, we have changed publishers from Sweet and Maxwell to Hart. A work as idiosyncratic as this did not fit well with Sweet's model of major textbooks and student specific works. They kindly let us go even though they had the contractual right to the next edition (though not the copyright!). Richard Hart's imprint will, we confidently expect, be a more appropriate home. Things have begun well – Rachel Turner of Hart never complained once that we were over a year late!

Huge thanks to Bryan Lewin MBE who knows more about criminal IP law in practice than anyone else in the country. We also give great thanks to Tom Leonard and Ryan Pixton of Kilburn and Strode who not only provided the information about official fees and the likely costs of patent and trade mark attorneys but also pointed out stuff in the old edition which needed changing.

Robin Jacob, UCL and 8 New Square, Lincoln's Inn
Matthew Fisher, UCL
Daniel Alexander, 8 New Square, Lincoln's Inn

CONTENTS

Part V Miscellaneous Matters

TABLE OF CASES

Table of Cases

Part I

Introduction

1

Imitation, Monopoly and Control

This book is about the law of commercial and industrial monopoly and imitation, and how it works: imitation by one manufacturer of another's products, imitation by one trader of the names and badges by which another's goods or business are known; imitations, deliberate or not, accidental or on purpose. It is about how the law deals with the appropriation of the fruits of other people's labour. And it is also about how people can acquire monopoly rights to do certain profitable things (such as make certain products or sell them under particular names), and how those monopolies are protected and kept from getting out of hand. Thirdly, it is about how people can control the use other people make of their creative work. These subjects overlap to the point of inseparability in much of what follows.

Kinds of Intellectual Property

'Intellectual property' ('IP') is the umbrella term now used to cover all the various rights which may be invoked to prevent imitations of various sorts. But contrary to quite a lot of current woolly terminology and thinking, actually the rights are quite distinct. For legal purposes they have to be considered individually. In practice, the kinds of imitation and the applicable rights often overlap. There are numerous examples of such overlap. The manufacture of a particular industrial item might infringe a rival's patent. But it may also infringe design rights of various sorts, some of which come into play if there has been copying, others even if there has not. For another example, industrial designs are given protection in theory to protect the work of the designer – to protect the artistic element in manufacture. In many cases, however, the main value of design protection is to supplement the manufacturer's trade marks by securing to him exclusive rights in the 'get-up' of the goods – a function that in legal theory belongs rather to the law of passing off or registered trade marks. For a third example, patent protection can be used in such a way as to build up the reputation of a trade mark for the patented goods such that the effect of the monopoly that the patent gave can be felt long after it has expired, because the trade mark has by then become so well established.

Exactly how to go about using, reinforcing and challenging the various monopoly rights to best commercial advantage is a matter for complex strategic assessment.

Quite often it is possible to do almost as much with an unchallenged monopoly (such as a granted patent) as with one that is secure (such as a *valid* patent) because the costs and risks for a competitor of breaking the monopoly by legal action are often very high. The mere possession of a patent, however rubbishy to a lawyer's mind, may be of real value for commercial purposes and it will encourage others to think of ways of 'designing around' the monopoly, rather than face an action for infringement, once substantial resources have been committed. Because of the substantial costs for people of finding out exactly what it is they can do by going to court to get a judge to tell them, a great deal of IP law in practice involves not squabbling in court over the existence or scope of rights, but getting into the best position for reaching agreement on who should to be allowed to do what.

Even a weak intellectual property right (or a collection of them) can often be licensed to a large company for a lot of money, partly because it can be cheaper to pay a modest licence fee per product than to risk any one patent being upheld and disrupting sales.

In the modern commercial world, considerations are rarely national. Because IP rights tend to be somewhat different in their effect in different countries, even if a right seems hopeless in one country, it might be different elsewhere. That difference can be used to try to obtain commercial advantage. So, one Court of Appeal judge who thought that a patent was clearly invalid in England referred to the fact that, in Holland, it had been upheld as an instance of 'quot homines, tot sententiae' ('there are as many opinions as there are men'). A patentee – and to some extent other right-owners – have a number of shots at a commercial rival because cases are judged by humans who sometimes have reasonably held differences in view. In some cases, maintaining a market in one country may be very valuable, even if the rest of the world is lost. The consequence is that it can really pay to have a go in obtaining the rights in question and, often, in enforcing them.

'Exclusive Rights'

Most of the legal rights with which this book is concerned are rights to stop other people doing things – what an old cynic once called 'the grit in the wheels of industry'. For some reason (or possibly none), Acts of Parliament and EU legislation do not put it like that; thus the proprietor of a registered industrial design is said by the Act to have 'the exclusive right' to do certain things with the design, and the other rights are expressed in similar language. But what is meant is, not that the owner of the design, or patent, or copyright concerned has, by that ownership, the right to do anything he could not otherwise do, but that he has the right – subject to questions of validity, the right *to exclude all others*. This is worth emphasising: the position is too often not understood. In particular, there are some people who take the trouble to secure patents for inventions who believe that, somehow, possession of the patent secures to them the right to manufacture their inventions without interference. It does nothing of the sort: the thing such an inventor wants to manufacture may well incorporate other people's patented inventions, and the only way the inventor can be sure that he or she has the right to manufacture is by searching to find what patents other people have. The inventor's own patent (if it is valid, and the specification is properly drawn up – points discussed later) confers the right to stop other people using the particular device that is the subject of the patent – and nothing else. In principle, the position is much the same with the other rights considered in this book, although ownership of a UK registered trade mark, exceptionally, gives a limited freedom from infringement of other people's UK registered marks.

A related misconception is that IP rights can readily be treated as items of property independent of the underlying business which they protect. IP rights can, of course, be bought, sold, or licensed. This has led to a tendency by accountants to want to value IP rights independently of any associated business, thereby 'increasing' net asset value. Such an approach overlooks the fact that the IP rights merely provide the business with protection from competition; so to value the rights and business separately is likely to involve a significant element of double-counting – absent the rights, the business would be worth less.

Another form of this misconception is that IP rights have some sort of inherent value in themselves. The notion is that IP rights are things that can be exploited in themselves. But that is not so – the value of an IP right is entirely dependent on what it protects, what it is for. If people want to do that thing (e.g. use a copyright work or a patented invention), then the right protecting it is valuable. If not, not.

That said, IP rights often have significant value for licensing or, in many cases, for securing reciprocal freedom to operate from others. A large patent portfolio (or even a small and good one) can be a key driver for persuading competitors to provide their own technology to you. One of the largest research-based companies in the world estimated some years ago that it obtained about 10 times more value from IP deals giving it access to the rights of others than it got from licensing rights for money. Since that company has a licensing programme worth about $1 billion pa, the access rights provide a serious benefit. It can really pay for large companies (and increasingly even small companies and universities) to have a reasonable arsenal of IP rights which can be deployed if necessary, sometimes to open up new markets. People sometimes talk about companies fighting their way into oligopolistic markets using their patent portfolio as a sort of IP battering ram. This has, to some extent, fuelled an arms race, particular with respect to patents. There is no sign of let up in the number of applications which are being made for patents and companies in countries which have historically not been so active in this area (such as India and China) are getting in on the act. The underlying problem here is that the costs of acquisition of rights are in a number of areas much lower than the potential benefits of having that right (and its utility as part of a portfolio of other rights). Whereas, in times past, companies might have simply given up on obtaining protection, it makes increasing sense to put even currently non-exploitable rights away, just in case.

Registered and Unregistered Rights

Most IP rights have to be applied for and registered to take effect, but there are some important ones which arise automatically as a matter of law. Of particular importance are: copyright and related rights; the right to prevent goodwill being undermined by deceptive conduct in the market ('passing off'); unregistered design rights; and the right to stop misappropriation of trade secrets ('the action for breach of confidence').

Foreign Law

This is a book mainly about UK law. In many cases this is now the same as IP law throughout the EU (and, in the case of patents, some other European countries too). Almost all foreign legal systems have something corresponding more or less to the various rights discussed in this book, but outside the EU the correspondence is seldom very close. Commonwealth countries, and to some extent the USA (though that has some bizarre aspects like jury trial in patent cases), have legal systems which work like ours. The patent laws of Commonwealth countries are generally like our old patent law, not the present one. Other countries, including European countries, have legal systems which work in a different way, so that even where their law is supposed to be the same as ours – as with European patent, trade mark and some design law – it sometimes works differently in practice from ours.

Spatial and Temporal Monopolies

Many IP rights are limited in time (e.g. 20 years for patents, 25 years for registered designs) and exist only for certain territories (mainly countries). The fact that the exclusive rights are limited by space and time causes a whole lot of problems of international and particularly EU law. For example: one of the key objectives of the EU is to create a single market. So the laws are designed to achieve free movement of goods and services by reducing or eliminating the effect of national boundaries. This objective stands in opposition to the structure of IP law because IP rights are largely national. Another key objective of EU law is healthy competition. But the right to exclude others, an IP right, is a right to prevent competition. Thus IP law has to be reconciled with these other objectives. The interface between the two is rather jagged.

Other Things

Although this book is mainly about exclusive rights themselves, it also deals other matters, for instance systems of licensing and the action to prevent threats of certain types of IP litigation.

Exclusive Licensees

An exclusive licensee is someone who has been given by the right-holder not only permission to work the subject matter of the right, but that permission *to the exclusion of the right-holder* as well as anyone else. An exclusive licensee is given special rights to sue. In the case of copyright and patents, an exclusive licensee of a copyright or the patent has concurrent rights with the right-holder to sue and can pursue an action as if he or she were the copyright-owner or patentee. There are certain formalities (registration at the UK IPO – Intellectual Property Office), which must be observed in the case of exclusive patent and trade mark licensees in order not to lose rights to some legal costs. If an exclusive licensee sues, the registered proprietor must be joined into the proceedings but the court can dispense with this requirement in the case of copyright. The point of making the proprietor join the proceeding is that he will be bound by the result – it would obviously be unfair if a defendant could be sued twice, first by the exclusive licensee and later by the proprietor.

The Scheme of this Book

This book is divided into sections broadly along the lines drawn by the main Acts of Parliament and EU legislation dealing with these branches of the law. The basic division is into three parts: the first is concerned with protection of the product and deals mainly with the law of patents and of industrial designs; the second is concerned with the way things are sold and deals mainly with the law of passing off, and trade marks and other rules preventing unfair competition or unfair selling techniques; and the third deals with the law of copyright (apart from its use to protect industrial designs) and certain related issues such as performance rights and 'moral' rights. It also deals with the law of confidential information.

This division into three parts is a consequence of the fact that the various sorts of IP right are governed by different legal rules. Commercial strategies and disputes often cut across these lines. It is one of the functions of this book to show the interrelations between the different subjects in a way that more specialised works cannot easily do. There is a large amount of academic writing, some of it by lawyers and some by economists, on the value of IP rights and the ways in which they are protected. For example, doubts are sometimes expressed by industrialists as to the value of patents at protecting the competitive advantage that their innovations produce, and some companies prefer to keep their inventions secret rather than disclose the details to the world, albeit in exchange for a limited monopoly. Often these concerns are industry-specific; depending in part on how fast innovation occurs and can be commercially exploited. So a form of protection that might suit the biotech industry might be useless for heavy engineering. For another example, doubts are also sometimes expressed by economists and industry analysts (not nearly so much by those in industry) concerning the importance of the IP system in providing incentives to research and innovate. The importance of providing proper incentives is one of the (several) justifications most frequently offered for giving people IP rights in the first place. As with most laws affecting business, the legislation which is the source of most of the law with which this book deals, is a mishmash of compromise, some of it the result of effective lobbying by particular interest groups, some a result of muddled thinking or questionable drafting by legislators and some which is actually sensible and practical. There is insufficient space in this book for detailed consideration of those arguments or of the empirical work (often of a limited or over simplistic nature) which has been done to support them.

2

Courts, Remedies and Legal Actions

Civil and Criminal Law

The enforcement of IP rights is largely by action in the civil courts. This must be started and paid for (at least until he wins and gets and enforces an order for costs) by the right-owner or exclusive licensee. In some cases (particularly with 'counterfeits' – near exact copies of things such as CDs, DVDs, perfumes and 'designer' clothes) criminal enforcement is used. Generally the prosecutions are then paid for by the public – either via local authorities or, exceptionally in the case of big dealers, by the DPP. Criminal courts have the power to punish by fines and/or imprisonment, but not to order payment of damages.

The Civil Courts – their Functions and Acronyms

A violation of a perceived violation of an IP right brings its owner into conflict with an infringer. If the violator will not stop after being notified of the right (care must be taken to avoid 'threats', in the case of some IP rights), ultimately he must be sued. It is a fact of life (sometimes ignored by competition lawyers and politicians) that many IP rights are rather indistinct at their edges (e.g. what is a 'substantial part' of a copyright work?) or uncertain in their very nature (e.g. the value judgement as to whether a development said to be an invention is so close to a prior idea that it is 'obvious'). So where there is a lot of money at stake, it may be rational for both sides to fight. Even weak cases may be worth a longshot if there are many millions at stake. It is principally in the civil courts that such fights take place.

For patents and registered designs there are specialised courts for England and Wales (where most IP disputes take place). These are the Chancery Division of the High Court (which has within it an even more specialised group of judges who form the 'Patents Court' for patent and registered design cases) and the Patents County Court, which deals with small IP claims of all sorts. There is now a special, truncated, procedure for dealing with these cases and a rather strict legal costs regime which means that a party will not have pay a fortune if he loses (usually the maximum is £50,000 in costs – still a tidy sum for most businesses, but much less than the £1 million which is quite common in heavily fought patent cases). These courts have specialised judges – the principal patent judges having spent their careers in IP and have science degrees. It is possible to sue in Scotland too – this occasionally happens. There the judges (and lawyers), though very good indeed, are less specialist, so cases can take longer. Northern Irish cases are very rare.

Of ever-increasing importance is the Court of Justice of the European Union ('CJEU') in Luxembourg, the EU's top court. Back in the '70s and '80s, its IP activities were only about the jagged edges between IP law and free movement and competition law. But, increasingly, substantive IP law has been based on EU law.

The Importance of EU Law

One key theme of recent years is how important EU law has become in every area. This has happened in phases. Following the EU harmonisation of trade mark law in the early 1990s, there was a lot of activity in the CJEU working out what that law actually required. That took a considerable time, and there are still cases in the system examining things as fundamental as whether the use of metatags is infringement, and the outer boundaries of trade mark law. The more recent focus of the CJEU's attention has been copyright, with numerous cases dealing with fundamental questions such as the conditions for subsistence of copyright and what constitutes infringement. One can tell this area of law is still in need of clarification when our own Supreme Court is unable to be sure whether it is an infringement of copyright to read articles on the internet. In the future, as a result of more intensive harmonisation of the patent system, it is likely that the CJEU will have to grapple with a number of issues in that area too: so far, its attention has been confined to specific areas of law relating to biotechnology patents and supplementary protection certificates.

The Court of Justice

If there is a problem with the meaning of the law based on a 'Directive' (an EU legal requirement to bring national law in line with what the Directive requires), then a national court can 'refer' a question of law to the CJEU. And some IP laws are now made directly by EU Regulations. These take effect directly (e.g. the EU trade mark and designs regulations which create EU-wide rights). So CJEU cases have been happening a lot and will happen more and more. Many of the cases which we mention were decided on a reference from a national court or on appeal from a court deciding EU law. A reference can take up to two years – the case has to pause meanwhile. If, as sometimes happens, a lot of other cases depend on the same point, they are often paused (the lawyers say 'stayed') at the same time. So the system is ponderous and cases are often prolonged.

To add to these difficulties, the CJEU, when it is asked to clarify the law, often does not come back with a very clear answer. This is not always its fault. The CJEU is composed of judges from many different countries and legal traditions, some of whom have had limited exposure to intellectual property law before coming to the Court. They have to reach a consensus on difficult issues: they are obliged to give unanimous judgments. EU legislation in this area is sometimes not very well drafted because it reflects political compromises; quite often such legislation has a very large number of recitals which lobby groups have managed to have slipped in to the text and which then need to be taken account of in interpreting the legislation. Even when the legislation is well drafted, the changing nature of technology makes it hard to apply in new situations. The CJEU therefore has to feel its way, more or less tentatively, in providing clearer definition to the law. Sometimes the Court does this almost on a case-by-case basis, or devises tests which depend on national courts and tribunals taking a large number of factors into account. So, the system which, overall, was intended to provide greater certainty at EU level, has wound up with a court that is often blamed for creating uncertainty.

Forum for Disputes

It is also possible for some sorts of disputes, essentially about whether a right should be or has validly been granted, to take place in offices which grant IP rights. Thus oppositions to EU trade mark registration can take place before the European Trade Mark Office. This forms part of the Office for Harmonization of the Internal Market ('OHIM'), based in Alicante. OHIM has boards of appeal, from which one can appeal further to the General Court (i.e. first instance court) of the EU with a possible appeal to the full CJEU or a chamber of it. Appeals from OHIM concerning applications for cancellation of registered designs go the same way. The UK IPO can hear trade mark oppositions to the grant of UK trade marks, or even attacks upon the validity of patents – the former is used a lot, the latter hardly ever. And the European Patent Office ('EPO') has its own elaborate and ponderous system for dealing with post-grant disputes about the validity of patents.

The Action for Infringement

Most IP rights are enforced in essentially the same way – by an action in the courts for infringement of the right. Although most cases do not go to a full trial (being settled on the way, or effectively resolved by an interim order), it is against what they assess would happen at a potential full trial that everyone judges their respective positions. A full action to trial will normally take about a year (which is very fast by international standards). Broadly, the process involves the following stages: a claim, a defence (and often a counterclaim if the validity of a registered right is challenged), disclosure of relevant documents by both sides, witness statements of fact, and expert reports. Ultimately there is a trial when each side's witnesses and experts give evidence, which is tested by cross-examination. There can be many incidental disputes on the way.

The usual procedure in any action for infringement is that the issue of liability is decided first. If the plaintiff wins, he will normally get an injunction and be entitled to a financial remedy as well as his legal costs. If he loses, he must pay the defendant's costs.

Remedies

'Remedies' is the English lawyers' word for the type of order which can be made by a civil court. We write about these and the practicality of the legal process for obtaining them early on in this book because ultimately it is what orders a court can make which governs how people behave. What courts can order is what IP is mainly about. Broadly there are two sorts of 'remedy': interim and procedural on the one hand, and final on the other. But sometimes interim remedies as a practical matter decide the case without more.

When to Sue

An action for infringement can be brought either when infringement has already started, or even earlier, when it is merely threatened; in general, the law allows one whose rights are infringed to choose when to sue. If infringement has already taken place, a successful plaintiff (we prefer this intelligible word to the trendy but official, 'claimant') will be entitled to damages for what has already occurred as well as an order for the future, and an order that any goods or materials whose use would infringe the claimed rights be delivered up or rendered innocuous. In many cases, instead of damages, it is possible to claim the profits the infringer has made from the infringement. However, litigation is expensive, and although the losing party will be ordered to pay the winner's costs, the amount paid will fall well short (typically 60–70 per cent) of covering the winner's lawyers' bills.

Even if damages are reckoned in with the costs the loser pays, there is seldom money to be made by this sort of litigation. Actions are often brought to punish the infringer, to stop further infringement by him or others, and to establish the legal position for the future; very seldom are they brought for the sake of the damages. It follows that, in almost all cases, the right time to start an action for infringement (if an action is to be started at all) is when infringement first starts – or even better, when infringement is first threatened. This is especially true of actions for infringements of trade or service marks and of actions to stop passing off, since in these cases the right to sue may be lost by delay.

There are other reasons why actions for infringement are best brought quickly if they are to be brought at all. The best way to win an action is not to have to fight, so it follows that the best sort of action to start is the sort that will not be defended. Whether an action is defended or not naturally depends in large degree on whether the case is important enough to the defendant to make it worthwhile going to the trouble and expense of fighting – and facing the uncertainty of not knowing what the result will be. The defendant in an infringement action faces the prospect of an injunction against continuing the offending business, and it is not easy to plan ahead not knowing whether such an injunction will be issued or not.

Accordingly, just as few people start infringement actions unless they feel they must, so few people defend them unless they feel they must. If an infringer is allowed to infringe in peace for years – to spend money advertising a new business or a new product, to develop a new market to the point where it becomes profitable, perhaps even to build a new factory or re-equip an old one – there may be no real option but to fight; yet if the action had been brought earlier on, before there was so much at stake, the offending activity would probably have been dropped, rather than waste time and money fighting. There are always other products and other markets. In trade mark cases especially is this so: it is very rarely worth fighting for a new mark, even if the chances are in your favour.

Time

Although the various rights with which this book is concerned are all enforced by actions of much the same nature, the cost and complexity of litigation varies widely between the different cases. Actions for infringement of patent are in a class by themselves – in complexity, in cost, in the time needed to bring them to trial. Few patent disputes are finally settled inside a year (though the courts are faster than they were); so that an infringement which will have ceased to be commercially important within a year or so is often hardly worth suing over at all, whilst an infringer who can be sure of stopping infringement within a year or so can often face the possibility of an action with comparative equanimity. This considerably reduces the practical value of patents for short-term products. A copyright, trade mark or passing off action may be brought to trial in a matter of months, and the cost and trouble are much less, too. Actions for infringement of industrial designs are intermediate in character; whether they are more like patent actions or more like copyright actions depends on how the parties (and the court) handle them.

Costs

The cost of litigation, particularly IP litigation, has always been a running sore with users. They want all of the following in combination: speed, low cost, and certainty. The last (which is often underrated) is very important – if both sides receive the same advice about their respective prospects, then there is room to settle. But if both sides think they are going to win, or that anything can happen, then settlement is much less likely.

That being said, the problem of legal costs has become even worse in recent years. It is not actually necessary to use a solicitor: the Patents County Court was created mainly so that patent attorneys could instruct a barrister direct, or even appear themselves. Recently, more use is being made of this court because it has new rules which cut down costs. However unnecessarily, clients, or perhaps their patent attorneys, are a bit frightened by the image of the big battalion law firms. They need not be – a good patent attorney with (and sometimes without) a good barrister can be a formidable fighting team for small or even medium-size cases. Even larger cases do not need more than the addition of a good solicitor and perhaps one assistant. Sensible businessmen will ask why their lawyers want to use so many people on their case. A slim team is usually more effective than teams twice the size.

Partly because of increasing costs, but also because of the increasing internationalisation of IP problems (with room for parallel actions in different countries and a patchwork of results) people are increasingly turning to mediation or arbitration as ways of dealing with their IP conflicts. There are even cases where English courts have 'punished' (by withholding some or all of an award of costs) a winner who has unreasonably refused to mediate – there are limits to this, however – if the parties have negotiated 'without prejudice' (i.e. so that their discussions cannot be used in court), then the court cannot tell whether one side or the other was unreasonable and thus 'punish' the winner (*Reed*, 2004).

The UK Intellectual Property Office came up with an idea (enacted in the Patents Act 2004) which helps a bit – the Office can be asked to give non-binding opinion on cases. This is quite cheap – it helps both sides (particularly small parties) to form a realistic opinion of their chances, thus helping them to settle. The system works with some effectiveness in small cases, though no one would say it is rip-roaring success. The UK IPO also offers a mediation service, but with limited success so far.

Final Remedies

The Final Injunction

This is the big one. IP rights are the right to exclude. The injunction is the court order enforcing that, requiring the defendant to keep off the protected territory on pain of punishment if he does not. The real point of most infringement actions is that in this country, once the owner of the right has made it clear that he or she insists on it and once the court (after appeals have been exhausted) has declared that the right exists and has been infringed, reputable business people will not want to argue the point any further. Although the owner of the right usually asks for, and usually gets (if victorious) an injunction against further infringement – a formal order, that is, from the court to the infringer, forbidding infringement for the future – it is the decision that really matters, not the formal order. Indeed, such an order is so rarely disobeyed in commercial cases (where the defendant is almost always a company) that effective methods of dealing with real disobedience are hardly ever invoked. In practice the thing to do against individuals who are determined infringers is to sue not only any companies which are controlled by them which are infringing for the time being, but also the individuals themselves. This prevents these individuals from forming new companies for the purpose of infringing – disobedience of an injunction by an individual means, ultimately, imprisonment.

Financial Remedies

The successful plaintiff has a choice: to be compensated according to the damage the infringement has done to his own business, or, instead, to have paid over to him the profits made by the infringer from the infringement. In either case, only the damage suffered or profits made in the six years immediately prior to the issue of the claim in the action and since the issue of the claim can be awarded. In exceptional cases, where the court for some reason disapproves of the plaintiff's conduct, profits can be refused, but damages can be refused only in special cases discussed below. Of course, neither problem may arise in some cases – for example, where the infringer merely made samples of an infringing article and was stopped by an interim injunction before he got any further. What happens in practice is this: the defendant must, if the plaintiff asks, make a preliminary disclosure of his infringing activities so that the plaintiff can make an informed choice about whether to take damages or profits *(Island Records,* 1995). The court orders a corresponding investigation. Before the investigation takes place (before, therefore, the plaintiff and defendant have seen each other's books in detail and sometimes at all) the infringer usually makes an offer (he may even have made this offer earlier, before the issue of liability was determined). If the plaintiff accepts, well and good; if the plaintiff refuses, the investigation takes place, but at the plaintiff's risk as to costs: if the amount found due is less than was offered, the plaintiff pays for the investigation; if it is more, the infringer pays.

Damages

Where the plaintiff elects to receive damages, the court orders an inquiry into just how and how much the infringement has injured the plaintiff. There is an exception to this, however, in the case of patents, designs and copyright, where an infringer can escape the payment of damages if, at the time of the infringement, he was not aware, and had no reasonable grounds for supposing, that the monopoly infringed existed. Such innocence is rare in patent and design cases: it is rarer still in copyright cases, since most 'works' of recent origin (i.e. within the last 100 years or so – see the copyright chapters below – are pretty well bound to be copyright. So the infringer who copies them ought to have known that. In any case, the infringer who goes on infringing after warning can no longer be innocent. And any manufacturer or importer is unlikely to have an innocence defence, because manufacturers are expected to make a reasonable check via the UK IPO that what they want to do is all right.

As to the measure (the lawyers' word for amount) of damages, the plaintiff is entitled to exact compensation for any monetary damage he has actually suffered that could reasonable be foreseen to be caused by the infringement. Thus, if an infringing book or machine has sales of so many, the author or inventor will have lost so many royalties. A plaintiff who is a manufacturer or publisher can ask the court to assume (unless the infringer can show that this was not so) that each infringing sale has cost him a sale, and so lost him the profit on a sale. There may be other heads, too: the owner of a trade or service mark which is infringed may have to pay for additional advertising to restore the position; the owner of an infringed patent or design may be forced, whilst waiting for the action to be tried, to reduce profit margins in order to retain any share of the market; a patentee may have lost sales of spare parts or other goods which normally are expected to follow the sale of a patented machine – so-called 'conveyed goods' (*Gerber,* 1996). All that can go in. Or the matter may be approached in a different way: pirating of a copyright work may render the work valueless, or passing off may partly or wholly destroy goodwill. Damages may be assessed by estimating the value of the copyright before and after the infringement, and taking the difference. Some cases are complicated of course; but it is seldom difficult to make a rough estimate of the sum likely to be involved. The key question, when dealing with a manufacturer-plaintiff, is: what is his profit on a sale? Very often, that will be simply the difference between his manufacturing costs and his sale price.

In the case of particularly serious infringements of copyright, the court may award a plaintiff additional damages. In deciding whether they are appropriate, particular regard must be had to the flagrancy of the infringement and any benefit accruing to the defendant by reason of the infringement. One example of a situation in which such damages might be awarded is where a journal publishes material believing that the profits (or enhancement of reputation) to be gained from publication would exceed the compensation which a plaintiff would be likely to recover.

Profits

When it comes to taking an account of profits, it is the infringer's profits that matter, not the plaintiff's. They are harder to assess. For one thing, it is difficult to judge the extent to which (in assessing the profit from infringement) that particular part of the business can properly be loaded with overheads. The basic rule is that general overheads do not count, unless the defendant can show that he had to spend them to make the offending sales (*Hollister v Medic*, 2012), but there obviously can be arguments about that. In addition it is the profits from infringement that matter: they may or may not be separable from other matters giving rise to profits. Take, for example, a book of which only part infringes; or a stocking, of which all that was patented was the way the toe was made. It may be very difficult in such cases to say what part of the profit is attributable to what. It is often even harder for a plaintiff to guess what the answer is going to be before he has seen the defendant's accounting books in fine detail. Accordingly, it is usually too risky to ask for an account of profits, and in practice this is seldom asked for. However, suppose that the inventor of a better way of making the toes for socks can show that making the toe in the patented way saves, on average, per dozen pairs of socks, so many minutes of an operative's time at so much an hour – then an estimate of the profit from the invention is directly available for comparison with estimates of damages before the plaintiff makes his election.

In copyright cases, innocence is no defence to a claim for profits. In other cases it probably is – based, no doubt, on the theory that profits is an equitable remedy. Equity acts on the conscience, and an innocent defendant would not have anything on his conscience for what he had done.

Other Final Remedies

In addition, the court can order delivery up or destruction of infringing goods, though the court will not order this if they can be rendered non-infringing. The defendant can be compelled to disclose the names of his customers and suppliers of infringing goods. And (this is a recent EU requirement) he can be ordered to advertise the fact that he was found to be an infringer. There is no EU requirement the other way around (i.e. ordering a plaintiff who has lost to advertise that fact), but there ought to be, so that the commercial cloud of uncertainty which may exist over a defendant's product while he is still being sued can be dispelled. The English courts have decided that they have the power to order an unsuccessful plaintiff to advertise that he has lost, if he has contributed to commercial uncertainty while the action was running (*Apple v Samsung*, 2012).

Interim ('interlocutory') injunctions

There are cases in which to wait a matter of months is to wait months too long. In these cases, the court may be asked to act at once, and to grant at the outset an injunction against infringement – not a permanent injunction, but an interim one, lasting until the trial of the action. In particular, many trade or service mark infringements, many cases of passing off (especially where there is a suggestion that the defendant is dishonest), and many infringements of copyright are best dealt with in this way. A plaintiff who is granted an interim injunction must give what is called a 'cross-undertaking in damages': he must undertake that, if in the end the action fails, he will compensate the defendant for the interference to the defendant's business caused by the injunction. In most cases, this is not an important matter; but an interim injunction in a patent case may well stop a production line, and the damage caused to the defendant may be very great. At the same time, the final result of the action is seldom entirely certain. So there is a risk to the plaintiff if he gets an interim injunction but loses a final trial. Whilst that risk must of course be assessed, an interim injunction is generally worth it even if the plaintiff ultimately loses. Whilst the trial is pending, he will be able to retain 100 per cent of the market and his price. That will generally result in more money than would be involved in paying on the cross-undertaking. Provided the plaintiff acts as soon as the infringement is brought to light (this is essential), an interim injunction may be granted to preserve the status quo until the trial. Unless the evidence fails to disclose that the plaintiff has any real prospect of success at the trial, the court will consider whether the balance of convenience lies in favour of granting or refusing an interlocutory injunction. An important consideration in weighing the balance of convenience is whether the plaintiff or the defendant will be adequately compensated in damages if an interlocutory injunction is either wrongfully refused or wrongfully granted. The court tries to make an order at the interim stage which will put the trial judge in the best position of being able to do justice at the end of the day. In reality, if a court grants an interim injunction that will be an end of the matter – it is seldom worth a defendant's while to take the matter to full trial to see if he can win and get compensated under the cross-undertaking. Generally there are better and less risky ways of making money. That is less so in the case of very large battles such as those in the generics pharmaceuticals industry, where awards for damages on a cross-undertaking can run into many millions of pounds.

Inspection and disclosure ('discovery') orders and freezing injunctions

Since about the 1970s, cases of piracy have become much commoner in many different fields of commerce. Partly in response to this, the courts have held that in extreme cases, orders can be made upon the application of the plaintiff alone requiring the defendant to permit the plaintiff's solicitors to inspect his documents and premises immediately. They are now formally called 'search orders' but the name *Anton Pillar* order is used, after one of the early cases in which one was granted. The purpose of this is of course that an unscrupulous defendant is given no time to destroy incriminating documents or evidence. The courts have also held that even innocent persons who have become 'mixed up' in the wrongdoing (e.g., the Customs, or innocent warehousemen and the like) can be compelled to disclose at least the name of the wrongdoer. Such persons (save, possibly, the Customs, who are in a special position) can also be restrained from permitting pirate goods from leaving their possession until at least there has been time for the case to come properly before the court. Defendants are protected against abuse of search orders by stringent conditions governing their grant and particularly by the appointment of a neutral 'supervising solicitor'.

Another remedy which is particularly useful in obvious piracy cases is the 'freezing injunction' (*Mareva* – after the first case when such an injunction was granted). This freezes a pirate's assets and bank account: it might not work against a dishonest pirate who is prepared to take a chance as regards contempt of court, but will be obeyed by honest third parties such as banks.

Customs Seizure

There are both a UK and an EU system in place whereby Customs authorities can be asked to seize infringing goods being imported. They are briefly detailed here. Broadly the scheme is that the right-holder gives notice to the Customs authorities of the existence of his rights, pays a fee and undertakes to indemnify Customs if anything is wrongfully seized and the owner claims damages from Customs. The systems have their limitations, for the obvious reasons that Customs cannot check anywhere near everything, and in any event are not exactly IP experts. They work best in the case of clear trade mark or copyright infringement – counterfeits. Even then, under the UK system, the owner must supply Customs with advance warning of the particular importation concerned, which means that he will probably have enough information to bring a civil action anyway. There are proposals under discussion for the EU system to be strengthened to combat counterfeits more effectively, including for instance, creating a power to seize counterfeits merely in transit through the EU.

Self-help for copyright infringement

There is a partial self-help remedy for copyright infringement to be exercised only with great caution. This is in addition to the inspection and discovery orders referred to above. After notifying the local police station, a copyright-owner can seize infringing copies found exposed or immediately available for sale (such as in a street market). Adequate notice must be left for the alleged infringer to challenge the seizure in the courts. An alternative, and safer route, is to apply to court for an order that the offending articles be delivered up.

3

Patent, Copyright or Design?

In considering the protection of a new product against imitation, the first question is whether the case calls for patenting, can be left to copyright or unregistered design right, or is one of the special cases where design registration is advisable

Patents

A patent is granted to protect an article that is essentially better in some way than what went before, or for a better way of making it. In an extreme case, a patent can be wide enough and represent a big enough advance over earlier ideas to give its owner a complete monopoly of a new industry. For instance, there have been patents giving for a time a monopoly of telephones, a monopoly of pneumatic tyres or a monopoly of transistors. Very few patents are as important as that, but the existence of almost any patent (if it is, or is thought to be, valid) will make it necessary for a competitor to do design work or even major research of his own, rather than copying the actual product he wishes to compete with.

When Patents Suffice

Whether in a particular case patent law can give a manufacturer the protection he needs depends on three things: how new his product is, how important it is, and for how long he needs protection. The degree of novelty will decide whether he can get a patent, and if so how wide a monopoly this patent will give him. The importance of the product will decide how much trouble it will be worth a competitor's taking to get over the monopoly and how big a risk of legal attack a competitor will be prepared to face. The time factor may decide whether it is practicable to carry out the design or research work needed to avoid a monopoly whose validity cannot safely be challenged.

If, then, a manufacturer needs freedom from competition while he builds up a new business of substantial size, only a patent of unusually wide scope with a really important invention behind it will do: any ordinary patent could be got over by competitors long before the business was firmly established. If what is wanted is a monopoly in a new line of goods not of great importance, a patent of comparatively narrow scope should suffice, for it will usually be less trouble for competitors to produce something different than to risk trouble with patents. In intermediate cases it may be very hard to get proper protection: where goods are markedly more successful than what was made before but without being very strikingly different, it is doubtful whether any patent can prevent imitation. This point is important and will be considered more fully in the course of the next two chapters.

Designs, Registered and Unregistered

Design rights are basically about rights over the shapes or decoration of articles. There are no less than four different sorts of right.

Unregistered Design Right

Unregistered design right is a useful short-term means of protection for designs for industrial articles. Like copyright, it arises without the need for any special registration or application. Although free in the sense of there being no official fees, a sensible designer will incur the internal costs of keeping records of all stages of the design process. This will include all drawings, models or prototypes as well as records as to who did what and, if they are employees, their employment contracts and if freelance the terms of engagement and preferably a proper assignment of all rights in the design. Like copyright, unregistered design right does not give a complete monopoly, it only prevents copying, so if others come up with the same design independently, they cannot be stopped. Almost unbelievably, there are now two sorts of unregistered design right, one arising under our own Copyright Designs and Patents Act 1988 and the other under an EU Regulation. They have different terms and somewhat different scope of protection.

Registration of Designs

The registration of a design involves some expense and must be done before the design is shown to anyone otherwise than in strictest confidence. But sometimes it should be worthwhile. In particular, the sort of design that someone else would be sure to come up with fairly soon may call for registration, to deal with competitors who arrive at the same design independently. A copyright is not infringed except by actual copying, but a registered design (if validly registered) is infringed by anyone using the same design even if he thought of it independently. Inevitably, though, it is much easier to persuade a court that someone else's design is the same as yours if you can show that he actually copied it. Unbelievably (again!)

there are two sorts of registered design, British and EU, with little difference in scope between them.

Copyright

Copyright is principally designed to protect literary, artistic, and musical works, as well as other products of what may loosely be called the entertainment industry – films, sound recordings, broadcasts and the like. It arises automatically as soon as a work is physically recorded, without the need for any formalities, application or registration. (Some people think that 'to copyright' a work you have to put © on it, but this is not so. But putting a © does serve as warning that the creator is copyright-savvy and may be the sort of person who knows how to sue.) Copyright does not play an important part in protecting industrial designs, though it once did.

Copyright gives a right to prevent copying. It does not give a complete monopoly in the sense that a patent does.

Computer Software

Computer programs are, in general, copyright. The copyright is infringed both when a listing of the program is copied (copied as a listing, or recorded as a runnable program) and when an object-code or assembly-code version is reproduced. Copyright protection, valuable though it is for preventing direct copying of programs, is comparatively narrow. Programming techniques or the ideas for programs, as distinct from actual programs, call for patent protection: but computer programs 'as such' are supposed not to be patentable. However ingenious patent attorneys, aided by enthusiastic Boards of Appeal of the EPO have in reality found ways in which this can be done. There was a long debate about whether the exception to patentability of computer programs should be removed, but this is unlikely in the near future The Americans do not have an exception, but there is not much evidence that allowing programs to be patentable has done much good – except, of course, to lawyers and perhaps the big companies such as IBM and Microsoft. The same goes for patents for business methods; indeed, even more so.

Periods of Protection

The periods of protection given by patents, copyrights and design registrations are all different.

Patents

A patent lasts – provided renewal fees are paid – for 20 years from the date of filing of the application at the Patent Office. Patent protection, however, does not become fully effective until the Office grants it, though once granted, damages can be claimed from the point at which the publication of the specification occurred (publication takes place 18 months after the date of application – which may be months, or even years, before a patent is granted). How long it takes to grant depends partly on the applicant (how quickly he responds to queries from the Office), but mainly on the Office. In this respect the British Office is much faster than the European Office. But whichever Office one uses, patenting of a quickly produced and short-lived line of goods will normally be near useless: the patent may have lost its importance before it comes fully into force. Additional problems occur in certain fields that require regulatory approval before marketing, as the wheels of motion there may turn even more slowly. Accordingly, it is not unusual for a new pharmaceutical product to face delays of many years before it is allowed to enter the hands (and bodies) of patients. During all this time, the patent life is slowly ticking away. To remedy this, the EU and some other countries provide so-called 'supplementary protection certificates' which, in effect, extend the period of monopoly for pharmaceutical and agro-chemical products protected by patents which have suffered regulatory delays in getting them to market.

Copyright

Copyright in an artistic work arises when the work is made so that the owner of the copyright gets immediate protection and there is no period of waiting for registration. In general, the period of copyright is the life of the author plus 70 years, but there are exceptions. Many think that this is far too long, but the laws are made by those who listen to powerful lobbyists, such as the publishers and the record and movie industries.

Unregistered Design Right

UK unregistered design right lasts for at most 15 years from the year in which the design was made. But it expires after 10 years, if the design is first marketed within the first five years of the life of the design right. Also, five years after first marketing by the designer, it is possible to apply for a compulsory licence. An EU unregistered design right lasts for only three years from first marketing of the product. That is enough to enable its owner to assess its market success and to judge from that whether he should apply for the longer period given by design registration (his prior marketing does not count for a novelty attack on such a registration).

UK Registered Designs

The registration procedure for a design may take about six months, and until then there is no registration and no protection. (So, with articles that are very quick and easy to copy – many Christmas 'must-have' toys, for example – registration ought to be applied for some six months before they are first shown to the trade, and then copying can be stopped at once.) The registration lasts for five years from the application, and can be kept alive on payment of further fees for four further five-year periods; 25 years in all. Few design-owners find this worth doing.

EU Registered Designs

These also last for 25 years on payment of renewal fees. They are quite cheap. And can be registered almost instantaneously online.

Registered Trade Marks

Shapes can also be trade marks. There are certain restrictions on the type of shapes that can be subject of registration, but if successfully granted a trade mark can last indefinitely provided renewal fees are paid. They can be lost, however, if they are not used (see later).

'Imitations' and Copying

In an action for infringement of a patent or a design registration, it makes, in theory, no difference whether infringing goods are copied from those of the owner of the patent or design, or the makers of the infringements worked entirely on their own. Essentially the main questions to be decided are, first, whether the patent or design registration is a valid one; and, secondly, whether the monopoly given by it is wide enough to cover the alleged infringement. Even if the 'infringer' did not know of the existence of the patent or registration concerned this will not make any difference to the giving of an injunction against him; nor even in some cases to his liability to pay damages and to pay the costs of the action. In an action based on copyright the position is different: the action will only succeed if it can be shown that the alleged infringement was copied (directly or indirectly) from the copyright work.

It follows that a new product, developed entirely by the staff of the company that makes it, may well be an infringement of patent or registered design rights belonging to a competitor. Throughout this book, when we speak of 'imitations', we mean to include such independently developed products. In the case of registered designs, the risk is not usually very serious and can be easily avoided by a proper search. The risk of innocent infringement of patents, however, in any industry where there is appreciable technical progress, will usually be a serious one if the new product is noticeably different from the old. There is no way of avoiding this risk except thorough acquaintance with or thorough search of all existing patents in the branches of industry concerned; in fields such as electronics these may number thousands. No attempt is made in this book to suggest any other way, and discussions in later chapters on avoiding patents refer only to patents whose existence is already known. A thorough search of a field of any size is difficult and rather expensive; a good patent attorney will do it as cheaply as it can be done. And not even a genius can find patents until they are published – so you are always at risk from an inventor who is slightly ahead of you.

The essence of a patent is that the inventor gets a monopoly in return for full disclosure of his invention in the specification which he files at the Patent Office and that the Patent Office publishes. (These published specifications are an extremely valuable source of information in many fields; in some fields they are almost the only reliable source of information about recent developments.) Sometimes, however, technical knowledge is best protected by not publishing it at all. Even where an invention is patented, those who work it soon acquire special knowledge of how to work it. The law will sometimes protect such unpublished information. It is discussed in Chapter 26.

Part II

Protecting the Product

4

Patents and How to Get Them

The European System of Patent Law

The current European system of patent law started in 1978. Before that, each European country had its own patent office and its own independent laws. By the EPC (European Patent Convention) of 1973, the participating countries (now 38, not just the 28 EU countries, and with further expansion planned) agreed to bring their own laws into conformity with the Convention and to set up a common system for granting patents. Each country then enacted a new national patent law to bring it into line with the EPC. The UK Patents Act 1977 was part of that process. No country was willing to give up its own patent office, and so a compromise was reached: an inventor can apply for his patent either through a national patent application ('the national route') or through the EPC route. The EPC route involves an application to the European Patent Office ('EPO') in Munich, the inventor choosing ('designating') the European countries in which he wants a patent and paying the relevant fees. Subject to one complication (so-called 'oppositions' – see below), once a patent is granted by the EPO it takes effect in each designated country just as if it had been granted by that country's national patent office. We call a patent granted by this route a 'European Patent (UK)', but it is not, as its name might suggest, really European. It is a British patent, with corresponding sister patents in other European countries.

The EPC deals only with issues of patentability. For infringement, the original countries of the Convention turned to another source, and based their laws on a separate instrument that it was anticipated would share the European patent throne: the Community Patent Convention 1975 (CPC). This was an EU (or EEC, as it was then) endeavour, which was intended to bring with it the jurisdiction of the CJEU (ECJ as was) as the senior court. Unfortunately the CPC proved to be a somewhat sickly child, and by the early 1980s it was clear that it had succumbed to fatigue and died. Various attempts were made at resurrection, but these ultimately came to naught – although it must be noted that more recent endeavours at creating a Frankenstein's monster from some of the body parts look far more likely to succeed (see below).

There is, accordingly, no common European patent court and you can get different results when the 'same' patent is litigated in different countries. This is not just because the facts might come out different in different courts; there is no 'top' patent court for Europe, and so the views of the 'top' courts of each country as to what the EPC actually means can, and do, differ. Most notably this is the case in relation to the rules for deciding what is the scope of a patent (see below). In recent years however the judges from the main 'patent countries' (Germany, UK, France and Holland) have come to know each other with a resulting convergence of approach. Differences are less than they were.

We must also mention the PCT ('Patent Cooperation Treaty'). This is procedural only: although an application made by this route is called an 'international application' it in fact leads to parallel national patents in different countries. An application is made to our own Patent Office or the EPO, the office checks formalities and then sends the application to the appropriate searching office for that type of invention (this will usually be a foreign office). If the applicant wants (he generally will), the searching office will reach preliminary conclusions on novelty and obviousness. Some countries' patent offices are apt to accept these. Thus the applicant is able to get a fairly early indication of how good his patent might be, and, if things do not look good, quit before he has spent too much money. If all is well, the application is then passed to the patent offices of the countries where he wants patents and proceeds as ordinary applications there. The system is administered by the World Intellectual Property Organisation ('WIPO') in Geneva, a UN agency. The procedure is complex (with some risk, therefore, of things going wrong), but patent attorneys have now got used to it and it is increasingly being used. Sometimes it has financial advantages: for instance, it treats all the EPO countries as one, which saves fees at an early stage. They have to be paid later, of course, but then the application may never get that far. Most countries are now parties to the PCT.

There is a more ambitious plan, which may well come to fruition in the next year or so. After over 50 years of discussion a scheme for a true European patent – a single EU-wide patent in effect – has been approved by the EU Commission and Council The scheme is rather complex, representing a series of compromises. The general idea runs something like this. There is to be a 'Unified Patent Court' with jurisdiction for at least 25 of the 28 member states of the EU (Spain will not join; Italy, from being against, is now wavering; Poland has decided against). And there will be the opportunity for applying to the EPO for a single EU patent with unitary effect. Such a patent would be a lot cheaper than asking for national patents in all the EU countries. Many politicians have been seduced by this into thinking that there will be a saving. However that seems unlikely, for in reality most companies only patent in a few countries – UK, Germany, France, and Netherlands. That is enough for most practical purposes. No one knows what the official fees will be. As regards the Court, there is a complex set-up, and again no one knows what the fees will be. There are to be regional divisions and a central division. A regional division can be for a single country or more. Currently Germany is asking for four, the UK one. The 'central division' will be in three places – London, Paris and Munich. London will take chemical and pharma cases; Munich, mechanical. All the rest will go to Paris. You start an action for infringement in a regional division. The court can 'bifurcate' ie decide infringement (whether the patent scope covers the accused produce or process) alone and send the question of validity to the central division, or it can decide the whole case. This is a compromise because Germany has a bifurcated system (one court for infringement, another for validity) and they like it. The regional division sits in panels of three – one of whom has to be a foreign judge. You can attack the validity of a patent in the central division. On top of this there are complex rules about language; and there is appeal to a court in Luxembourg. Currently it is proposed that the new court not only has jurisdiction over the new unified patent, but also over existing parallel European Patents – whose owners are to be given an option lasting for seven years to keep their patents out of the system.

There are lots of unknowns – particularly official fees, and who the judges will be. The fee problem is acute, because the court is supposed to reach a self-funding state. The current authors think the whole thing is too complex, and does not satisfy the acid test of 'Is it better than what we have now?' Whether it will really happen remains to be seen (it has to be ratified by 13 countries, including the UK, France and Germany, and there are some legal challenges by Spain).

What route: European or British?

Since he can get a patent here either via the EPO in Munich or via the UK Patent Office (in Wales – now operating as the UK Intellectual Property Office (UKIPO)), an inventor can choose which system to use. Indeed he can, initially, choose both, though once the EPO grants a patent with the UK as a designated country, any British patent (at least of the same scope) evaporates by operation of law. A number of factors will influence the inventor's choice of route. And he can possibly use the 'international route' of the PCT, rather than applying directly to the EPO or UKIPO.

First, cost. Obviously there are official fees. Official fees are not the only factor, however. If one uses the EPO, one can use a single patent attorney to draft the application – which is significantly cheaper than employing up to 38 for the national route in all EPC states. Moreover there is no need in the EPO at an early stage for translations. The application can be filed in just one of the official languages (English, French or German) and the whole application proceeds in that language. Only later, when and if the patent is granted, is there need for some translation into other European languages. The burden was reduced by the so-called London agreement of 2000. You have to translate the claims into the other two official languages, but most countries do not require more – the detail is a bit complicated. If one uses the national route, then translations are needed from the beginning of applications for protection abroad which, under the Paris Convention (mentioned in the next chapter), will be a year from the initial application. Generally speaking, if a patent is wanted in more than three countries, then the EPO is cheaper. Three countries are about break-even. The following is a rough indication of cost for a reasonably simple-to-explain, invention. A patent attorney's fees for an initial draft would be about £2,000. Then come official fees, along with further attorney's fees, depending on what happens. In the UK there is a small application fee (which covers preliminary examination – i.e. checking to see that the application is all in order); the typical cost to go all the way to grant is currently £230 to £280 (depending on whether you file electronically or use paper). In the EPO, official fees to grant are €4,350 (slightly less if you apply online). There will also be the translation fees if the patent is granted – and also on the way further attorney's fees, typically about £2,000. Obviously if the case is complex, the attorney's fees will be significantly higher, for instance £5,000. Patent attorneys have devised ingenious ways of delaying the time when fees need to be paid. This can be important, since it gives the inventor more time to see whether what he has got is actually a good idea commercially, and whether his patent is likely to be any good.

Next, speed; the UKIPO is markedly faster than the EPO. For instance, in the early '90s an infringement and validity action about the patent for the first hepatitis C testing kit was decided by the UK High Court and Court of Appeal within two-and-a-half years of grant by the British Office. The corresponding EPO application (made at the same time) was still pending several years later, and the opposition in the EPO was still going some eight years after grant. The position is largely the same now (e.g. a similar thing happened in the case of the patent about packing lie-down seats in aeroplanes, *Virgin v Contour*, 2009). The EPO Boards of Appeal can sometimes speed thing up a bit, at least as far as the appeal goes, but overall that has not had much effect. The lesson is obvious: if you think you will need to enforce your monopoly soon, go British.

Thirdly, validity and scope; a patent drawn up to suit the practice of one country will seldom be fully suited to others. So international applications (for the whole world) using a single specification for all countries may not be as good as individually tailored applications.

Fourthly, there is the 'eggs in one basket' verses the 'gap in protection' choice. If the inventor goes the European route and something goes wrong (e.g. the Office holds the patent invalid and an appeal fails), then he loses it for all EPO countries (unless he has also gone via national routes also). This is particularly important in relation to 'oppositions' in the EPO – see below. On the other hand, if he goes only via national routes then, if the application fails in one country, he will have a gap in his European protection. If he goes via both routes it will cost a lot more, but he will have the maximum flexibility and security against things going wrong, even though he will ultimately have to choose between the patent granted by the EPO and that granted by the British Office – if he does not choose, the British patent will be the one to suffer.

Who Applies

Anyone can apply for a patent. However, it may only be granted to the owner of the invention – the inventor himself, or anyone who can claim the invention from him. Other people can join in the application. If anyone applying is not the inventor, then they have to fill in certain forms for the UK IPO explaining why they are entitled to the patent.

Most inventions are made by employees, as part of their job: in such cases, the employer owns the invention (see the end of this chapter) and can apply to patent it (or claim entitlement to it if the inventor has already done so). Or they may both apply together (when the inventor will be a sort of trustee of his half share).

The Specification and the Claims

The applicant must file at the Patent Office a document called a specification. This must contain a description of the apparatus or process or article, or whatever is to be the subject of the patent. It must contain instructions which will enable a skilled man to work the process, or make the apparatus or article, as the case may be. Most important of all it must contain what are called 'claims': that is, statements defining the precise scope of the rights of monopoly that the patent will give. There is only one way of finding out whether the owner of a patent can prevent the manufacture and sale of a particular imitation of his patented product, and that is by reading his specification and seeing whether the words of the 'claims' describe that imitation. Note that the form of the specification which matters is the 'B' specification (the one with 'B' after the patent number). The specification with an 'A' after the number is the application as filed by the patentee. In other words, the 'A spec' is what he asked for, the 'B spec' what he got. Claims are usually written in special jargon (to make them as general as possible), and a good deal of practice is needed to understand exactly what they are saying. Likewise a good deal of practice is needed to write them. The heart of a patent attorney's craft lies in claim drafting.

Most patent disputes include an argument about the meaning (what the lawyers call 'construction') of the claims. Generally the patentee says they are wide enough to cover the thing he is complaining about, and the defendant denies it. Often the defendant adds that if they are wide enough to catch him they also cover something old or obvious and so are bad. We in Britain are reasonably careful about patent claims. After all, they are there for telling people not only what they cannot do but also, conversely, what they can. And it is the patentee (or at least his patent attorney) who draws the fence (to mix metaphors) in the first place. Although foreign countries have claims in their patents and in theory might seem to use them as we do, this is seldom so in practice. Parties to the EPC are indeed supposed to treat claims in exactly the same way and there is a special 'Protocol on the Interpretation of Art 69' which tries to achieve this. But all that says is that the claims should be construed in the context of the description and drawings (which we have always done anyway) and not used as a 'guideline'. In practice it seems that some Continental countries still treat claims rather more liberally than we do, particularly in relation to so-called 'equivalents' (i.e. the court making the patent cover something which is not, but which is very close to, what the language of the patent claim means). Quite how that is reconciled with the requirement that the invention be specified in the claim, we are not sure. An amendment to the Protocol was made in 2000. It says courts are to take equivalents into account in applying Art 69. Typically, this being a diplomatic comprise, it does not say how. For instance you could take the view that if a patentee uses a specific term ('screwed', say) then he must have meant what he said and intended to leave out equivalent methods of fixing, e.g. nailed. Or you could take the opposite view. The Americans also have a more liberal doctrine of equivalents, but no one seems to know exactly what it is. In recent years the uncertainty it leads to has been caus-ing the courts to apply the doctrine more and more restrictively, both in the US and on the Continent, albeit in different ways. It may end up as just covering equivalents unforeseeable at the time of the application – working on the princi-ple that if you could have claimed it but did not, then the doctrine of equivalents will not save you.

Two examples

The patent in *Catnic v Hill & Smith*, 1982 was for a 'box lintel' – a building com-ponent for going over the openings for doors or windows. Old lintels were formed of reinforced concrete, steel girders or (the very old ones) bits of trees. The Catnic idea was to use a hollow steel box appropriately shaped. The patent claim called for two horizontal plates 'substantially parallel' to each other, an inclined support member, and a 'second rigid support member *extending vertically*' from one hori-zontal plate to the other. The row was over the meaning of 'extending vertically'. What the defendant did was to use a support member which was 6° off true verti-cal but which was good enough to work. He said that the claim meant true vertical – emphasising his point by contrasting the way the claim dealt with the horizontal plates. It was enough for these to be 'substantially parallel', whereas the word 'ver-tical' was not qualified. The House of Lords had no difficulty in dismissing this argument as a lawyer's quibble. A practical man would regard any member verti-cal enough to work as 'vertical'. The only wonder of the case is how the Court of Appeal ever thought otherwise.

On the other hand, in *Improver v Remington*, 1989, the patent was for a device for removing hair from women's legs – in the refined language of the patent, a depilator. The patentee had the idea of using a helical spring bent in a curve. One end was fixed to a small high-speed electric motor and the other to a fixed bearing. The spring rotated at high speed and its windings opened and closed rapidly, catching and pulling out the hairs. The patent claim called for a 'helical spring.' The wily defendant substituted for this a rubber rod with transverse slits. When this was rotated the slits opened and closed just as in the case of the windings of the helical spring. But, both here and in Hong Kong, the courts held there was no infringement. True it was that the rod had all the necessary properties of the helical spring (it was appropriately 'bendy' and 'slitty'), but it was not a helical spring. To find infringement it would have been necessary to ignore the word 'helical' altogether, or regard it as no more than a kind of shorthand for a component having the necessary properties.

Interestingly, the corresponding German court took a different view, applying the then German view of a doctrine of infringement by exact and obvious equivalents of items specified in a claim. It is not clear the case would be decided the same way now – as we said, there has been a narrowing of the concept of infringement by equivalents. From the point of view of a student of comparative patent law (apart of course from the lawyers involved), it is a great pity that this case was not fought all over the world, because its facts are easy to understand and the legal approaches of different countries would have been easy to study. From the point of view of a British lawyer or patent attorney, the case is an excellent example of the danger of being too specific in the widest patent claim. If it had said in Claim 1 'means for removal of hair' and by a Claim 2 'wherein said means is a helical spring', there would have been no difficulty. But then it is always easy to be wise after the event. Some good patent attorneys do favour the 'means for' approach. It forces the patentee to think about the function of each item making up his invention. On the other hand some patent offices (e.g. the US) do not like this type of approach, holding that it is apt to give the patentee more than he really invented.

Securing Priority

Preparation of a specification is usually a long job, and it is often important that the patent should be applied for at the earliest possible moment. But the law allows the applicant to secure a right of priority by filing an informal application in the first place (here or abroad); he then has a year to prepare and make a proper application. So long as the invention is well enough described in the original application to 'support' the claims of the final one, the novelty of his invention will be judged as of the earlier date. The original application can simply be dropped: but there are snags; see 'Delay in application' below. If it is dropped, the penalty for getting the original specification wrong is loss of priority which may or may not matter depending on what information has been made available to the public meanwhile. The specification of the application that is finally proceeded with, however, not only has to pass detailed scrutiny by expert examiners at the Patent Office, but also must be proof against the destructive criticism of hostile lawyers and experts: for if the patent is ever the subject of legal proceedings, the wording of the specification may determine the validity and scope of the patent.

Just what is necessary for an earlier specification to 'support' the claims of a later one is not clear; as is coming to be more usual in IP legislation, the draftsman has been careful not to use words that mean anything very definite, either to a lawyer or to anyone else.

Inherent Patentability

Not every bright idea is patentable. A patentable invention has to be 'capable of industrial application' – including exploitation in agriculture, but excluding plant or animal varieties and 'essentially biological processes for the production of animals or plants'. Microbiological processes, though, can be patented; they are rather important, since many antibiotics are made by fermentation, as are many drinks. And although genes as they are in nature cannot be patented, stretches of DNA containing the essential code can be – a matter of controversy, both because some of the patents are particularly important, and because it is normally impossible to design around. It has been decided that you can have a gene (and corresponding protein and antibody) patent if you have discovered a gene and its code and have only a slight idea what the protein or its antibodies do (or can make an educated guess as to such) (*Human Genome Sciences*, 2011). This is controversial, for it means in practice that you have patented a research programme, rather than anything which is immediately, or even remotely, practical. The Americans would not allow it – calling such a patent a 'hunting licence'. Medical and veterinary treatments are not patentable; but drugs are (even if the materials used are old; see Chapter 6).

There is also a list of matters excluded from patentability as being essentially intellectual: scientific theories, mathematical methods, computer programs, aesthetic creations of all sorts and business methods. Patents for computer programs have caused a lot of difficulty. They are not patentable 'as such'. But what does that mean? Both our courts and the EPO Boards of Appeal have grappled with this. In a series of cases (UK: *Aerotel/MacCrossan*, 2006, *Symbian*, 2008; EPO: *Duns; G03/08* and many others, none of which are easy to read) the general answer is this: it depends on whether the claimed technical contribution to the state of the art can be said to be the excluded subject matter itself. Thus in *Symbian* a patent for a program which speeded up the operation of a computer was allowed as being technical, whereas in *MacCrossan* a program for helping fill in the form to be used for forming a company was refused because it was for a business method. But whether a program is 'technical' can be close to a metaphysical question. In practice it is generally possible to 'dress up' a claim to a computer program as some sort of device claim (a computer loaded to run the program for instance). Borderline cases in this area will always be improved by ingenious framing of claims, another reason why the services of an experienced patent attorney can be so valuable. The American system currently adopts an 'anything goes' approach, both for computer programs and business methods; but the Supreme Court is showing signs of discomfort, so change may be in the air.

Another area where controversy raged until recently is the patentability of genetically engineered animals (there is no problem over bacteria). The EPO took ages over the point in the 'Harvard Onco-Mouse' case – a mouse which develops cancer so it can be used in cancer research. The EPO finally (July 2004) decided in favour of patentability. Astonishingly, the patent was applied for in 1984 and took until 1992 to be examined and granted. Then the EPO 'opposition' ran until 2004. The patent was very nearly expired. For the particular case the delay hardly mattered, because the 'onco-mouse' was a commercial flop but, more generally, the case shows the EPO 'opposition' procedure at its worst. The argument about animals is largely over, but possibly could flare up again for it raises emotion and debate which is not always entirely rational – see for example the split Canadian Supreme Court decision refusing the onco-mouse patent. More recently, stem cells have taken up the limelight. The CJEU has waded into the arena (biotechnology being one of the few areas where the EU has currently legislated in the field of patents). It has proclaimed that even if a patent's claims do not directly concern the use of human embryos, the patent may still be refused where the invention requires the destruction of human embryos at some point in the past (*Brüstle*, 2011). Accordingly, even inventions using 'off the shelf' stem cells derived, at some point, from the destruction of a human embryo, are unpatentable. The chilling effect of this decision on stem cell research remains to be seen, but is likely to be significant.

Search, Publication, Examination

If it is intended to proceed with a patent application the next step is to request (and pay for) a preliminary examination and a search of earlier patents. The preliminary examination goes to the formal correctness of the application and specification; the search, in the first place at least, will be through earlier published specifications for the same sort of invention. At the same time, the application and its specification will be published, at the latest 18 months after filing. This means that if the inventor wants to avoid publication (as he may: see below, under 'Delay in application'), the application must be withdrawn.

The next stage is for the applicant to request (and, as usual, pay for) a full examination. Here the examiner considers whether what is claimed is the sort of thing that is patentable at all; whether the specification is clear and complete enough to enable a skilled reader to work the invention; and above all, whether when compared with what appears in earlier publications the invention appears new and not obvious. In theory, all publications of all kinds count for a possible novelty objection, but in practice examiners largely – although not always – confine their searches to earlier patent specifications. It is reasonably easy to decide whether a supposed invention is new – normally the examiner has only to read the claims of the specification and look in the earlier documents for anything falling within those claims. Deciding whether an invention is obvious, on the other hand, is always difficult, and with nothing to go by except what appears in earlier documents, becomes almost impossible. Naturally, then, examination for obviousness produces some odd objections: the only thing an examiner can do is turn the application down and see whether the applicant's patent attorney can produce a convincing answer to the objection.

When examining for obviousness, the examiner considers only documents published up to the date when the application was filed (or the date of an earlier application giving priority, if there is one). But in considering whether the invention is actually new, he must look also at specifications published after but already on file at that date: in relation to novelty only, these are treated as if already published. This makes things complicated; see below.

Delay in Application

If a reasonable specification was filed with the application for a patent (either the application actually proceeded with, or an earlier one made here or abroad – see above, 'Securing Priority'), nothing after that counts in deciding on the validity of the patent. This is the main reason for getting an application in as soon as enough is known about the invention for a specification to be drawn up. If there is delay, some competitor, here or abroad, working along the same sort of lines may in the meantime publish some description, or market something, or make some patent application, which will make it difficult or impossible to get a valid patent. Or the inventors themselves may let out enough information to invalidate their own patent: by samples shown to the trade, perhaps, or by some note in a trade journal. Too often, inventors let the cat out of the bag too soon. Even a single non-confidential disclosure to one person anywhere in the world is enough to destroy a subsequent patent. And a single use from which it is possible without undue effort or skill to work out the nature of the invention is also enough. There is a particularly acute problem in the case of inventions which need some sort of public trial. There is no special protection for such trials, so if you can work out the nature of the invention from such a trial, there will be prior disclosure. Public trial which does not enable a skilled man to know the secret of the invention is, in itself, all right (*Quantel,* 1990). There are proposals to ameliorate this rule – so that the inventor has a 'grace period' following disclosure by him in which he can file for a patent – his prior disclosure not counting for this purpose. The trouble with this is some uncertainty – the Americans prior to March 2013 had a similar (and even more generous) scheme in place. Under their 'first-to-invent' system, provided an inventor applied within a year from the time he had 'reduced his invention to practice', no intervening disclosure counted. The rules led to much litigation, quite apart from meaning that trade rivals might not know for several years (the one-year period plus Office processing time) about the patent. The Americans have recently changed to a 'first to file' system, albeit ameliorated by a one-year grace period for publication by the inventor himself. There is rather a lot of uncertainty about how this will work out. Prudent inventors never rely on grace periods.

The problem of priority can be dealt with (as has been explained) by getting on file an informal patent application that is good enough to support the claims in a proper application filed in due course. But getting priority in this way will not stop a competitor working along similar (but not identical) lines – and it is remarkable how often competitors are found to have been working along similar lines – from getting his own patent. If a competitor has a patent covering essentially the same thing, it may be impossible to work the invention without a licence from him. To invalidate rival patents, it is necessary either to have made the invention public or to have filed a patent application (in this country, or an international or European one 'designating' this country) which is in due course published. But it will seldom be safe to allow publication of an application intended only to give priority: it might anticipate the inventor's own later application too. So: not only should the first, informal application be filed as soon as practicable, the formal application should be filed as soon as practicable too.

Examination Procedure

If an examiner sees an objection to the specification or the claims (or considers the whole thing unpatentable) he writes to the applicant's patent attorney stating his objection. The applicant must show the examiner is wrong, or alter the specification or claims, or abandon the application. (If examiner and attorney cannot agree, the matter will go to a Principal Examiner, and if necessary the applicant can appeal from him to the Patents Court.) This is for a British application. The position is similar in the EPO, the appeal going to a 'Board of Appeal'.

Grant and Revocation after Grant

If and when all objections have been overcome, the applicant must pay another fee, and the patent will then be granted. Its owner may then start to sue for any infringements that have occurred since that application was published. The patent may still be revoked, however, either by a procedure in the Patents Court or in the UK IPO, if anyone can show (in effect) that it should not have been granted. (Such an attack on the patent is almost certain to be made if the patentee sues for infringement, as part of the defence to the action.) To attack a patent in the UK IPO will be much cheaper than attacking it in the Court, mostly because of the different way in which the evidence is provided; but an attack in the UK IPO will often be less likely to succeed and is liable to be slower. In practice, people wanting revocation of a patent use the Patents Court or Patents County Court.

EPO Oppositions

There is one feature of the EPO system which calls for special mention: the misnamed 'opposition'. Within nine months of grant, anyone can 'oppose' the patent in the EPO, that is to say, seek its revocation. If successful, an opposition will knock out the patent at its roots and it will shrivel and die in every state. Unfortunately the opposition procedure (which has one tier of appeal, where, oddly, fresh arguments and evidence are common) is extraordinarily slow, leaving the fate of the patent or the scope of eventual claims uncertain for many years. (Of course this may operate to a patentee's advantage – uncertainty often puts competitors off). Moreover the procedure is, at least to those used to the Anglo-Saxon system, crude and uncertain. It proceeds almost exclusively on paper with oral hearings seldom lasting more than a morning. There is no real method of assessing evidence – assertion of technical fact by an advocate is common and accepted. 'I discussed the case with an engineer yesterday and he said . . .' seems to do as well as a sworn statement. There is no cross-examination or discovery of documents. Quite often parties are permitted to take the other by surprise at a hearing, for instance by producing an exhibit 'out of the hat'. The slowness of the opposition system can have serious effects on enforceability too. In many European countries the courts will not enforce the patent or hear revocation proceedings whilst there is an opposition pending, though there is the later advantage that considerable respect is given in those countries to a patent which has survived EPO opposition. Until recently our courts would only stay proceedings pending determination of an opposition, if the final result of that opposition (on appeal) was imminent. But this may change because of a recent Supreme Court case, *Virgin Atlantic v Zodiac*. Moreover a patent which has survived an EPO opposition is not treated differently from any other patent by our courts, which decide the case using their own judgment on the evidence. The possibility of an EPO opposition is a factor in favour of a national application. Some companies, particularly US companies, avoid the EPO route for patents in Europe precisely because they do not trust the EPO opposition procedure. The EPO has said that it will hurry things up in urgent cases (both before grant or in oppositions). However, to a patentee wanting his patent granted, or to an opponent wanting his opposition determined, the Office's sense of urgency seems rather like that of the man who thinks that *mañana* conveys too great a sense of haste.

Cost and Period of Protection

A patent granted by the UK IPO covers the whole of the UK, and proceedings upon it may be brought in the English, Scottish or Northern Irish courts, as may be appropriate. The patent is kept in force by annual renewal fees, increased from time to time to keep pace with inflation, for a total period of 20 years from filing. The inventor has also to pay the fees for filing, search, examination and grant already mentioned. There will also be the modest charges made by the patent attorney who drafts the specifications and negotiates with the Patent Office. Foreign patenting will add very greatly to the cost.

Money can of course be saved by not paying renewal fees and letting the patent lapse, but patents that are not kept up for their full term are seldom much use: since all a patent can do is to stop other people using the invention, it will not be of value until the invention has reached the stage where other people want to use it. Few inventions are profitable quickly enough to tempt others to infringement in their first years; indeed, many inventions of importance seem seldom to be very profitable until quite late in the life of any patent covering them. Of course, it is often impossible to tell at the beginning what an invention is likely to be worth and, in doubtful cases, it will be better to take out a patent just in case; even so, the published figures suggest that many applications which turn out to be useless are filed. And actually that is what you would expect.

Grant and Ownership

Subject to what is said below concerning employee inventions, the general principle is simply stated: the inventor is usually entitled to the grant of a patent. The Patents Act also presumes, for eminently practical reasons, that the person who applies for a patent is the person entitled to its grant – this presumption may be rebutted.

Once a patent has been granted, it can be bought and sold much like other property, provided the disposition is made in writing and the transaction is registered at the IPO. The name of the current owner can usually be found from the Register, because failure to register could lose him some of his rights to costs if he has to sue on the patent. The names of the applicants will appear on the copies of the specification found online. All details of the patent – including applicant, owner, and whether it is in force or not – can be found online on UK IPO's rather good website.

A sale or other disposition of the patent may be effective in law if made by those whose names appear on the register of proprietors, whether or not it 'really' belongs wholly or in part to someone else. If, therefore, the inventor (for example), or the promoters of a company intending to exploit the invention, wish to retain some control over a patent, it may be wise for them to arrange to be registered as part proprietors.

Inventions by Employees

As noted above, inventors these days are usually employees of some company. It would be rash to conclude, however, that all inventions made by employees belong to their employer: it depends on the circumstances. Unless the employee's service agreement makes some special arrangement more favourable to him – an agreement less favourable to the employee is ineffective – what governs the matter is broadly whether or not it was the employee's job to make that sort of invention. If so, it belongs to the employer (just as a workman may be employed to make boots, which then belong to the employer, not the workman). If not, it belongs to the employee (even though he may have made it in his employer's time and misappropriated his employer's materials for the purpose). Thus an eye doctor whose job was essentially to treat patients owned the patent for an invention of a device which could be used in eye treatment (*Greater Glasgow Health Board's Appn,* 1996). There is no halfway house, except by special agreement; so that if the invention does not belong to the employer, the employee can demand a royalty for its use or even refuse permission to use it. Inventions made before the employment began, or after it stopped, do not belong to the employer.

In deciding what the employee's job was, his general position is naturally crucial. An engineering draughtsman, for instance, is normally expected to improve the design he is drawing out if he can (although a radically new idea may be outside the scope of his employment, even though sparked off by something connected with his work). A factory hand is not normally expected to invent at all. Directors are generally in a position where anything which might reasonably be connected with the company's business belongs to the company: by and large, a director must never profit at his company's expense. (The English agent of a foreign engineering concern has been held to be in that sort of position, too.)

Sometimes, there is a special agreement, under which an employee-inventor not merely applies for a patent jointly with his employer (which in itself means nothing) but actually owns his share of the patent. Inventors should note (a) that sort of agreement is best put into writing, and (b) the owner of a half-share in a patent cannot (unless the agreement specially says so) do anything with it except himself work the patent – something his employer may be able to do but he will not. (Forming a company to do it is not working the patent: the company will need a licence from both patentees.) Such agreements should be vetted by a solicitor – on both sides.

If the employer does particularly well out of a patented invention made by an employee, the employee can apply (to the Court, or to the Patent Office) to be awarded a fair share of any 'outstanding benefit' the employer has got from the invention; unless the rewarding of employees for that sort of invention is already covered by a collective agreement. People who were employed mainly abroad when they made their inventions cannot apply. In practice this provision had little effect until recently. One of the problems was that the Act originally spoke of the *patent*, rather than the invention, being of 'outstanding benefit'. Thus if an employer merely saved himself some money by using the invention, he had not received any benefit from his patent. The provisions were so unsuccessful that they were amended in 2004 so that inventors can get a reward if their employer gets a benefit from the patent or the invention or both. More recently the courts have begun to make the provision work. Thus in *Kelly v GE*, 2009, two inventors were awarded £1½m between them where the judge thought their employer would make at least £50m profit from their invention.

Patent Attorneys

In practice, the work of negotiating with a Patent Office (UK or EPO) is done by patent attorneys, whose profession it is. They also draw up nearly all specifications and are concerned in nearly all Patent Office proceedings and so on. It is theoretically possible for an inventor to do everything himself without professional help, but if a patent is worth applying for at all, the difference made by practised drafting of the specifications and skilled negotiation with the examiner will be worth far more than a patent attorney's fees.

Furthermore, current application procedure, both national and international, is so complex that it is best left to experienced professionals. A good patent attorney may (literally) be worth his or her weight in gold.

The Grounds on which a Patent may be Declared Invalid

These are of great practical importance. It should always be borne in mind that while it is generally not too difficult to decide whether a patent is infringed or not, it is very seldom easy to decide whether a patent is valid. Thus whenever there is a question of enforcing a patent by court proceedings, the question of validity may be the most important one in the case. It will be seen that while some of the grounds set out below affect the patent as a whole (insufficiency of instructions, for instance), others affect only the claims as such. Where this is so, it is possible for some of the claims to be valid (or even, to be partly valid) although others are invalid. Such a position gives rise to difficult procedural problems, but for most purposes the important question then is: is any claim that has been (or will be) infringed a valid claim? The other claims matter much less.

These are the grounds:

1. **Lack of novelty**   That a claim of the specification includes something which has been 'made available to the public'. This means that somehow the public have been able to learn what the invention is before the priority date. Most often that is by reading an openly published prior document which clearly describes something in the claim. But there are other ways – for instance blurting it out in a public lecture, or even to a single individual (provided it is not in confidence). Selling a product which can, without 'undue difficulty' be analysed, or even using it in public in circumstances where it can be analysed or dismantled to find out how it works will do – see below. What is not enough is selling a product which cannot be analysed – the public then has access to the product of the invention but not the invention – the idea itself. In the past public (and even in some cases secret) prior use of any sort was enough to invalidate, but that is no longer so. The prior use or document must 'enable the public' to work the invention (*Synthon*, 2006). Where this is so, in the jargon of patent law, the claim is said to be 'anticipated' by the prior publication or prior user (the 'prior art').

A couple of further points are worth noting: first it is sufficient if the prior art gives at least one member of the public a means of finding out what the invention is. It does not actually matter whether or not anyone did. Thus in one case a patent for an invention about portable traffic lights was lost simply because the inventor tried his invention out at night at a junction and it was shown that a skilled man could have worked out what the invention was by standing around and observing what happened – though of course no one did stand out all night doing that (*Lux v Pike*, 1993). Nor does it matter whether the member of the public is here or abroad.

2. **Obviousness**   That the claim includes something that was obvious, at its priority date, in view of what had already been made available to the public. Obviousness is also called 'lack of inventive step'. It is one of the most important, yet one of the

most uncertain, grounds. In principle it is only common sense that any more or less self-evident variant of an old idea does not deserve a patent. The trouble is that in practice it is often very difficult to decide after the event (sometimes many years after) what would have been obvious to the 'skilled man' – an ordinary worker in the field. A lot depends on the court's feeling as to whether the invention was a good idea. Sometime the patentee wins by asking, 'If it was obvious, why was it not done before?' (A good example is *Schlumberger v EMGS*, 2010.) That is particularly effective if, once the invention was made, lots of money was made from it.

3. Insufficiency That the specification does not disclose the invention clearly enough and completely enough for it to be performed by a person skilled in the art. It is possible for there to be insufficient instructions to carry some claims into effect, but sufficient for others; but, generally speaking, a specification tends to be sufficient for all claims or insufficient for all. It has now been decided that this ground can apply where the 'disclosure' is not as wide as the claim – so that you cannot perform some part of the claim (*Biogen*, 1997). This is one of the ways the courts have dealt with the problem of a claim which is too wide – where the patentee has claimed more than he has really invented. The other way is to use a combination of obviousness and insufficiency in rather a tortured way – to say that a claim which covers an obviously desirable thing is obvious unless there are sufficient instructions on all ways as to how to make it. The law here is not particularly satisfactory because it is not often easy to apply these general notions to particular cases. The trouble is that there is no explicit ground of undue width of claim (as there used to be), so the courts have had to concoct one.

4. Obtaining That the patent was granted to someone not entitled to it. This objection is seldom raised not least because if an invention is stolen and patented the victim usually brings a claim for the patent to be transferred to him (or invokes a special procedure before the Patent Office to the same end). Invalidating the patent on this basis really is the nuclear option. Only the man who is really entitled to the invention can run this ground, and then only within two years from grant.

5. For excluded matter That the alleged invention is not the sort of thing that should be patented at all. This covers things like methods of medical treatment, immoral inventions and those things deemed not to be inventions at all (such as computer programs and business methods), see above.

6. Incapable of industrial application As noted, this ground has recently been hugely restricted by the Supreme Court. Now even an educated guess as to a product's function will avoid invalidity on this basis.

7. Wrongful amendment There are two sorts: that the specification has been altered by amendment so as to disclose something not disclosed in the specification when it was first filed, or that it has been altered since the patent was granted to make the claims cover something they did not cover before.

History of Patents

The English patent system, from its earliest foundations in the Middle Ages, has been based on the principle of incentivising technological development with monopoly. In the fourteenth and fifteenth centuries, grants of letters patent were made to encourage European skilled workers to come to England and teach industrial methods to the (largely agricultural and mercantile) English. Often the grant of letters patent was conditional on the grantee providing practical training for a number of native apprentices in the working of the inventions. Until the early seventeenth century it was very difficult to challenge these monopolies in the courts, since to do so was regarded as evidencing a lack of proper respect for the sovereign's authority. The royal prerogative to grant patents was widely abused as a source of crown patronage (the famous *Case of Monopolies*, 1603, was about a patent for playing cards – hardly a new invention by that time). The Statute of Monopolies (1623) confined the legitimate exercise of the prerogative power to grant patents to the true and first inventor in respect of the sole working or making of 'any manner of new manufactures . . . which others at the tyme . . . shall not use.' It also set a limit to the time for which the monopoly could be granted, at 14 years. That statute said that the grant of letters patent shall be permitted provided also that 'they be not contrary to the law nor mischievous to the state, by raising prices of [commodities] at home or hurt of trade, or generallie inconvenient.'

It was not until the eighteenth century that the specification (i.e. the description of the invention) became important as providing the educational function of the patent and also in defining the scope of the monopoly claimed. Until then, the subject matter of the patent was usually described in very broad and general terms and the patentee was probably in a relatively strong position to beat off infringers (for whom the punishment could be imprisonment). During the eighteenth century it was established that the grant of the patent would be made conditional upon the patentee's filing a specification of his invention within six months of grant, which would show that the invention existed, telling the public how to work it, and showing what the claimed invention was. At the time, getting a patent was very expensive – as Dickens so well explained in his cynical (but accurate) description in *The Tale of a Poor Man's Patent* (patents have always been an expensive business – there is nothing new about that). The system whereby a potential patentee had to file a specification upon application for a patent dates from 1852. The official search to determine whether the invention had already been published was introduced in 1902. The system remained largely unchanged until the new European system started in 1978.

5

Important Inventions

Introduction

Every now and then, somebody makes a really important invention. As a rule, nobody knows this has happened until too late, and it is found either that the man who made the crucial step did not bother to apply for a patent at all, or that his application was considered just as a matter of routine, so that he got a patent that would do very well to cover some minor improvement, yet withstand neither a determined challenge to its validity nor a determined attempt to invent around its 'claims'. In that case, the invention can be used by any one prepared to spend a little time and money upon research and rather more upon litigation. Sometimes, though, the inventor – or the inventor's employer – knows he is on to a good thing. What should he do about it?

Where Others have Tried

If the invention is one that a lot of people have been trying to make there may well be very little to be done about it except get whatever patent the Patent Office will grant and hope for the sympathy of the court in due course. For in that case the files of the Patent Office will contain dozens or even hundreds of specifications dealing with the subject, and some of them may well have come too close to the right answer for there to be much left to patent. In theory, of course, the failure of many other workers to make the invention is strong evidence that it was a good and patentable invention, rather than something obvious; but in practice, the drafting of valid claims that are broad enough to give real protection for the invention may be impossible where there have been too many earlier proposals. Some big firms, especially, make a point of patenting every slight advance in research into some subjects; partly in the hope that if one of their competitors finds the answer, they will have patents of their own that are important enough to bargain with, partly for the very purpose of making it difficult or impossible for competitors to get valid patents. (Economists, many of whom cannot grasp how the patent system works and has always worked, are apt to express concern about this – referring to it as 'patent thickets' and talking about 'hold-up' even in industries as fast-moving as the mobile phone business.) The independent inventor, hoping to make a large fortune by research in competition with the research departments of such large firms, is for this reason almost certainly wasting his time unless he makes a truly important advance. He would probably make more money by research in a field that is specialised enough for his success not to be a serious challenge to his bigger rivals.

An Important Invention

Let us consider then the case of a manufacturer who is in possession of an invention that he believes is important, and that is unexpected enough to offer a chance of a really valuable patent. It will have to be a valid patent, for it is sure to come under hostile scrutiny as soon as its importance is understood; and it must have 'claims' that are wide in scope, so that competitors cannot escape from it except by spending large sums upon research. It follows that attention will have to be paid to legal technicalities, which means extra trouble and extra expense in applying for the patent – though they will be trifling compared with the trouble of fighting a lawsuit later on, and the expense that will be incurred even if the suit is successful.

The initial application

The first step will be the filing of an application accompanied by a specification. This will not be the ultimate specification: its real purpose is to provide priority for the invention. It will be worth giving more care than usual to drafting this, so as to be certain that it both includes as much detailed information as possible and also foreshadows the claims that will be incorporated in the final specification. Those claims will have to be broad: they must cover not only the actual machine or process that the inventor would like to see used commercially, but also any alternative form of the invention that competitors may want to use – or that competitors may be prepared to use if compelled to do so by the need to avoid the patent. In order to be sure that such broad claims will hold, as much basis as possible for them must be laid in the original specification: both by indicating the general principles of operation of the invention, and by suggesting alternatives to whatever is actually described in detail in the specification. Many inventors dislike trying to think of and describing alternatives that they believe to be inferior, but it ought to be done. They should be encouraged to think of as many variants of their basic idea as possible – good, bad and indifferent. It is a good idea to ask them to put themselves in the mind of someone trying to pinch their idea. If the alternatives later turn out to be hopelessly inferior, they can be abandoned when the final specification is drawn up.

If, as often happens, the inventor later thinks of a development of the ideas in the original preliminary application it will be desirable to file another application, so as to get the best priority for the development. It will not get the original priority date even if it is within the general ideas disclosed in the first application. So also with any later new developments. The application on which the patent will ultimately be based will have to be filed within a year of the first application anyway.

Protection Abroad

It will soon be necessary to consider patenting abroad: even a company not able to contemplate manufacturing abroad, or bringing infringement actions abroad to protect an export market, may want to license foreign manufacturers and get something back that way. (Even a foreign manufacturer who is mainly interested in 'know-how' will often be unwilling to sign a satisfactory agreement, unless there are patents in his home country to hang the agreement on.)

First: Europe. The initial application can be filed here; a British application can found priority in Europe as well as a European one can. But before any application is filed that is meant to be proceeded with, a decision will have to be taken whether in Europe to seek separate national patents, or a European patent – or both. (See Chapter 4; and note that if both British and European patent applications are wanted, either a single international application must be made for them – see below – or both applications must be filed on the same day; otherwise one will anticipate the other.) In the case of a really important invention where patenting costs are only a minor factor, the sensible thing to do is to go via both national and the EPO routes. This provides the maximum flexibility downstream (although as noted in Chapter 4, if the EPO application designates the UK then eventually you must choose which application to take to grant as there cannot be two patents on the same invention. If no choice is made, the EP(UK) patent will prevail.) You can often adjust the application which is trailing behind (almost certainly the EPO application) using the experience gained from the earlier one – though there are limits to this. Adopting this double-barrelled approach may also be a sensible precaution given the uncertainties of the potentially forthcoming Unified Patent Court and the fact that it may no longer be possible to agree on an EP (UK) while an EPO opposition is pending.

In countries outside the European system, the initial British application (or applications) can again be used to give priority. Almost all industrial countries are parties to an international convention (the 'Paris Convention', going back to 1883 with revisions every 20 years or so until the end of the 1970s) concerning IP, which allows residents of any such country to file a patent application at home, and then within a specified period (normally 12 months) to file corresponding applications in the rest of such countries 'as of' the date of his home application. The normal practice is consequently to make foreign applications by means of Convention priority, and ignore the few small countries not party to it.

As we said in Chapter 4, it is possible to avoid the trouble and expense of preparing and filing separate applications for all countries where patents are wanted by filing an 'international application' under the PCT. So the inventor must choose whether to use this route for his application rather than separate national routes.

The specification

The final specification must be filed within 12 months of the first application (assuming priority is being claimed), in any case, and unless foreign patenting is to be handled entirely by an international application, it will have to be ready long enough before then for specifications based on it to be filed at Patent Offices abroad within the 12-month period. Before the filing, the inventor should set to work to discover the secret of his own success and, when he has, should put the answer into a further specification.

It was explained in the previous chapter that for a patent to be fully effective, the distinguishing features of the 'invention' (as listed in the claims of the specification) must all be features that play a real part in the success of the new device. The system of guessing which features matter is too risky when the patent will be important: so the specification must be drawn up by someone who knows what the vital points are.

The Patent Office Examination

The applicant will not know at this stage whether his patent is going to be a satisfactory one. Indeed, he will not know this until his invention has been compared with those in earlier publications, and it usually pays in practice to leave the job of searching for these earlier documents to the examiners at the Patent Offices concerned. The claims of the specification will also be unable to take on their final form until the examiner's comments have been received. If the specification has been well drawn up the examiner may not have any serious objection to make: although he will almost certainly find something to comment upon in its wording. It does sometimes happen that his search produces nothing. This is inconvenient since it leaves the patent attorney handling the case in the dark as to what earlier documents there are. To avoid this, the draftsman will sometimes 'draw a search' by including initially a broader claim than he considers himself entitled to. Further, it may be advisable to make even the most half-hearted objection by an examiner an excuse for quite large alterations in the 'claims'; for the claims are being framed less with a view to satisfying the examiner than with a view to what a judge may say later on. It may also prove desirable sometimes to frame the specification in a way to which the examiner will object; examiners are not trained lawyers, and have a lot of work to get through, and naturally tend to prefer standard patent jargon and standard forms of claim to anything new. This is fine for doubtful inventions, since the incomprehensibility of the jargon makes it harder for the patentee's competitors to decide whether the claims mean anything or not, or are anticipated or not. A court less conditioned to the jargon may take a different view of it. Besides, sooner or later new sorts of claim become desirable: claims for important biotech inventions and suchlike. There has to be a first of such things, and any good examiner will probably notice and question it. Finally we should mention an amusing ploy used by one wily old patent attorney when he wanted to ensure that he could have a second look at the application before it was accepted – he used to include a claim to a 'Wellington Boot'. The examiner would have to object to this – and thus was prevented from just accepting the application.

If necessary, disagreements with the examiner must be disposed of by obtaining a 'hearing', that is, by going to the Patent Office and arguing the point out with one of the higher officials. If she in turn is not persuaded, it will be necessary to appeal to the Patents Court or the EPO Board of Appeals depending on which patenting route has been taken.

Amendment after Grant

The examiner's search usually uncovers a representative collection of the published documents on which later attacks on a patent might be based, while the applicants themselves will usually know what sort of thing was made and used up to the date of the application. Sometimes, however, a publication or other disclosure, which was not considered when the specification was drafted, will turn up later, and which seriously threatens the validity of the patent. Or it may turn out that something too close to the claims of the patent was publicly used, either in this country or abroad, before the date of the application – the applicants not knowing of it (or omitting to mention it to their patent attorney). The validity of the patent can then only be secured by 'amending' the specification: that is, by altering the claims so as to narrow them down until they no longer include whatever it is that has turned out to have been unpatentable. It is nearly always far better to amend as soon as the patent is found to be invalid; amendment is easier then (for it is less likely to be opposed), and fewer problems will arise afterwards. In the case of a patent whose specification was drafted without especially full investigation of the invention and its potentialities for future developments, the specification is likely to be defective anyway by reason of matters not known to the draftsman, so that amendment is worth considering as soon as the patent is found to be important enough to be worth spending money on.

Amendment of the specification post-grant requires the permission of the Patent Office or, if the patent is the subject of an action pending in the court at the time, of the court. Permission to amend is not very difficult to obtain provided the amendment complies with the law by not going too far. Thus widening the claims is not allowed (nothing can be made to infringe after amendment, if it did not before). Nor is it permissible to add new information about the invention – 'new matter', as it is called. So it is not possible, for instance, to cure by amendment a failure to give adequate instructions to carry out the invention, nor to add a new feature which was not mentioned in the specification and has since been found essential to the working of the invention. One may properly cut a claim down, to exclude something old or obvious, but it is dangerous (though sometimes useful) to try to include an explanation of the reasons for what has been done – the explanation may in itself add new matter. Furthermore, amendment of the specification may make it impossible to recover damages for infringements that took place before amendment. The result is that while the power to amend is very useful, it is a poor substitute for successful drafting of a specification in the first place.

If the patent has been granted by the EPO, then it and its sister patents in other designated countries can be amended by a single application in the EPO. Also if it is being 'opposed' in the EPO it can be amended in those proceedings. The amendment takes place 'centrally', that is to say it applies in all the countries designated in the application.

'Improvement' Patents

If a patent proves really profitable, its owner will want to go on profiting from the invention for as long as possible after his patent expires. There is a way in which a monopoly in an important invention may effectively be kept alive after the patent has come to an end, and that is by patenting large numbers of minor improvements to the original invention. Provided the patented improvements represent genuine developments, and provided they are patented with determination and persistence, by the time the original patent expires, a would-be imitator should be faced with this situation: that the article described in the original specification is too inferior to contemporary designs to be commercially saleable, while he cannot equal the newer models without risking an action for infringement of so many of the improvement patents, that he would almost certainly lose in respect of some patent or other. Even if he were to win the action on enough of the patents to let him go on manufacturing without any fundamental change in his design, the cost of fighting and losing the action as a whole would still take much of the profit out of his venture. For this reason the existence of a mass of improvement patents is often a sufficient deterrent to would-be imitators. The original manufacturer's position need not deteriorate with further lapse of time: he should always be some years ahead in design, so far as patentable improvements are concerned, while the longer he keeps the field to himself, the greater the advantage he has in manufacturing experience. His monopoly will last until some competitor comes along with the skill needed to 'design around' the more dangerous patents and the courage to fight a patent action if necessary; how long this will be will depend as usual on the importance of the market covered by the monopoly, as well as on the rate at which he continues to devise new patentable improvements. In the past, such monopolies have sometimes lasted a very long time indeed.

Where the owner of the original patent is himself the manufacturer, the patenting of improvements presents no particular difficulty. Where, however, the main patent is exploited by licensing someone else to manufacture in return for payment of a royalty on production, the patentee will find it difficult not to lose control as soon as the original patent expires. In such a case the developments on which improvement patents can be based will be made by the manufacturer, who will also have the practical experience; the new patents will naturally belong to him and the monopoly given by them will belong to him too. Sometimes the manufacturer can be persuaded to agree that the original patentee shall become the owner of the improvement patents, but such arrangements are mostly illegal under EU competition law.

It is in general very difficult for an inventor who is not actively engaged in an industry to keep any substantial control over it by means of patents. Cases do still occur from time to time of inventors making large fortunes by using their inventions to build up large manufacturing businesses, while other inventors do well enough by selling their patents to existing firms and at the same time getting important posts with those firms as consultants or designers. The inventor who makes any large sum simply by the sale or licensing of his patents seems to be very rare.

Action for Infringement or Revocation

The ultimate testing ground for a patent is the court. Generally only important patents are litigated, those of minor scope can be invented around, and unless there is a lot of money at stake, litigation will probably not be worth it for either side – they reach a business arrangement instead. The first case in which a patent is involved is vital for that patent – there is normally just one fight about the validity and scope of a patent. Normally such a fight is started by the patentee suing for infringement, the common response to which is a counterclaim for revocation. However, the potential defendant can start things off by claiming revocation – to which the patentee often responds by counterclaiming for infringement. If the patentee loses, it means either that his patent is found invalid and the grant is revoked or that the claims of the specification are declared to be too narrow to cover the articles the defendant is making. In the former case there is no longer any patent, in the latter everyone in the industry now knows how to get around it. If he wins, on the other hand, the patentee's competitors will probably respect that patent in future: there are always other things to make and sell that do not involve a patent action. Furthermore, if the patent is held valid, the patentee will receive a 'certificate of contested validity', which, while not forbidding others to challenge the validity of the patent or to claim they are not infringing it, will make it extra expensive for them if they lose. (The actual effect of a certificate is to entitle the patentee, if he wins another action on that patent, to ask for 'indemnity costs' instead of 'standard costs' for the action. 'Standard costs' are supposed to correspond to the reasonable amount it would be possible to spend in fighting the action (any doubts being resolved in favour of the paying party). 'Indemnity costs', by contrast, are far closer to the actual costs incurred by the party defending the action. The Patents Act itself refers to 'his costs or expenses as between solicitor and own client', but no one has ever claimed that it was clearly drafted.)

Delayed Actions

It was emphasised in Chapter 1 that, in most cases, if a patent action is going to be fought at all, the sooner it is started the better. Equally, there are cases where an action should not be started at all. For example, a patent of dubious validity may be of considerable commercial value, being respected by most competitors. If someone does pluck up enough courage to infringe it, it may be better to buy him off, with a licence at low rates (or even free of royalty), rather than risk suing. It may be better thus to buy off a whole series of competitors – a sort of game of sardines. If, on the other hand, the patent is probably valid, and infringers are not of great importance compared with those who respect the patent or pay royalties, it may be worth while waiting until the patent has almost expired and then cleaning up by demanding damages from infringers – rather than upsetting things by suing earlier. (In any case, where an infringer is not sued right away, consideration should be given to notifying him of the existence of the patent, to stop him pleading innocence later.) Again: suppose a competitor finds a way around the patent, and tries to patent his alternative. The immediate reaction of most businessmen is to attack his patent. Often this is the wrong reaction. The right thing to do may well be to encourage him to have his patent, to stop other rats using the same hole.

From the point of view of an intending imitator of the patented article, there is a serious risk that he may be allowed to make his imitation for several years and may then be faced with a claim for a very large sum in damages. He can bring an action before he starts manufacturing, asking the court to declare that the article he proposes to manufacture will not infringe the patent concerned. He may also ask the court to revoke the patent on the ground that it is invalid. The proceedings in either case are nearly as expensive as ordinary actions for infringement, and may be rather easier for the patentee to win, especially if there is no very precise definition of the proposed article.

6

More About Patents

What Amounts to Infringement?

The Act contains a list of the kinds of activity which amount to infringement. Most of those which amount to 'direct' infringement are what one might expect: making, selling, importing, using a patented article; working a patented process, or selling, importing or using products obtained directly therefrom. But it is also an infringement to 'keep' the article or product. This really means 'stock for commercial purposes', so a mere carrier is not liable (*Smith Kline v Harbottle*, 1980). And 'making' can involve a question of degree. Thus where a patent claim was for an ingenious cage holding and supporting a large standard plastic bottle, a party who simply replaced old bottles for new was held not be to 'making' the claimed product (*Schütz v Werit*, 2013).

There are also various forms of what is called 'indirect infringement'. Thus a supplier of a 'means relating to an essential element of an invention' for putting an invention into effect will infringe if he knows or it is obvious to a reasonable person in the circumstances that those means are suitable for putting and are intended to put, the invention into effect in the UK. A defendant who made and sold a patented potato harvester was caught in this way. The patent claim required the use of a rubber roller. What the defendant did was to sell a machine with a steel roller, and to sell a rubber roller for the farmers to replace the steel roller with. The end-users were the ones who 'made' the invention, but the defendant was still supplying the means essential (*Grimme v Scott*, 2010). There is an exception to this rule, where what is supplied is a 'staple commercial product' – and even then, it is infringement if the supplier is intended to induce the recipient to infringe.

On the other hand, there are general exceptions: for things done privately and not commercially (it is not at all clear what 'privately' means here: probably, 'privately as distinct from commercially'); for experiments with the invention; for methods of medical treatment (e.g. the making-up of individual medical prescriptions); for use by foreign ships and aircraft (which includes regular ferries for instance between England and Ireland (*Stena v Irish Ferries*, 2003). There is also a special provision protecting those who used or prepared to use the invention before the priority date of the patent: they may go on doing what they did or prepared to do before. (This last provision is necessary, because use of an invention only invalidates a subsequent patent for it if the use makes the invention public in the sense that the public can find out how to do it. Manufacturing processes may well not be made public or a product may be incapable of analysis. It is a fundamental tenet of patent law that it should not be able to prevent a person doing what they did openly before it was applied for.)

The infringing act must be carried out within the UK (or its continental shelf – added for the oil industry). However, use within the UK is read widely by the courts; for instance, an online bookmaker who had UK punters using their computers as terminals could not escape infringement by keeping his computer abroad – he was still in substance using the patented system (computer, program and terminals) within the UK (*Menashe v William Hill*, 2003).

Threats

A threat of proceedings for infringement of patent can be very worrying to the recipient. Naturally, a manufacturer who infringes, or the importer of an infringing article made abroad, should expect the patentee to say, 'If you do not stop I shall sue you.' But threats to a person's customers are another matter: they are unlikely to want to become involved, and will usually quietly stop buying his goods rather than face an action. So it is provided that anyone aggrieved by threats of an infringement action can sue for damages and for an injunction preventing further threats, 'unless the defendant . . . proves that the acts in respect of which proceedings were threatened constitute or, if done, would constitute an infringement of a patent' – and the patent is not shown to be invalid. However, even if the patent is invalid, the defendant may still get away with things if she proves that at the time of making the threats she did not know oir have reason to believe that this was the case. There are other exceptions too: where the only threat is to sue for making or importing something (or for using a patented process) or doing anything with a product so made or imported, no action lies.

Since it is very seldom possible to be certain of proving that any particular act is an infringement of a patent, or to be sure that any claim in a patent specification will not be found invalid, this provision is a dangerous trap for unwary owners of patents. On the other hand it is actually very difficult – near impossible – to get damages for unjustified threats – the problem is that it not so much the threat as the existence of the patent action which puts people off buying the goods (*Carflow v Linwood*, 1998).

Patents Protect a Trade

The essential function of a patent is to keep others out. So, in the case of a manufacturer (or importer), it is an adjunct to a trade. The value of the patent depends on how valuable that trade is – and the mere fact that others cannot compete does not guarantee the patentee a profit or anything of the sort. Whether a patent is valuable depends upon the importance of the underlying invention and how well the patentee can exploit that invention in the market place. So in a sense a manufacturer does not exploit a patent at all – he exploits the invention, relying on the patent to keep that exploitation to himself.

The Importance of Validity

Of the patents that are challenged before the courts, some are found to be invalid. Since most lawsuits about patents cost at least £100,000 per side (and generally a lot more), and the larger part of the cost falls on the loser, this is a serious matter for patent-owners. (The owner of a patent can insure against the risk of having to sue infringers, and some do.) It does not, however, follow that patents are useless; rather this is a measure of success that patents have. It is expensive to challenge the validity of a patent, even if the challenge succeeds, and it is hardly ever possible to be sure beforehand that the challenge will succeed. In the ordinary way, therefore, it is a better proposition commercially to make something unarguably outside the 'claims' of the patent, than to risk an action for infringement. As a rule, it is only the most important patents that are attacked, and even then the attacker will try to find a design that escapes at least the more impressive claims as far as possible. The great majority of patents go through their lives in peace, with nobody really convinced they are valid, but nobody prepared to take the risk of infringing them. Commercially they are just as useful as if they had been valid. Thus, even an invalid patent is often valuable enough to make it worthwhile keeping on bluffing until the bitter end. And there is a lot of truth in the old adage 'a weak patent in strong hands is worth more than a strong patent in weak hands'.

Evading Patents

By 'Designing Around'

A more serious problem is that of the competitor who avoids infringement of a patent. It is much easier to say why a particular patented device is successful, and, critically, what else would be successful, when a product using that device has been on the market for some time than it was when the specification of the patent was drawn up. So the patent attorney who makes out the specification must foresee what, up to 20 years in the future, other manufacturers are likely to want to do, and must frame his 'claims' so as to include all these future activities – while at the same time excluding anything that has been published before. (The inventor who creates a crystal ball for patent attorneys to use will make a fortune.) In practice, what he does is to estimate which features of the new product are going to be important to its success, and make the claims cover whatever combinations of those features are not present in the earlier specifications found by the examiner at the Patent Office. If he gets it right, the patent should be valid and fairly hard to 'design around'. If he gets it wrong (or some unknown piece of 'prior art' is unearthed), it will be found later on either that he has 'claimed' something only trivially different from the subject of an earlier disclosure – in which case the new patent will be invalid for obviousness – or that he has confined the monopoly to things having some feature that is not essential – in which case competitors may be able to avoid infringing the patent by omitting that particular feature. Though the courts may disregard features shown not to be practically significant, this cannot be relied upon to happen. Indeed mostly the courts say that the patentee must have regarded the feature as significant, for otherwise he would not have put it into his claim. The more and better information the client gives to the patent attorney, the better she can estimate. That is why it is important to get a good patent attorney – one who can really understand the technology, and who has the vision to frame claims which both are wide enough and can stand up. A good working relationship with one's patent attorney is a valuable asset indeed.

By Making Something 'Old'

A list of the earlier specifications considered by the Patent Office examiner when the patent was being prosecuted is published on the patent. Other possible pieces of 'prior art' may be found by employing a private searcher. One way of avoiding a patent is to go back to one of these earlier ideas and use that, or something only trivially different. The owner of a patent is then in a dilemma: if the rival product is within the 'claims' of his specification, his invention is not sufficiently different from the earlier idea and his patent must be invalid. If it is not within the claims, then there is no infringement. A defendant who says his product is old or an obvious development of what is old is said to be raising a 'Gillette' defence, named after an old case (*Gillette v Anglo-American*, 1913). There, the defendant's razor closely resembled an old razor, and the judges said there was 'no inventive step' between the defendant's and the old razors.

If the owner of the patent has made a real technical advance and his specification is skilfully drawn, his product should have a sufficient commercial advantage over earlier designs and his patent will protect that advantage. If, however, as so often happens, he is only the first to interest the public in an idea, and not the first to make it technically successful, then competition based on earlier designs may be very damaging. *Hallen v Brabantia,* 1989, is a good example of this sort of thing. The plaintiff had been the first to put the 'non-stick' material PTFE ('Teflon') onto a type of corkscrew called a 'self-puller': when you go on turning, the cork rises up out of the bottle. But self-pullers were old, and a Frenchman had put PTFE onto another type of corkscrew to help get the screw into the cork. It was obvious thereafter that PTFE would improve the 'getting-in' of any kind of corkscrew, including self-pullers. So even though the plaintiff was the first to make PTFE self-pullers commercially attractive, he had no valid monopoly in them. No system of patents can stop competition of this sort: the commercial innovator of this kind must rely upon the commercial advantages of being first, ideally a good trade mark, and helped perhaps by patents on minor features and design rights to make it impossible for rival products to look the same as his.

As ways of avoiding patents go, this method of digging up an old design is reasonably safe. It also has the advantage in theory that there is no need to do any patent search to see if what is being done is safe. Sadly, in practice things are rarely this simple. If what is now made is exactly what was made (or described) before the patent, then certainly any claim that covers it must be invalid. Nearly always, however, some alteration of the old design will be needed, if only to make it suitable for production. Then a quite different question arises, whether the changes to the old design were obvious changes to make before the date of the patent. The answer may easily be that they became obvious changes to make only when the owner of the patent had shown that there was a market for something close to the old design. But if that is so, it is possible for the patent to be both valid and infringed.

Most firms will prefer not to take this risk unless the matter is of real commercial importance, so that in the ordinary way the patent will be almost as useful to its owner as if the earlier design had never been published. As we saw in Chapter 3, the value of a patent may depend greatly on its not being too important – like a chess pawn.

Licensing

The General Principle

So far we have only considered patent monopolies as a means of keeping imitations off the market. There is another way of exploiting a patent: the grant of licences. If the patent is valid, the manufacture, importation, sale or use of a patented article (or of articles made by a patented process or machine) are each only lawful if the patentee gives permission for them. Such permission is what is known as a 'licence'. Subject to the exceptions mentioned below, a patentee can charge what he likes for the licence, and make what rules he likes for its exercise. For those who do not wish (or cannot afford) to manufacture under the patent themselves, this is the normal way of making money out of a patent.

Permission to use and sell is implied where the patentee made the product himself or licensed its making, but even so the permission may be subject to express limitations or conditions. Anyone who buys the article knowing of these conditions must either comply with them or risk being sued for infringement of the patent.

Limits on what can be done by Way of Licensing and Exploitation

Not every sort of limitation or condition, though, is allowed. First, there are the EU rules about 'free circulation' – also called 'exhaustion of rights': once a patented article has been put on the market anywhere in the EU, by the owner of the patent or with his licence, he cannot stop its subsequent sale anywhere else in the EU. This means, in particular, that although it may be allowable to restrict a licensee to manufacturing under the patent in only one EU country, the patent cannot be used to stop the things he makes being sold throughout the EU. Even a licence to manufacture in a single country only has to comply with some complex and not very comprehensible regulations in order to satisfy the EU. Next there are the limits which competition law imposes on what can be done with patents (and other IP rights). Competition law has two sources: EU (for which inter-state trade must be affected) and our own. Our own (in the Competition Act 1998) now follows EU law, though it is enough that trade within the UK may be affected. Very broadly anti-competitive agreements and abuses of monopoly are caught. A good example would be where a patentee, as a condition of a licence (or the sale of a patented product) required the buyer to purchase wholly unrelated unpatented items from him ('If you want to buy my patented running shoes you must also buy my shorts'). This area of the law is complex and often uncertain. For a really important patent, a refusal to licence on reasonable terms may amount to an abuse of monopoly. Some violations of the EU competition licensing rules may each give a defence to what would otherwise be an infringement of a valid patent (*Intel v Via*, 2002). The EU Competition authorities are currently pursuing a case against Samsung and Motorola, saying that even to ask for an injunction in respect of a patent which has been declared essential for mobile telephones is an abuse of monopoly. That may be going too far for it does not follow that an injunction will be granted unless the patentee has made a fair offer of a licence and the defendant has refused it.

Compulsory Licensing

The owner of a patent ought to make use of his invention if he can; certainly he ought not to use his patent to prevent all use of his invention. In the hope of preventing such misuse of patents, provisions of one sort or another have for many years been inserted in the Patents Acts; in particular there have been provisions by which anyone who wants to use an invention and can show that the patents covering it are being misused in certain ways can apply to the Patent Office for a compulsory licence, enabling him to use those patents upon payment of a proper royalty. The application cannot be made for three years after the patent has been granted. Compulsory licence provisions have never proved effective, and the present ones are hardly ever used.

Patents are not in practice used for suppressing new ideas: the difficulty with anything really new is to get anyone to take it up. Stories about patents for everlasting lightbulbs or petrol engines which work on a mixture of water and petrol, and the like, being bought up by existing manufacturers to protect their existing business, are apocryphal. The few applications for compulsory licences that are made are not concerned with inventions that have been suppressed, but with inventions that have already proved profitable – where the patentee wants to keep the profit to himself and the licensee wants a slice.

Supplementary Protection Certificates ('SPCs')

Most of the life of a patent for a medicine or agrochemical may be exhausted before the safety authorities give permission to market. So the patentee may have spent a small fortune yet have very little monopoly period to recover his costs and make a profit. To deal with this problem there is an EU Regulation and scheme. Under this, a certificate can be obtained which extends protection for a patented medicine or agrochemical (the one actually sold, not everything covered by the original patent) for up to five years from normal expiry of the patent. The amount of extension is the period between application for the patent and first permission to market anywhere in the EU less five years. Although the rules for the grant of SPCs were meant to be simple, they are not (partly because those who wrote the SPC Regulation seemed to know little about either patents or regulatory rules) and there have been and continue to be lots of references to the CJEU about them.

Taxation and Patents

Patents are subject to special rules as to tax. As one might expect, the costs of inventing and patenting an invention are normally regarded as deductible expenses when computing profits. Royalties are not allowable as business expenses of a manufacturer who pays them (so that they have to be paid out of taxed profits, if he has any profits to tax); instead, whoever pays the royalty out of taxed income should deduct tax before paying and may then keep it. (If he had no profits (i.e. no taxed income) to pay the royalties out of, he must deduct the tax and hand it over to the Revenue.) Furthermore, capital sums paid for patents and patent licences (but not sums paid for know-how) are treated as income of the seller spread over a six-year period; this being balanced by allowing the purchaser annual allowances on what he has paid. (This is not quite as hard on inventors as it seems; for a professional inventor must reckon the proceeds of sale of patents as income anyway. It is hard on purely amateur inventors, but they have too few votes to matter.) The position of foreign patentees needs watching here: they naturally tend to demand that a British licensee agree to pay royalties (and even more, capital sums) free of tax. There are agreements in force with most foreign countries under which a foreigner can get payment in full (in the case of royalties, the payer is compensated for the tax he would otherwise have deducted and kept); but the foreign patentee has to make the request, and licence agreements ought to be specially framed accordingly. VAT is payable on most patent related transactions, e.g. royalties. On a brighter note there is no stamp duty on IP transactions.

Coming into force as we write is the so-called 'patent box'. The general idea of this is to reduce corporation tax to 10 per cent of the profits made from patented inventions, where those inventions were made by the taxpayer. The notion is that this will encourage research: you cannot get the benefit unless you played a significant part in the research leading to the invention. There are lots of complications (e.g. to allow for research by a group company). Quite how it will all work out remains speculative. One likely consequence will be that companies may apply for patents of minor scope just to get the benefit of the box – and of course the Inland Revenue will not be able readily (or at all) to assess the quality or scope of any patent claimed by the taxpayer to justify the reduced rate.

Drugs, Similar Chemical Compounds, and Genetic Engineering

Problems

The effective patenting of newly invented drugs and the like presents special difficulties. The fundamental problem is this. If the drug concerned is an entirely new chemical, its discoverer will be entitled to patent it; but because it is entirely new, he will be unable to tell what related substances will be so similar in their effects as to be just as good. If he attempts to guess what other substances will work, he may well guess hopelessly wrong; if he confines himself to those he really knows about, his competitors (who have been told by his success what sort of thing to look for) will be able to market some related substance not covered by him. The preparation and trial of any new drug is a long job, and even the biggest research laboratories can try out only a few likely compounds at a time. To a certain extent the difficulty can be overcome by the power of amendment, but this is seldom a completely satisfactory answer. The inventor's main safeguard is the cost of testing and marketing a related substance; but if the drug is profitable enough, that may be worth doing.

Even worse difficulties face the man who discovers how to prepare a substance that already exists in nature (a vitamin, for instance, or something like penicillin); for there are bound to be other ways of doing the job that he cannot cover. Further, the man who discovers a new and valuable property of an old substance must be very clever to get any sort of patent at all, even to cover the stuff as sold. What he does, for instance, is to claim 'a pharmaceutical dosage form' containing the old compound. And he is allowed to have a claim in the form of 'X [the old substance] for the treatment of A [a disease for which X has not been used before]'. The EPC fictionally treats 'X for a new purpose' as new even though X is old. Similar dodges can be devised for other types of invention. He should also be able to get a patent to cover a process of using the stuff (not, though, use in medicine); but collection of royalties or finding out about infringements may be very difficult.

It might be thought that such inventions were particularly valuable and need to be especially encouraged; but some people (a sort of alliance of competition lawyers, some economists and cheap medicine campaigners) advocate restricting such patents, rather than with encouraging them. The reality is that there is a strong emotional reaction amongst many who ought to know better against patents for new medicines. The stronger their voices the more patent law may be restricted, and the less likely is it that new medicines and better forms of old ones will be found.

'Selection' Patents

There is a special sort of invention that turns up fairly often in the field of chemistry, and leads to what are called 'selection patents'. When a new and valuable chemical compound is discovered – a new drug, perhaps, or a new sort of dyestuff – it will usually at once be apparent to a skilled chemist that innumerable other closely related compounds may be as good or better. But there is usually still room for invention in making those compounds, one by one, and finding out which really are as good or better; and even more room for invention in seeing without making them all others which will be as good or better. This picking-out of the useful ones, from a large class which is already known in general terms, is known as 'selection', though the word has no technical meaning in patent law. In practice, if an inventor finds a compound which is better or different from the earlier, known, large class, he will get a valid patent (e.g. in *Dr Reddy v Eli Lilly*, 2009, a claim to a specific compound was held to be valid against a general disclosure of a class of 1019 compounds which included the one in question).

Genetic Engineering Patents

When recombinant DNA techniques were first developed in the late 1970s it became possible to identify particular genes or the DNA codes and structures of viruses. Much speculative money went into 'biotech' companies, which scrambled to find these in the hope of obtaining valuable patents. And by and large, quite a number of such patents have been granted. One can take the view that any new information, even if obtained by routine techniques, can be the basis of a patent (as in the US where any new isolated gene stretch of DNA has been considered patentable). Or one can be stricter and require that the technique used has some novel and unexpected twist to it. Broadly that is the position in Europe. And in either case there is only a minimal requirement that the patentee not only identifies a gene, but also must say what it is for, before he can have a patent – although here, even an educated guess will do (*Human Genome Sciences*, 2011). Genetic engineering patents create great controversy, not only of a purely emotional kind ('How can you patent life?'; 'Such patents are monopolies over God's creation', etc.) but also of a more practical kind, in that they are apt to give the patentee a total monopoly over anything to do with the gene, whether by way of research, diagnosis or even treatment. Currently, for instance, one company claims that by virtue of its patents it has a monopoly on tests for certain types of breast cancer. And of course there is no way of 'designing around' this sort of patent.

Rights in New Forms of Plants

There is an ongoing case before the EPO Enlarged Board about whether ordinary patents can be granted for new and inventive forms of plant (Case G2/12 – tomatoes). Not surprisingly there is some heated controversy about this. However there is a separate system for protection of 'plant breeder's rights'. It works a bit like patents but the procedure for obtaining them is separate from the patents system. The Plant Varieties Act 1997 is the basic legislation through which plant breeders' rights are administered, and there is a special Plant Variety Rights Office.

For a variety to be protected it must be new, distinct, uniform and stable. By 'new' is meant 'not previously commercialised'. The Plant Variety Rights Office, part of the Food and Environment Research Agency, examines applications for plant variety rights, and will only allow them to be granted in respect of those varieties for which a special scheme has been made for the relevant genus or species to which the variety belongs. There are different periods of protection for different species (ranging from 25 to 30 years), and all are subject to periodic renewal within this time.

The plant breeders' right prevents others from commercial use of the protected plant variety for production or reproduction, sale or offering for sale, conditioning for the purpose of propagation, exporting or importing, or stocking for any of the foregoing purposes. There are specific exceptions for private and non-commercial use, experimental use and use for the purpose of breeding another variety. There are also express provisions allowing farmers to use farm-saved seed for the payment of a 'fair fee', which should be lower than the royalty charged on the sale of the certified seed. Compulsory licences are available to prevent abuses of monopoly, and special provisions govern the names of new varieties. A parallel Community Plant Variety Rights (CPVR) scheme exists that covers the entire EU. The CPVR and the UK Plant Breeders' Right are mutually exclusive and cannot be held simultaneously.

The Government's Right to Work Patented Inventions

Any government department may use, or authorise others to use, any patented invention 'for the services of the Crown'. Mostly, this means for the armed forces – although some drugs for British hospitals were procured under these powers in the 1960s. The patent-owner is entitled to compensation for any use in this way, but he cannot prevent that use. If the invention was one that any government department knew about (otherwise than because its owner told them about it in confidence) before the patent was applied for, this does not of itself make the patent invalid, but it disentitles the owner to compensation for any government use.

Surplus patented articles, originally made for government use, may be freely sold. So may articles confiscated by the Customs and Excise. So may medical supplies. During a war and for war purposes, or for national purposes during a period of emergency, or in respect of inventions concerned with atomic energy, government departments may authorise anyone to sell such articles, whether originally made for government use or not – subject to the usual rights to compensation. The Government may also have weapons and munitions made here for allies, or the UN, and sell them to the government or organisation concerned. Except in these cases the Government has no right to authorise the sale of such articles without permission from the patent-owner.

If the patent-owner has licensed a firm also authorised by the Government to use an invention, the royalties fixed by the licence need not be paid so far as government use is concerned. Such a licensee may still be liable to make some payments to the owner: guaranteed minimum royalties, for instance (*No-Nail Cases v No-Nail Boxes*, 1946). In general, however, the owner must rely on his right to demand compensation from the Crown. The amount of compensation, if it cannot be agreed, will normally be settled by referring the whole matter to the High Court. The Crown is supposed to let inventors know that it is using their patents, but it tends not to (especially, but not only, where military secrets are involved). One of the inventor's main problems tends to be finding out what use, if any, is being made of his invention. The problem is at least in part caused by the fact that it is the Crown which is first supposed to decide whether it is using an invention. It will not 'own up', even where it knows of the patent, if it decides the scope of the patent does not cover what is being done or that the patent is invalid. Naturally the patentee might take a different view, but he does not get the chance to complain unless he finds out some other way.

There are similar provisions allowing Crown use of registered designs and design rights, though in practice this will not matter much.

Keeping Inventions Secret for Security Reasons

There are special provisions about patents containing information which relates to national security and which, if published, might be prejudicial to that security. If an application is made to patent such an invention, and if and for so long as the Secretary of State (really the appropriate service department) considers that it ought to be kept secret, the application for a patent will not be published. In addition, although it will be examined, it will not proceed to grant. Similar provisions apply to designs (but whoever heard of or even imagined a design prejudicial to national security!) and similar provisions apply to all inventions involving atomic energy, whether of military character or not. Military inventions that the armed forces think good enough to use are precisely the ones they will want to keep secret. So the provisions giving inventors the right to be compensated for Crown use applies in such cases as if the patent were granted in the ordinary way. In addition, the Crown can, if it likes, compensate the inventor for the damage the secrecy does to him.

It would of course be useless to keep such inventions secret here if they were published abroad. So it is made a crime for anyone resident in the UK to apply for a foreign patent if the application contains information which relates to military technology or might be prejudicial to national security, unless an application has first been filed here and six weeks have then elapsed without any direction being made that the invention should be kept secret. This is all very well in theory, but since people can apply direct to the EPO or foreign countries, it is essentially academic. The prospect of a criminal prosecution for breach of this rule seems pretty remote.

7

Industrial Designs

Introduction

For many years, our law has included protection for industrial 'designs'. Originally the general idea was to protect the artistic element in mass-produced articles (shape or applied decoration or the like). The main mechanism for protection was supposed to be by a system of designs registered at the Patent Office – like a patent for an invention. But over the years, both Parliament and the courts managed to produce a convoluted system as a result of the interaction between the law of registered designs and that of ordinary copyright. The problem arose because ordinary copyright in drawings could be infringed by indirectly copying an article made from them. This is easy enough to understand where a truly artistic drawing is concerned (e.g. of 'Popeye', *King Features Syndicate v Kleeman*, 1942) but seems odd in the case of purely mechanical items, such as an exhaust pipe. The whole business got out of hand: not only was the law complicated, it was unsafe to make things which were copies of, or based upon, really quite old articles. For instance Lego were using (successfully, until final appeal) copyright to maintain a monopoly in their system, even though the basic brick was designed (actually by an Englishman, who was originally copied by Lego) in the 1940s. Absurd arguments as to eye appeal or otherwise of a Lego brick were deployed in all seriousness (*Interlego v Tyco*, 1989). In the case of spare parts (exhaust pipes) it took the House of Lords to say: never mind ordinary copyright, you are allowed to make them (*Leyland v Armstrong*, 1984).

So in 1988 Parliament tried to sort things out. It created two systems for design protection: one in registered designs and another (lesser system) for unregistered designs, the right in which arose automatically without the need for registration. It was pretty complicated in detail. Now the EU has added its half-euroworth, too. Pursuant to the Designs Directive, the UK expanded its registered designs law so that it corresponds with the new EU approach. In addition, the EU has introduced its own, EU-wide, system of registered designs. From April 2003 it has been possible to register these at the Office for Harmonization of the Internal Market (OHIM) in Alicante, Spain. On top of that the EU has created an EU unregistered design right, which arises automatically. Finally there is scope for ordinary copyright to play a part – a part which, as of writing, seems destined to grow further in future months – see below. On top of that, some designs can be registered as trade marks or protected by passing off.

The upshot of all this is that things are pretty complex – four different sorts of right especially for designs, or five if you include ordinary copyright, or seven if you also include registered trade marks and passing off. No one could, or does, call it rational – but no one seems to be in a position to simplify things either. Broadly, however, the position may be rather simpler than it seems – it is unsafe to copy anything that has come on the market within the last 10 years. If you do, then you are likely to fall foul of an unregistered design right. Even simple things, such a rectangular floppy case for a flat folding umbrella, can be the subject of such a right (*Fulton v Totes*, 2003). And the sensible thing to do, even if you have not, or your supplier has not, copied, is to check whether an article you make or import bears a resemblance to a design registered either in the UK or at OHIM. A good patent attorney can organise this for you.

UK and EU Registered Designs

Almost anything visual can be a design which is registrable: 'the appearance of the whole or a part of a product resulting from the features of, in particular, the lines, contours, colours, shape, texture or materials of a product or its ornamentation'. It is the design, as applied to any product, which is protected. And 'product' is widely defined too, covering even such things as 'graphic symbols', whatever that may mean (probably computer icons, for instance – or graphic trade marks). A design can be registered at the UK IPO (for a UK design right) or at OHIM in Alicante (for an EU design right). It must be new (i.e. not the same as any design which has already been made available to the public) and have 'individual character' (i.e. the overall impression it produces on an informed user of the design must differ from the overall impression produced on such a user by any design which has already been made available to the public). In assessing individual character the freedom of the designer in creating the design is taken into account. 'Made available to the public' does not have the clear, brightline, meaning it has in patent law. For the latter it is enough if one person has the prior information and is entirely free to use it – that is why blurting out your invention before you have applied for the patent will prevent it being novel. But for design law, a prior disclosure is not regarded as making the disclosure 'available to the public' 'if it could not reasonably have become known in the normal course of business to persons carrying on business in the EU and specialising in the sector concerned'. This is dreadfully vague – and particularly odd, given that for infringement there is no 'sector concerned'. The CJEU will have its work cut out trying to make sense of this. Moreover there is a 'grace period' – a disclosure by the designer himself or with his consent does not count, if he applies for registration with one year of his disclosure. This means he can test his product in the market first – only applying for registration if it seems successful enough for others to want to copy. Apart from the question of novelty, there are certain other specific exclusions from registrability – components of a complex product which are not visible in normal use of the complex product, features of appearance 'solely dictated by the product's technical function', and 'must fit' or 'must match' features of designs are the most important. Again, these are vague concepts, bound to lead to litigation. Under our old law, for instance, 'appearance dictated solely by function' had to go the House of Lords (*Amp v Utilux*, 1972). The same battle will have to be fought all over again, with what result remains to be seen.

Registration gives a true monopoly so, unlike copyright or unregistered design right, a defendant infringes if he makes or deals in a product having a 'design which does not produce on the informed user a different overall impression' from that of the registered design, degrees of freedom of design again being taken into account. But, as always, it helps if the defendant copied. The significance of registration could be very great for a successful design. You get up to a 25-year monopoly in your design (upon paying renewal fees). For something like a classic furniture design, that could be very important. (Do not ask us why registered designs get 25 years whereas patents only get 20 – it is one of life's little mysteries.)

Registering a design involves much less effort (and cost) than a patent. Normally some good photographs (from all angles) of a prototype three-D design are all that is needed. Two-D designs (e.g. a wallpaper or textile) would only need a sample. The biggest defect of the domestic system used to be that it took a while (about six months) for the registration to come through; and in the case of certain fields, such as some toys, the craze would have been over before protection was obtained. Nevertheless, things have become a lot faster in recent years. The UK IPO now works on the basis that a design will usually be registered within two months of application. OHIM is potentially even quicker, and often grants registration on the same day as you apply. In any case, this sort of design (i.e. one that could be registered) will be protected by the EU unregistered design right immediately upon creation – see below. Official fees for a UK design application start from £60 for a single design; for an EU registration the fee is higher (€350), but you do get coverage in 28 states. In both cases an attorney, if one is used, will have further fees (perhaps £500), and will obviously have to charge more if he has to prepare the drawings; however, good photographs will generally do. It is possible in simple cases to make the application without an attorney, but, unless the applicant makes regular applications and knows what to do, it often is best to use one: there are some bureaucratic technicalities, such as something called the seven representation rule, that only confuse the unwary.

Another advantage of the design registration system is that it can be used to claim priority in other countries (the applications abroad have to be made within six months, rather than a year as in the case of patents). The international protection of designs will probably grow with the increasing trans-border nature of goods and markets. At present, most other countries have design registration schemes, though the variation from country to country is quite marked; noticeably more so than in the case of patents.

The principal difference between an EU and a UK registered design is that the former gives EU-wide rights. As in the case of EU trade marks (see below), the system of enforcement is by courts designated as Community Design courts – for England and Wales, these are the Patents Court and Patents County Court. Third parties are able to apply to OHIM for declarations of invalidity of community design registrations. As in the case of EU trade marks, there are Boards of Appeal, from which appeals can go on to the General Court of the EU, and on a point of law on to the CJEU itself.

In the last edition we forecast that as the new system takes effect, the uncertainty of the law and the complex and uncertain litigation system, will lead to much work for lawyers and much cost for industry. Thus far, there has been less litigation than we expected. We have had only a few cases reach the Court of Appeal, and only one case of note has reached the CJEU, *Pepsico v Grupo Promer*, 2011. This case is important, deciding that the scope of protection of a registered design is comparatively narrow. The test set out in the Regulation is whether the alleged infringement produces a different overall impression on the 'informed observer'. The Court held that this notional person 'knows the various designs which exist in the sector concerned, possesses a certain degree of knowledge with regard to the features which those designs normally include, and, as a result of his interest in the products concerned, shows a relatively high degree of attention when he uses them'. And when he makes the comparison he will make 'a direct comparison between the designs at issue'. This means that, normally at least, a merely general resemblance between the design and the accused design will not be enough. English cases to the same effect are *P&G v Reckitt*, 2007 (toilet airfresheners) and *Apple v Samsung*, 2012 (tablet computers: note that the Apple registered design sued upon was not the same as the actual iPad).

UK Unregistered Design Right ('UDR')

This is essentially a right born of frustration. It started in 1988 as a way of replacing the over-powerful protection which was given by ordinary copyright to functional designs (then life plus 50 years of protection). It only protects against copying, and has a limited term as compared with a registered design. A designer is automatically given a UDR in 'any aspect of shape on configuration' (internal or external) of the whole on any part of an article. The design must be original (in the copyright sense of being the designer's own work, not copied), and must additionally be 'not commonplace in the design field in question' – a fuzzy notion, which the courts have had some difficulty in dealing with. In *Farmers Build v Carrier*, 1999, the court said it should be construed narrowly and that a comparative exercise to find out how similar the design is to those of other similar articles is involved. And in *Lambretta v Teddy Smith*, 2004, the court said that 'design field in question' covers the sort of designs with which a notional designer of the article concerned would be familiar. Both of these explanations are a bit helpful but hardly precise – blame the legislator, not the courts.

Designs must also have been recorded in a design document or a physical article. There are special modifications (both as to the extent of the night and the nationality of origin) in relation to design rights in the topography of semiconductor products, following our implementation of an EU directive on the subject. There are exceptions to UDR: none can exist in a method or principle of construction, or in a design which must fit some other article (e.g. a spare part), or must match some other article so as to form an integral whole (e.g. a body panel), or in a surface decoration.

The UDR is extremely powerful and pervasive. Almost any piece of design work will give rise to one. But a UDR only lasts, at best, for 15 years from the end of the year when the design was first made. Earlier expiry occurs if the first marketing of the design takes place in the first five years of its life. Then expiry is at the end of the 10th year in which first marketing occurred. So in practice all a designer can get is 10 years from first marketing; he is unlikely to be copied before then in any event, and his protection is cut down even more because, after five years from first marketing by the designer, his rivals can obtain a compulsory licence. So there may be quite a few cases where, when the copying starts a few years after first marketing, it will be doubtful whether a case could be brought to trial before the end of the five-year period during which an injunction can be had. In such cases the crucial question will often be: can the designer obtain an interim injunction meanwhile?

In practice, UDR is valuable to protect against slavish imitations early in the life of a product. So it helps in fast-changing fashion trades, such as toys and garments. It also gives initial protection to a designer who has applied for registration of his design but is still waiting for grant. UDR cannot be used as a basis for claiming priority for foreign applications. Indeed unless a foreign country (outside the EU) recognises a similar right, their nationals are not entitled to UDRs here.

It will obviously be important to keep drawings and prototypes for future enforcement. A well-advised design based company would have a standard procedure for this, and for ensuring that the employment records of the design employees (and assignments from outside designers) are kept.

EU UDR

This is based on the British idea – again, protecting only against copying for a limited term – but in this case only three years from when it was first made available (in the design sense) in the EU. The definition of infringement is not the same as for a British UDR, on its face at least being confined to making or dealings in products 'in which the design is incorporated or to which it is applied.' The British definition covers the use of 'any aspect' of a design or part of a design, which is really rather wide; see *Fulton v Totes*, 2003. The practical distinction between the two, however, may well be narrower than it seems – the CJEU is well capable of saying that the definition of infringement is of practically the same scope.

But in other respects the EU UDR is wider than a British UDR. Thus a British UDR does not extend to just the choice of colours of the panels of an old design of garment (*Lambretta v Teddy Smith*, 2004) whereas an EU UDR would do so.

Ordinary Copyright

Up to now, the scope for protection under copyright of industrial designs for most artefacts has been limited. It is not an infringement to make a three-D article directly or indirectly from copyright design drawings or models, provided that the design or model is not for an artistic work (e.g. a sculpture, work of artistic craftsmanship, etc.). As of the time of writing, works for surface decoration, all two-D designs, such as fabric designs, and works which are designs for artistic works (e.g. drawings for a sculpture on a sculpture itself), may be copied in three-D after 25 years from the first industrialisation of the work. Prior to then, it will be an infringement to copy. So, if the copyright drawing is for making an exhaust pipe, then you can copy at once (subject, of courses, to UDR), but if the drawing is for a textile design or for a sculpture, or is of a cartoon character, then you must currently wait 25 years to do so. However, this is all about to change, as a Bill has just passed through Parliament which removes the 25-year limit of protection for such industrially exploited designs – putting it up to the usual copyright period of life of author plus 70 years. The Government seems to think it has got to do this to comply with EU law as a result of a CJEU case, *Flos v Semararo*, 2011. It is probably wrong about this, but the wheels are now in motion.

Use of other Rights to Protect Designs

Some designs can be protected in other ways: for instance, a design may in some cases also be a trade mark, e.g. the back of a playing card (*US Playing Card's Appn*, 1907) or the scheme of coloration of medicinal capsules (*Smith Kline & French*, 1976). However, the courts are careful to prevent these other forms of protection (which may be perpetual) from straying too far into the field of designs proper, so, for example, the shape of the Philips razor was not registrable as a trade mark (see later chapters). Similarly, plaintiffs sometimes try to use a passing off action to protect a design, but generally fail. An example of this is *British American Glass v Winton*, 1962, where the plaintiff failed to protect the design of his glass animals by passing off, because he could not show that the customers cared which make of glass animal they were buying and so were not cheated. On the other hand in the *Jif Lemon* case (*Reckitt v Borden,* 1991) the plaintiff successfully stopped a rival plastic lemon containing lemon juice precisely because it did prove that a substantial number of customers did care about the maker, and would be deceived by the defendant's lemon.

Part III

Trade Marks, Passing Off and Unfair Competition

8

Trade Marks and Passing Off

Introduction

Most European countries have some sort of general rule of law forbidding unfair competition. The United Kingdom does not: but most of the activities that such a rule would discourage run contrary to specific rules of English law.

In particular, English law has rules – some of them judge-made, but a large part from statute – which prevent the filching of a competitor's trade by misleading conduct. As we shall see, these have expanded quite significantly in the last 20 years so as to prevent various kinds of competition which are stigmatised as unfair; even, in many cases where it does not mislead the public.

The judge-made rules have existed for many years and have been adapted to meet modern conditions. Their original object was largely to protect the so-called 'goodwill' of a business. It is difficult to define goodwill, but it has famously been said to be the 'attractive force which brings in custom' (*IRC v Muller*, 1901). It can be thought of as the reputation that a business enjoys as a result of having actually traded using a particular name and therefore having become known by the public. In order to protect this goodwill, the law forbids any trader from so conducting his trade as to mislead customers into mistaking his goods or business for someone else's.

This sort of deception is known as 'passing off'; anyone who suffers financial loss as a result of it is entitled to bring an action in the courts, claiming compensation for the loss, and asking for an injunction against continuance of the deception. Its nineteenth-century origins lie in the tort of 'deceit'. It makes no difference whether it is other traders or the general public that are deceived; nor whether the deception is fraudulent or merely mistaken or accidental; not how it is brought about. Passing off does not extend to non-deceptive encroachments upon a business: it is not passing off to say honestly 'my cola is as good as Coca-Cola but half the price'. Nevertheless, where there is deception, passing off can be a powerful and effective remedy.

Passing Off and Registration of Trade Marks

However, the problem with passing off is that it relies on a claimant showing that it has actually traded using a mark and as a result has built up a sufficient goodwill. It also relies on showing that the conduct of a rival is deceptive (we discuss later how much trade and what kind of deception must arise for the law to intervene). This makes it a potentially cumbersome tool in practice, and of more limited utility for several reasons.

First, if a business has just started up or has not started trading at all, it may not have established enough goodwill to stop a rival from adopting the same or a similar mark. In an action for passing off, the plaintiff must in practice prove that he has sufficiently extensive goodwill for his goods or services to be recognised by members of the public; otherwise it will hardly be possible for people to be deceived when they come across similar goods or services put out by the defendants. It follows that the law of passing off will protect established businesses from imitation of their names or trade marks, but will not provide a shield behind which a new goodwill can be built up.

Second, proving cases of passing off, except in obvious situations where a defendant is using the same mark plainly to steal a claimant's business is not always easy. Cases depend heavily on the evidence and can turn on finding sufficient numbers of actual customers who were confused (see e.g. *Chelsea Man v Chelsea Girl,* 1987 where customers of the claimant came to court, and *Neutrogena,* 1996, where a number of deceived customers were located via various sorts of opinion poll).

Third, because it is not necessary to show that a defendant intended to pass off, a trader can be taken by surprise by someone else asserting prior rights to a mark.

So, for over 100 years, there has been a system of trade mark registration: in fact, there is now more than one. Undertakings can apply for trade marks at both the UK and EU level (the latter effective throughout the EU). If and when granted, these marks are then recorded in public registers. Registration gives rights which, by and large, are more powerful than the rights given by passing off, and the costs of obtaining registration are modest.

Registration generally makes it much easier for a claimant to prevent the sort of deception which involves imitation of trade marks or brand names. However, this is not always so. First, registration of a mark is not always possible because, as might be expected, there are some policy and practical limits placed on the type of things that may be registered (see Chapter 9). Second, and partly as a result of the fact that it is now easier to register a trade mark, enforcement in some cases has become more difficult and uncertain. Nevertheless, it remains the case that traders are well advised to obtain full registration of all their trade marks, since it will generally make legal disputes over trade marks and brand names simpler and cheaper to resolve. Perhaps even more important than that, it will generally warn rivals off altogether – why look for trouble when you are considering what mark to use? Things are different once a business is committed – it may feel it has to stand and fight.

Critically, therefore, it is normally possible to register a mark before there has been any use of it at all (the exception is in the case of very descriptive marks – see later). Since registration gives almost an absolute right to stop others from using that mark or a mark like it, goodwill can be built up behind the shield of protection given by a registered mark. That is why prudent businesses register (or at least seek registration) before starting use. Even if unused, it is in practice virtually impossible to remove a mark from the register for at least five years. The natural consequence of this, particularly in the last 10–15 years, is that trade mark registers, especially at EU level, have become clogged with huge numbers of marks, often making it difficult for rival traders to find marks suitable for use.

What does Passing Off do that Registration of Marks Cannot?

It may be questioned why, if registering a trade mark carries so many benefits, does anyone sue for passing off? There are several reasons.

First, many businesses do not keep their trade marks fully registered, so that resort to a passing off action may be necessary to cover flaws in their trade mark position. Second, passing off can occur in cases that have nothing at all to do with trade marks: e.g. by the marketing of goods whose get-up is the same (in everything but the wording on the package) as that of an old-established line; in cases of reverse passing off (see later); celebrity endorsement; and so on. Thirdly, the fact that enforcement of registered trade marks has become more difficult and uncertain, means that a claim to passing off may be included in proceedings as a back-up in the event that the case on the trade mark infringement fails.

And there is one particularly overriding reason for suing in passing off where this is possible – judges are very apt to stop anyone who is actually doing something deceptive. The converse is also likely to be true – mere technical infringements of a registered mark do not invoke judicial sympathy in the same way, and so judges are apt only to stop clear cases.

Kinds of Registered Trade Marks

Readers who have persevered this far will not be surprised to learn that this area of law, like patents, has increased in complexity as a result of EU action. There are two types of registered mark enforceable in the UK: the UK national registered mark (obtained from the UK Trade Mark Registry under the provisions of the Trade Marks Act 1994); and the Community registered trade mark ('CTM') (obtained from OHIM under the provisions of the Community Trade Mark Regulation). The CTM can also be enforced in the other EU countries. For most purposes, the substantive law relating to UK marks and CTMs is the same. This is because the Trade Marks Act 1994 is itself based on European legislation, namely the European Trade Mark Directive, which tracks the Community Trade Mark Regulation very closely. For this reason, the UK must take into account decisions of the CJEU on the Directive and the Regulation. Many of the cases referred to in the following chapters are decisions of that court.

A claimant who sues on a UK or a Community trade mark must satisfy one of three different tests, depending on the relevant facts. Which test applies is crucial, since it will affect how easy it is for the claimant to win. If the mark used by the defendant is identical to the claimant's registered mark and is being used by the defendant for identical goods or services to those for which the claimant has registered his mark, then the case is straightforward. To succeed, the claimant only has to prove that the marks are identical and that the goods or services are identical (assuming that the trade mark is valid and that no relevant exception applies – these issues are discussed in Chapters 11). It is in this situation (identical mark/ identical goods or services) that it is a major advantage to the claimant to have a registered trade mark, since there is no need for him to prove that he has sufficiently extensive goodwill to be recognised by the public, or that the public has been deceived, as there would be in a passing off case.

If, on the other hand, the defendant only uses a similar mark, or uses an identical mark but only for similar goods or services (or both), the test the claimant must meet is more onerous. He must prove that, because of the similarity of the marks or the goods or services, there is a likelihood of confusion. This is rather like the requirement to prove deception in a passing off case and so can make the case much more complicated. The test goes further than passing off in one respect: the claimant does not actually have to prove he has a goodwill – his mark is taken to be in use, and to have a goodwill (*Reed v Reed*, 2004).

Finally, if the facts are that the defendant is using a sign which is identical or similar to the claimant's registered mark in relation to goods or services which are identical, similar or dissimilar to those for which the mark is registered, the claimant can still succeed in a case for infringement if he can prove two things. First, that his trade mark has a reputation (again this is very similar to the requirement in passing off). Secondly, that the defendant's use of the mark, 'being without due cause, takes unfair advantage of, or is detrimental to, the distinctive character or the repute of the trade mark'. Despite attempts at clarification by the CJEU, exactly what is required for this aspect of infringement is still uncertain. The matter is discussed further in Chapter 10.

Trade Mark Conflicts

Where a potential plaintiff has a registered trade mark and the potential defendant uses a mark that is identical to the plaintiff's mark for goods or services identical to those for which it is registered, the case is usually clear. A complaint by the potential plaintiff will usually result in the potential defendant stopping the offending activity, which is very likely to have been inadvertent. It is relatively easy for a trader contemplating using a new mark to check the trade marks register (this can now be done with a fairly high degree of accuracy online, at http://www. ipo.gov.uk and http://oami.europa.eu) to find out whether it can be safely used or not. Having a patent or trade mark attorney or solicitor do a trade mark search or, at the very least, doing one yourself online, is obviously the best way to avoid disputes.

Litigation is much more likely to arise where there is no registered trade mark (and the potential claimant therefore relies on passing off), or where there is a registered trade mark but the potential defendant is not using an identical mark, or is using an identical mark but only for similar or dissimilar goods or services. In this situation, the difficulties in proving the case are likely to mean that the outcome will not be certain for either side. And, unless there is a plain case of passing off, the uncertainties of the law caused by a failure of the legislation to address most if not all of the basic problems of trade marks, coupled with appalling drafting, further encourages litigation. The CJEU, which is regularly called upon to clarify matters, has not always succeeded in doing so, and on some occasions has made matters worse.

9

Trade Mark Registration

Introduction

Here we explain what sort of thing can be registered as a trade mark, discuss the conditions required, and give an outline of the procedure for both registration and opposition. It must not be forgotten that registration is not the be all and end all of a mark's existence. A mark which has been registered can, at a later date, be revoked or invalidated, which we describe in Chapter 12.

What Kind of Sign can be Registered?

The types of things which can be registered as trade marks were much expanded by the Trade Marks Act 1994 and the Community Trade Mark Regulation.

In addition to the obvious things such as words, logos and pictures, it is now possible, in principle, to register three-dimensional shapes, e.g. the shape of the Coca-Cola bottle for non-alcoholic beverages; colours, e.g. the colour orange Pantone 151, being the predominant colour applied to the visible surface of packaging and/or advertising and promotional materials for certain telephone handsets etc. (*Libertel*, 2003), or a particular shade of purple for chocolate (*Cadbury's*, 2012); combinations of colours (*Heidelberger Bauchemie*, 2004); and sounds, e.g. the Direct Line jingle or 'Für Elise', the latter held registrable for various services, by the ECJ in *Shield Mark v Memex*, 2003.

The only limit is that the mark must be capable of being represented graphically and must be identified precisely. On this basis it is currently impossible to register signs consisting of smells. The ECJ (as it then was) decided, in relation to a 'balsamically fruity scent with a slight hint of cinnamon' that the requirements of graphic representability are not satisfied by a chemical formula, by a description in written words, by the deposit of an odour sample or by a combination of those elements (*Sieckmann*, 2002).

Of course, just because a sign is the type of thing capable of being registered does not mean it necessarily will be. In particular, the mark must be distinctive, not descriptive (as discussed below), and not otherwise excluded for policy or practical reasons. Distinctiveness is likely to be much more difficult to prove in the case of exotic marks such as shapes, colours and sounds: these are far less likely to be regarded by members of the public as indicating the source of the product than conventional marks such as words and logos.

Registrable Marks

Since the fundamental function of a trade mark is to act as a guarantee of origin for the public, in order to be registered, the mark must serve this purpose. To ensure that this is the case, the Act and Regulation impose a series of requirements which any mark applied for must meet. In the case of a Community trade mark, it must meet each requirement in a sufficiently large part of the Community.

The mark must be distinctive, not descriptive

Distinctiveness is a crucial concept in the law of trade marks and passing off. A distinctive mark is one which is suitable for differentiating the goods of one trader from those of another. The contrast is with a descriptive mark: one that describes the goods in question or is otherwise unsuitable for distinguishing the goods of one trader from those of another, because it would be applicable to all of them or would not be regarded as denoting origin at all. The first thing that must be noted in this connection is that trade marks are not registered in the abstract; they are registered for specific goods and/or services. Accordingly, a mark that might be perfectly acceptable for certain goods may be wholly unsuitable for others. Furthermore, distinctiveness and descriptiveness are not black and white concepts. In general, marks are spread along a spectrum, with completely descriptive marks at one end and completely distinctive marks at the other. A made-up word (Kodak, for example), is ideal, from a trade mark lawyer's point of view, for distinguishing goods. But, from a marketing point of view, at least initially, the opposite may be true. Here, there is a strong increasing tendency to prefer at least somewhat descriptive marks, since they are more likely to tell the public something about the attributes of the product or service in question. The tension is clear.

To be registerable, a mark must reach a certain threshold of distinctiveness. This can be achieved by the nature of the mark itself, or by the use made of it having turned it into one the public now recognises as denoting trade origin (or perhaps by a combination of the two). Quite where the threshold lies is a matter of debate and some fluctuation. On the whole, however, its level seems to have been decreasing of late. Much excitement (admittedly only amongst trade mark lawyers) was caused by the registration as a Community trade mark of *BABY DRY* for nappies. The decision of the ECJ (*Procter & Gamble v OHIM*, 2001) was widely criticised as applying too low a threshold, it being said that the mark was descriptive for nappies and that other traders were likely to wish to use it in this way. The Court thought that BABY DRY was a 'lexical invention': no one else did.

Although a defendant using such a phrase may have a defence (as to which, see Chapter 11), the problem is that registration of descriptive marks of this sort hands a weapon to large and wealthy companies who are more likely to have the resources to pursue extensive trade mark registration and enforcement programmes against smaller, and poorer, traders. Accordingly, despite in theory having a defence, in reality defendants are likely to back down when threatened with a registered trade mark like this held by a big company.

Perhaps in response to the furore over its *BABY DRY* decision, the Court has now visibly (but without the grace of admitting it got *BABY DRY* wrong) backed off. It held that *DOUBLEMINT* for chewing gum was too descriptive and that the rights of other traders should be taken into account when registration is being considered apart from any defences which may exist once the mark is registered (*Wrigley's Appn*, 2003).

In addition to considering the inherent distinctiveness of the mark, that is the capacity of the mark to distinguish goods from those of other traders in itself, a further important consideration in assessing whether a mark is registrable is any distinctiveness which the mark has acquired through use. Whilst some marks (such as *SOAP* for toiletries) could never in practice acquire distinctiveness through use, many other descriptive marks may, on being used extensively for a particular product or service, become sufficiently well-known that they achieve what is known as 'acquired distinctiveness'.

There is no hard and fast rule for assessing whether a mark is sufficiently distinctive and not too descriptive to be registrable. If the mark is already customarily used in the trade for the goods of the application, then it will almost certainly not be registrable. Further, if other traders might legitimately wish to use the mark to describe their product or service, it is likely not to be registrable, notwithstanding *BABY DRY*. Certain categories of mark are generally more difficult to register, in particular, geographical marks (e.g. *CHIEMSEE*, the name of a Bavarian lake, for clothing (*Windsurfing Chiemsee v Huber*, 1999); laudatory marks (e.g. *TREAT* for dessert sauces and syrups, found invalid in *British Sugar v James Robertson*, 1996); and names of famous people (e.g. *ELVIS* for toilet preparations, soaps etc., refused under the old law (*Elvis Presley TMs*, 1997)).

The mark must not be contrary to public policy or morality

This requirement covers a multitude of sins. In particular, a mark is likely to be refused if it would cause offence or offensive behaviour. Three examples give a flavour of the type of marks which are likely to be refused on this ground. In *Ghazilian's TM Appn*, 2002, *TINY PENIS* for clothing, footwear and headgear was refused on the basis that the mark would cause offence to 'right-thinking' members of the public if used on, say, advertising bill boards or on the side of a bus. The irony here, of course, being that refusal to register the mark would not prevent this from happening – all that it prevents is the use of the term in connection with certain goods/services falling under the control of one undertaking. Nevertheless, the judge stated that 'correct anatomical terms for parts of genitalia should be reserved for serious use and should not be debased by use as a smutty trade mark for clothing'. Whether this is a generally accepted moral principle, or indeed a relevant concern, is subject to debate. By contrast, an attack on the validity of the trade mark FCUK was rejected in *French Connection v Woodman*, 2006. Here the court considered that there was nothing inherently objectionable in the mark; the fact that it could easily be rendered offensive by switching round a couple of the letters was irrelevant. King Cnut (he of commanding the tide fame) would no doubt be relieved. Finally, in *CDW Graphic Design's TM Appn*, 2003, www.standupifyouhatemanu.com for various goods, including car bumper stickers, mugs and t-shirts, was refused on the ground that it was likely to function as a badge of antagonism and to increase the incidence of football violence or other offensive behaviour.

The mark must not be deceptive

A mark cannot be registered if it will deceive the public, for instance, as to the nature, quality or geographical origin of the goods or services. The classic example is the *ORLWOOLA* case: the mark was registered for various articles, including clothing. The Court of Appeal decided that it should not remain registered, since if the goods were made wholly of wool, the mark was descriptive, and if they were not made wholly of wool, it was a misdescription that was certain to deceive ('*Orlwoola*', 1909).

The mark must not be a specially protected emblem

Certain emblems are specially protected. Thus trade marks consisting of or containing various emblems such as Royal arms, representations of the Royal crown and the Royal family, flags, national emblems of Paris Convention countries, emblems of international organisations, coats of arms and Olympic symbols are subject to special rules relating to registration.

The mark must not be applied for in bad faith

The requirement that an application must not be made in bad faith applies to UK trade marks only at the application stage, although in the case of a Community trade mark, bad faith can be relied upon as a ground for invalidity of the trade mark. In the case of UK trade marks, the requirement is of rather uncertain scope.

The Court of Justice has said that it involves an evaluation of all of the circumstances. Mere knowledge of a third party's claimed rights is not enough; however it could be bad faith to apply for a mark knowing it was in use by a third party so as deliberately to interfere with that person's legitimate use of the mark.

There is considerable uncertainty as to what type of behaviour may be covered and as to how reprehensible the behaviour must be for the application to be refused. Nevertheless, the ECJ has indicated that the test requires consideration of two things: what the applicant for the mark knew; and (separately) whether a reasonable and honest person would regard the applicant's conduct, in light of his knowledge, as being in bad faith (*Lindt & Sprungli*, 2009).

Where someone else is entitled to the mark

This is sometimes referred to as trade mark misappropriation or theft. It occurs when the applicant knows or ought to know that the trade mark belongs to someone else, but nevertheless proceeds to make an application for the mark in his own name. Consider, for example, *Harrison v Teton Valley*, 2004. The mark applied for was *CHINA WHITE*, for cocktails. Registration was opposed by the owners of the well-known nightclub Chinawhite. The nightclub sold a house cocktail known by the name *Chinawhite*. It had been developed by employees of the opponent, including the bar manager. The bar manager approached the applicant and told him that he was working at Chinawhite nightclub and had developed a cocktail called *Chinawhite* to be sold at the nightclub. The applicant proceeded to make the trade mark application in his own name. This was found to fall short of the standards of acceptable commercial behaviour observed by reasonable businessmen. Consequently, it was held that the application had been made in bad faith.

The applicant has no intention of using the mark at all or for some of the goods/services applied for

This is a trickier issue. An applicant for a UK trade mark must sign a form stating that the trade mark is being used by the applicant or with his or her consent in relation to the goods or services stated or there is a bona fide intention that it will be so used. On this basis, it has been said that if the applicant has no intention to use the mark at all, the application is made in bad faith and should be refused. Similarly, in cases where the applicant intends to use the mark but only for some of the goods or services for which it has been applied for, the mark should be refused for those goods and services for which the applicant does not intend to use the mark. For this reason, whilst it is important for a trader to make sure that he applies for a mark which will cover all the goods and services for which he may use the mark, too broad an application may well be cut down. Having said this, the legal justification for refusing or restricting the scope of a mark on grounds of lack of intention to use is somewhat dubious: the law provides a specific ground for revocation of a mark where it has not been used for a period of five years (this is discussed in Chapter 12). For this reason, OHIM has taken the view that lack of intention to use should not, of itself, be regarded as bad faith when considering the validity of a Community trade mark (*Trillium,* 2000). However, specifications much wider than the scope of use will inevitably help clog up the Registers and bring people who have no real commercial conflict into pointless trade mark disputes.

Special requirements for shape marks

As has already been explained, signs consisting of the shapes of goods are now registrable as trade marks. However, in order to ensure that a trade mark proprietor cannot thereby monopolise shapes which other traders have a legitimate interest in using, the registration of such marks is subject to certain special restrictions. In particular, a sign cannot be registered if it consists exclusively of the shape which results from the nature of the goods themselves, the shape of goods which is necessary to obtain a technical result or the shape which gives substantial value to the goods. It should not be forgotten that these requirements are in addition to those which apply generally to all types of trade marks, in particular, the requirements that the mark be distinctive and not descriptive. If any mark falls foul of the special requirements for shape marks, it is very likely that it will also be insufficiently distinctive to be registered.

The case of Philips' three-headed rotary shaver illustrates how the special requirements for shape marks operate in practice (*Philips v Remington,* Court of Appeal 1999 and ECJ, 2003 – note how long it took). Philips' mark actually consisted of a drawing of its three-headed rotary shaver, consisting of three circular heads with rotating blades in the shape of an equilateral triangle. In practice, everyone treated this as a registration of the shape itself. It relied on this mark to sue Remington for trade mark infringement by the sale of its three-headed rotary shaver, which also used three rotating heads forming an equilateral triangle. Remington argued that Philips' trade mark was invalid on various grounds, including that it did not comply with the special requirements for shape marks.

As to the first requirement, Remington's case was that because the shape registered resulted from the nature of a three-headed rotary shaver, it should not have been registered. However, the Court of Appeal took the view that the purpose of the requirement was to exclude from registration basic shapes that should be available for use by the public at large. In this case there were other shapes of shavers and, in particular, other possible shapes for three-headed electrical shavers, therefore there was no reason to exclude this particular shape from registration. As to the second requirement, Remington argued that the essential features of the shape shown in the trade mark were designed to achieve a technical result and therefore should not be registrable. The Court of Appeal agreed, rejecting Philips' argument that because there were other ways of achieving the same technical performance (for example, using four heads not three, or arranging the heads in a different configuration), the mark was valid. This point was also referred to the ECJ, who came to the same conclusion. So Philips lost. As to the third requirement, Remington's argument that the shape registered gave substantial value to the goods and, therefore, was not registrable, failed. The Court of Appeal held that there was a distinction between the second requirement which excluded functional shapes and the third requirement which excluded 'aesthetic-type' shapes. Only if the shape, as a shape, had substantial value should it be excluded from registration on this ground. On the facts, the Court found there was no evidence that this was the case. An attempt to register the form of the LEGO bricks foundered in a similar way (*Lego Juris*, 2010).

Earlier Marks and Rights

In order to be registered, a mark must comply with the requirements of registrability set out above. But even if all these requirements are complied with, a mark may still fail to achieve registration because it clashes with an earlier registered trade mark or other unregistered right. Note that, in the case of a UK trade mark application, if the applicant can get the consent of the proprietor of the earlier trade mark or other earlier right, then the mark applied for can be registered. In the case of a Community trade mark application, the following grounds for refusal of an application only apply if they are raised in an opposition by the proprietor of the earlier mark or right.

Earlier Trade Marks

In the case of an application for a UK mark, the earlier trade marks which need to be considered are those UK trade marks, international trade marks (UK) and Community trade marks with earlier application dates and, in addition, any earlier well-known marks (international marks and well-known marks are discussed in Chapter 13). In the case of an application for a Community trade mark, the earlier trade marks which need to be considered are Community trade marks, trade marks registered in any Member State and trade marks registered under international arrangements with effect in a Member State with earlier application dates and any earlier well-known marks.

The question of whether or not there is sufficient similarity between one of these earlier trade marks and the mark applied for, such that the mark applied for should not be registered, is assessed by a series of three tests mirroring those which apply in cases of infringement. Accordingly, if the mark applied for is identical to an earlier trade mark and the goods or services for which it is applied for are also identical with those for which the earlier trade mark is protected, the mark will not be registered. If, on the other hand, the mark applied for is identical to an earlier trade mark, but the goods or services for which it is applied for are only similar to those for which the earlier trade mark is registered, or the goods or services are identical but the marks are only similar, the mark will not be registered only if, because of the similarity of the marks or the goods or services, there is a likelihood of confusion. Finally, if the mark applied for is identical or similar to the earlier trade mark and is applied for in relation to goods or services which are identical, similar or dissimilar to those for which the mark is registered, the mark will not be registered only if the earlier trade mark has a reputation and the use of the mark applied for without due cause would take unfair advantage of, or be detrimental to, the distinctive character or the repute of the earlier trade mark.

These tests are discussed in detail in the context of infringement (see Chapter 10). Since the same principles apply, that discussion will not be anticipated here. In addition, it should be noted that where the grounds for refusal of registration exist in relation to only some of the goods or services for which the mark is applied for, the mark should be refused only in relation to those goods or services, permitting registration in respect of the other goods or services applied for.

Other Earlier Rights

A trade mark application may also be refused if use of the mark applied for is liable to be prevented by the exercise of a law protecting an earlier unregistered mark (in the UK, this would be the law of passing off). In the case of UK trade mark applications, this principle is also extended to marks whose use may be prevented by virtue of any other earlier right, e.g. copyright, design right etc. (For example, if the mark applied for consisted of a logo or device which infringed someone else's copyright, registration would be refused.) Where Community trade mark applications are concerned, other earlier rights can be relied upon as a ground of invalidity once the mark is registered, but not as a ground for opposing the application. Invalidity is discussed in Chapter 12.

As far as earlier unregistered marks are concerned, the position for a UK trade mark application is that if it can be shown that, at the date of the application, a third party could have prevented any normal and fair use of the trade mark applied for by relying on its rights in passing off, the mark will be refused (see Chapter 15 for a discussion of passing off). In summary, it will have to be shown that the third party had a reputation in respect of the earlier trade mark at the date of application and that use of the trade mark applied for at that date would have resulted in members of the public being deceived into thinking that the goods or services for which the mark is applied for were the goods or services of the third party. Unlike in a standard passing off case, the use of the mark applied for will be considered in the abstract, by reference to anything which would be considered normal and fair use of the mark, but without reference to any particular surrounding circumstances. As with earlier trade mark rights, if this ground can only be made out in respect of some of the goods or services, the mark should only be refused in respect of those goods or services. In theory, it might be possible for the mark to be limited in geographical extent, if the ground can only be made out in some parts of the UK. However, this approach could create practical problems in defining the area in question.

In the case of Community trade mark applications, the position may be rather different, because the law protecting the earlier unregistered mark could be the law of any Member State, not necessarily the English law of passing off. In addition, there is an added requirement that the earlier unregistered mark be of more than local significance. The CJEU has recently stated that this has two elements: first, it must actually be used in a sufficiently significant manner in the course of trade; and second, the mark must be used in a substantial part of the territory in which it is claimed it is not merely local (*Anheuser-Busch v Bud jovický Budvar*, 2011). At present, therefore, it is not entirely clear what this requirement entails. This said, evidence of use in three cities in France in this case was not considered to be sufficient to support an argument that this use was of anything other than local significance.

Applications and Oppositions

An application to register a UK mark must be made to the Registrar of Trade Marks. The Registrar's office is at the UK Intellectual Property Office (the operating name of the Patent Office), which he administers under the alternative title of Comptroller-General of Patents, Designs and Trade Marks. The office is in Newport, Wales. Applications are normally made by trade mark attorneys, but it appears to be increasingly common for members of the public to apply without using an attorney. If possible, it is wise to employ an experienced attorney to make the application, since this can prevent problems with the application and registration in the long run. However, the UK IPO now has an excellent website (at www.ipo.gov.uk) which offers plenty of information for those wishing to go it alone. Using the services of an attorney the costs of applying for a registration are of the order of £550, of which £200 is the official fee (£170 if filed electronically). If there are problems leading to significant correspondence with the Registry, the costs will be higher. The registration must be renewed (fee currently around £200) every 10 years.

Applications for Community trade marks are made to the Office for the Harmonization of the Internal Market (OHIM) which is based in Alicante, Spain. These applications are dealt with in Chapter 13.

The Classes of Goods and Services

Goods are divided into 34 classes for trade mark purposes, services into another 11. Typical classes of goods are: machines and machine-tools; fuels, industrial oils and lubricants; vehicles; clothing; games and playthings; wines, spirits and liqueurs. The 'service' classes are fewer and broader: e.g. 'Telecommunications'; or 'Treatment of Materials' (such as 'engraving,' which could be of jewellery or of tombstones). An application may be made for goods and services in more than one class, although each additional class requires payment of an extra fee.

The scope of the goods and services applied for is particularly important. Obviously, it is in the applicant's interest to apply for all the goods and services on which he uses or potentially wishes to use the mark (note, care should be taken to include spare parts and accessories, or ancillary services). So far as OHIM is concerned, undue width of specification is not currently an objection (and indeed is positively welcomed) – however, broad claiming in the specification is not without its problems: it does increase the potential for partial revocation for non-use later (as to which, see Chapter 12). In addition, OHIM's *laissez faire* approach to broad specifications has come in for criticism from the Court of Justice recently in *IPTRANSLATOR*, 2012.

The Applicant

The application should be made by the person, firm or company actually using or intending to use the mark. An agent or representative of an overseas proprietor should not apply for a mark without the authorisation of the proprietor, otherwise the proprietor can oppose the application or, if the mark is granted, can apply for a declaration of invalidity of the registration or ask for his name to be substituted as the proprietor. A mark can be applied for by two or more applicants and, in theory, each is allowed to use the mark for his own benefit, without the permission of the other. However, there is a danger that two proprietors using the mark independently could make the mark deceptive and liable to revocation (see Chapter 12).

Examination of the Application

Every application is examined to see that it complies with the basic requirements as to registrability. In particular, the Registrar will consider whether the mark is adequately graphically represented, whether it is distinctive, not descriptive and not otherwise excluded, and has not been made in bad faith. In the UK, if the application meets these requirements for registrability then it will be accepted, and subsequently published in the *Trade Marks Journal*. Since October 2007, the Registry performs searches for prior conflicting marks and notifies the applicant of these, but no longer raises such conflicts as objections to registration. Instead, it informs the proprietor of the earlier right, who then has two months following the application's publication in the *Trade Marks Journal* to launch an opposition (see below). The same sort of search and inform process is also performed by OHIM in respect of applications for Community marks. If the Registrar or OHIM, as the case may be, considers that any of the criteria are not met, then he will inform the applicant, who has a chance to respond in writing. In the UK, if the applicant so wishes, he can have a hearing. The applicant may need to file evidence in order to try to overcome any objections. Most commonly, if it is suggested that the mark is not distinctive, the applicant will need to file evidence of the use made of the mark in order to try to prove that it has acquired distinctiveness through use. A final decision of the Registrar that the mark is not registrable can be appealed to the High Court or the so-called Appointed Person (someone with experience in trade mark law, usually a Queen's Counsel or an academic). Appeals from OHIM go first to a Board of Appeals and then on to the Court of First Instance of the ECJ in Luxembourg, then on to the full Court or a Chamber of it. In the UK, courts are apt to uphold the decision of an experienced trade mark official, whereas, at least until recently, the European courts in Luxembourg have not given respect to decisions below and have tended to be erratic.

In the UK it takes around nine months to obtain a registration if all goes smoothly. In OHIM things can take a lot longer – especially if there are objections to be overcome. Hence it is advisable to apply for registration well in advance of actual use, wherever possible.

Acceptance and Publication

In the UK if and when the Registrar has no further objection to the mark, the application will be accepted and the intention to register it will be published in *The Trade Marks Journal*. Once the application has been published, anyone who wishes to oppose the registration of the mark has two months to do so. Therefore, the mark will not be actually registered until after this period. Occasionally, even where there is no opposition, the Registrar may change her mind and refuse the application if new matters have come to her notice indicating that it was accepted in error. If this happens, the applicant should be given an opportunity to respond before the final refusal.

Things are much the same at OHIM – except slower.

Opposition

Anyone may oppose an application on any of the grounds for which the Registrar may refuse to register a mark, and they may also oppose on the basis that the application conflicts with an earlier right. The usual reason for opposition is that the new mark is too similar to a mark the opponents are using or have registered or hope to use or register. (Once they have decided to oppose the application at all, however, opponents will naturally raise any other objections to it that they can find.) The procedure for opposition commences with the opponent filing a statement of his grounds of opposition to the mark. The applicant responds with a counter-statement. Then each side files evidence in support of their case. If the parties wish, there will then be a hearing before one of the Registrar's hearing officers to decide the matter. An appeal from the decision of the hearing officer can be made to the High Court or the Appointed Person (as described above in relation to examination).

Oppositions are often bitterly fought, not only by opponents (who have often much to lose, since the new registration might reduce the value of their existing goodwill), but also by applicants. Nevertheless, the goodwill in a new mark will often not be worth the legal costs involved, particularly if the matter is appealed. Most applicants in such situations would therefore be best advised to simply drop the application and start again with another mark – it's rarely worth betting the farm at this stage.

OHIM too has an opposition procedure. It is much more paper-based, and is apt to be long and drawn out. Appeals go on the same route as for appeals from a refusal by the Office, i.e. to a Board of Appeal, then to the Court of First Instance and finally to the European Court itself. With such a four-stage procedure, and the flood of cases, it is not surprising things take so long – yet this sort of timing seems particularly inappropriate for the determination of trade mark rights where marketing men need speedy answers. Something needs to be done, but the EU thinks it has more important matters to attend to, so things will probably have to get much worse before they get any better.

10

Trade Mark Infringement

Introduction

How a trade mark can be infringed is closely linked to the more philosophical question of the function of a registered trade mark: accordingly, this latter element is discussed first. This chapter then discusses the three tests for trade mark infringement. Even if one of these tests is satisfied, a case for trade mark infringement may still fail if either the trade mark should not have been registered (the circumstances in which this may be so are addressed in Chapter 12) or the defendant has a defence (possible defences are discussed in Chapter 11).

What a Registered Trade Mark can Stop

The registration of a trade mark gives the owner the exclusive right to use the registered mark. This exclusive right is defined negatively by rules which set out what acts others cannot do – these acts, if done without the consent of the proprietor, amount to trade mark infringement. The prime rationale behind the rules is to ensure that the registered trade mark acts as a 'guarantee of origin' (a phrase used in the Trade Mark Directive). The 'guarantee' is to ensure that when a member of the public sees the registered trade mark used in relation to certain goods or services, they can be sure that the goods or services in question come from the registered proprietor or someone under his control. The point is to make sure that the public is not deceived. If the public buys a can of soft drink bearing the name *Coca-Cola*, they are entitled to assume that it is the famous soft drink, and not an imitation made by somebody else. The infringement rules are intended to prevent this kind of imitation.

In fact, as will be seen below, the rules go further than this, and prevent other kinds of imitation and even, in the case of goods imported from outside the EU, the use of marks on the genuine goods. Quite how far the law should go in protecting trade marks is a matter of extensive debate amongst lawyers. It is a subject not merely of academic interest: it can have a major practical effect on traders and consumers. The *Arsenal* case provides a useful illustration.

Arsenal v Reed, 2003, was about football merchandise. In common with other top clubs, Arsenal made a great deal of money by selling merchandise bearing the club's name and badge. The name and badges were registered as trade marks for things like T-shirts, scarves and hats. All the merchandise sold by the club was labelled 'official' and the club had invested a good deal of effort in trying to ensure that the public knew its merchandise was official and in attempting to prevent others from selling 'unofficial' merchandise. Mr Reed was an Arsenal fan and had been selling goods bearing the Arsenal names and logos from a stall near the Arsenal football ground for over 30 years. The vast majority of his merchandise was unofficial and was indicated as such by prominent signs on his stall. Arsenal sued Mr Reed for passing off and trade mark infringement. The case in passing off failed in the High Court, because the judge found that the club had not proved that fans buying from Mr Reed would be confused into believing that the merchandise came from the club or was licensed by it. In 30 years of trading, the club could not show a single instance of confusion which had come to light.

The case on trade mark infringement turned on the question of how far the protection given by a registered trade mark should extend. Arsenal argued that since Mr Reed was using their registered trade marks in relation to the goods for which those marks were registered, it was a straightforward case of trade mark infringement. Mr Reed maintained that mere use of the offending sign was not sufficient: in order to be an infringement, the use had to indicate trade origin. Mr Reed said, and the judge in the High Court agreed, that he was not using the Arsenal name and badge to indicate trade origin (i.e. to say that the goods had come from a certain source), but simply as a badge of allegiance. The public bought the goods for the Arsenal name or crest, not because they thought it was an 'official' club product. The tricky legal point was whether use of a sign as a badge of allegiance should be sufficient to amount to trade mark infringement.

The judge decided that this point of law should be referred to the ECJ for a definitive ruling. Arsenal and Mr Reed duly travelled to Luxembourg to argue over the function of a trade mark before the judges there. The judgment, which was given a year and a half after the reference was made (about the average time for a reference), provoked a storm of academic and judicial dispute. The Court repeated the mantra that the essential function of a trade mark was to guarantee the identity of origin of the marked goods or services, but found that it was immaterial to the question of infringement that the sign was perceived as a badge of allegiance. It concluded that, in the circumstances of the case, the trade mark proprietor was entitled to prevent use of the trade mark. As is usual following a reference, the case returned to the referring court, in this case the High Court, to allow the judge to apply the ECJ's guidance to the facts of the case. Normally that is pretty much a formality. But here it was argued on behalf of Mr Reed, that the European Court had exceeded its jurisdiction and, consequently, the conclusion it had reached should not be applied by the High Court. The excess of jurisdiction was said to arise from the fact that the ECJ is only able to give guidance on points of law, whereas in this case it appeared to have come to a conclusion on the facts and one which was contrary to the findings of fact made by the High Court, namely that the marks were just badges of allegiance. Although the judge considered it to be an unattractive outcome, he accepted Mr Reed's submission that the ECJ had gone too far and found that, despite its ruling, Mr Reed should win. This radical step, although considered to be justified by many intellectual property lawyers, was promptly stamped upon by the Court of Appeal, which held that the real basis for the ECJ's decision was that the use complained of was liable to jeopardise the guarantee of origin and that the High Court had made no finding of fact on this point. Consequently, it was open to the ECJ to conclude that the use by Mr Reed was liable to jeopardise the guarantee of origin of Arsenal's trade marks, since this was a finding of fact which was inevitable in the circumstances.

The Expanding Functions of Trade Marks

Thus the upshot for the law of trade marks is that although the essential function of the trade mark remains as a guarantee of origin, the acts which may be prevented having regard to that function have been stretched. Accordingly, trade mark infringement is not limited to preventing deception of the public as to the origin of the goods. It now extends to any use of the trade mark in the course of trade which, whilst it does not serve to indicate origin, may harm the trade mark's use by its proprietor as a guarantee thereof.

The result for Mr Reed and other traders like him is that they will be prevented from selling anything other than 'official' Arsenal merchandise (if they can get it) and for consumers that they will only be able to buy their shirts, scarves and the like from 'official' sources.

There are three postscripts. First, just a day after the decision of the Court of Appeal in *Arsenal*, the House of Lords, in a case called *R v Johnstone*, 2003 (for a little more about the *Johnstone* case, see Chapter 24), said that for infringement there had to be trade mark use by the defendant. The context was a criminal charge under the provisions of the Trade Marks Act. The defendant dealt in bootleg CDs (unauthorised recordings of live performances). The registered trade mark said to be infringed was the name of the band, Bon Jovi. (The astute reader may wonder why Mr Johnstone was charged under the Trade Marks Act, rather than under the Copyright Act, for the bootleg CDs undoubtedly infringed both copyright in the music and the performers' rights. The answer is almost certainly that it is much easier to prove title to a registered trade mark (just produce the certificate of registration) than to prove title to a copyright or a performers' right. For these the live evidence of witnesses of the creation or of the performance may be required, particularly in a criminal case.) Mr Johnstone said he was only using the name to indicate the performers – not as a trade mark. And he might have got off on that basis – whether the public took the use as only denoting the band or as denoting the band and a trade mark or just as a trade mark was never decided: by the time the case reached the House of Lords Mr Johnstone had served his sentence, so there was no point in a retrial. Some claimed this case put the Court of Appeal decision in *Arsenal* back into the melting pot.

Postscript two: the matter in *Arsenal* wasn't revisited directly – the parties eventually settled. However, in subsequent decisions, the Court of Justice has continued its discussion of the functions (plural) of the trade mark. Accordingly, in a series of cases, the Court has confirmed that guarantee of origin is only one (albeit the essential) function of the trade mark. In these days of sophisticated commerce, the trade mark also provides a consistent guarantee of the quality of the goods or services provided (as it demonstrates the trade mark owner's commitment to the consumer) (guarantee function). It provides a basis for publicity and advertising (advertising function), a focus for investment (investment function), and is a platform for communicating with the consumer (communication function). Accordingly, junior use that harms any of these functions may amount to infringement (*Google France*, 2010; *Interflora*, 2012).

The final postscript shows how copyright and trade marks can overlap. When the High Court judge found against Arsenal the first time and sent the case off to Luxembourg, Arsenal decided to do something about its badge. The old one, a splendid Victorian thing with a Latin motto, was out of copyright. Arsenal commissioned a new badge – in which there would be copyright. The copyright would last for ages – 70 years after the death of the author. Pirate copies could be suppressed by the use of copyright rather than trade marks. Legally the plan worked, though the fans did not like it, especially those with tattoos of the old badge.

We discuss the *Arsenal* case at length because it illustrates an important fact about modern trade mark law: it has broken free of its origins in preventing deception and now has just as much utility in protecting investment in creating a brand aura and identity. The debate on whether that is justified will doubtless continue for many years. In the meantime, we return to the current law.

The Tests for Trade Mark Infringement

As already outlined, there are three types of trade mark infringement, as follows.

(i) Identical Marks and Identical Goods/Services

This is the most straightforward type of case. The claimant only has to prove that the mark used by the defendant is identical to his registered mark and is being used by the defendant for goods or services identical to those for which registration has been obtained (assuming, that is, that the claimant's trade mark is valid and that no relevant defence applies – these issues are discussed in Chapters 11 and 12). The vast majority of cases of this type will settle unless, of course, there is some other issue at stake. This said, it is not always easy to say whether or not the marks and goods or services are identical.

In *LTJ Diffusion v SADAS*, 2002, a case referred to the ECJ from the French courts, the claimant's registered trade mark was *Arthur* in a fancy script; that of the defendant was *Arthur et Felicie*, in a device (picture) mark. On one view, the marks might be considered to be identical: after all, the defendant's mark does contain all of the claimant's. However, the European Court's view was that a sign could only be identical to a registered trade mark where there was reproduction, without any modification or addition, of all the elements of the registered trade mark or where, viewed as a whole, it contained differences so insignificant they would go unnoticed by an average consumer. Whilst the European Court did not have to decide the case on the facts, it seems pretty clear that under this reasoning the marks would not have been found to be identical. Following this guide, the English Court of Appeal held that 'Reed Business Information' is not identical to 'Reed' alone, noting that 'Business Information' added something significant to 'Reed' in the former sign (*Reed v Reed*, 2004). Nevertheless, the Court also stated that there may be cases where the added matter is effectively ignored by the consumer when comparing the marks: accordingly, 'Palmolive soap' might be considered identical to 'Palmolive' (as 'soap' adds nothing relevant to the mix, it would not be considered to have anything other than descriptive significance and so would not feature in the comparison).

Another facet of this latter point is that the courts compare the registered mark with the sign used by the defendant, ignoring extraneous matter. So it is not a defence where goods and/or services and the mark and the sign are identical, to say that there is other material which ensures that there is no confusion. One extreme example of this is found in the case of *BP v Kelly*, 2002. Here BP, which has a registration covering the colour green for petrol stations, successfully sued the operator of an Irish petrol station who had painted it green. Kelly's premises were prominently marked in such a way that no one could suppose that they were owned by BP, but this did not matter: he had used an identical sign in relation to identical services, and so infringed.

The Scope of the Registration

Working out whether the goods or services are identical is usually more straightforward. On the whole, the question will be resolved by deciding whether, in ordinary parlance, they might be considered the same. An example illustrates this principle: in *British Sugar*, 1996, the claimant contended that the defendant was using the mark on a dessert sauce or syrup, which fell within the scope of the claimant's registration. However, this argument was based upon comments made on the back of a jar of the defendant's product which said that it could be used with desserts. Nevertheless, it was primarily sold as a spread, and the court considered that no one would naturally call it a 'dessert sauce' any more than they would call a jam a dessert source. Therefore the action failed.

The position may be more complicated with services, which are often defined in trade mark specifications much less precisely than goods. Wary of this, the courts have said that specifications of services should be read narrowly. Thus in *Avnet v Iosact*, 1998, the court said that the defendant, an internet service provider, was not offering advertising and promotional services by providing customers with webpages on which they could publicise their products. And in the *Reed* case a sophisticated internet jobs site was not 'an employment agency service' because it did not actually put employers and employees in contact with each other.

(ii) Identical Marks and Similar Goods/Services, or Similar Marks and Identical Goods/Services

The second type of trade mark infringement case arises where the mark used by the defendant is identical to the claimant's registered mark, but the goods or services for which the defendant is using the mark are only similar to those for which the claimant has registered, or the goods or services are identical but the marks are only similar. In these circumstances, the claimant must show that because the marks are identical and the goods/services are similar, or vice versa, there exists a likelihood of confusion, including a likelihood of association, on the part of the public. Much judicial ink has been expended over the meaning of a likelihood of confusion/association and the correct approach to this category of cases. Many of the cases discussing these issues have been decided by the ECJ (*Sabel v Puma*, 1998; *Canon v MGM*, 1999 and *Lloyd*, 1999). It has come up with the 'global appreciation' test.

In a nutshell, this requires the court to take into account all relevant factors, such as the degree of similarity between the marks and the goods/services and the distinctiveness of the registered mark, to work out whether confusion is likely. It is important to note that the test requires marks and goods/services to be *sufficiently* similar for there to be a likelihood of confusion. Accordingly, these factors are interdependent. Therefore, a lesser degree of similarity between goods or services may be offset by a greater degree of similarity between marks, and vice versa. Similarly, the more distinctive the registered trade mark (either in itself, or because of the reputation it possesses on the market), the greater the risk of confusion. Conversely, the less distinctive the registered trade mark, the smaller the risk of confusion. So when *The European* newspaper sued *The European Voice* newspaper for trade mark infringement, the fact that 'European' was an ordinary English word in common use, which was not in itself distinctive of the plaintiff's newspaper, militated against a finding of a likelihood of confusion (*The European v The Economist*, 1998). (The concept of distinctiveness is discussed in detail in Chapter 9.)

When it comes to assessing the similarity of the marks, they must be looked at from the point of view of the average consumer. The average consumer is assumed to look at the mark as a whole and, in particular, its distinctive or dominant components, rather than analysing its details. In the case of composite marks – i.e. marks consisting of two or more signs – it will sometimes be the case that the average consumer, although perceiving the mark as a whole, will nonetheless appreciate that it consists of separate units and consider both to have continuing significance. Accordingly, in *Aveda v Dabur Uveda*, 2013, the High Court considered that DABUR UVEDA would be perceived as a house mark (DABUR) plus a secondary mark (UVEDA), and that the average consumer familiar with the claimant's mark AVEDA would be likely to mistake UVEDA for AVEDA and thus there would be a likelihood of confusion.

Although the average consumer is assumed to be reasonably well-informed, observant and circumspect (*Lloyd*, 1999), account has to be taken of the fact that a consumer rarely has a chance to make a direct comparison between the marks and is, therefore, likely to have an imperfect recollection of the registered mark. One of the problems in the law of trade marks is that the average consumer is an entirely fictional construct. The law of passing off looks at things somewhat more realistically and asks whether a significant proportion of the relevant population would be confused.

Confusion as a concept is satisfied if either there is direct (actual) confusion, or indirect (thinking the goods/services come from an economically linked entity, or that the trade mark owner might have expanded their lines). This, and the imperfect recollection of the average consumer, is well illustrated in the case of *Wagamama v City Centre Restaurants*, 1995. The claimant ran a Japanese-style noodle restaurant under the registered mark *Wagamama*. The defendant started an Indian restaurant called *Rajamama*. The judge found that because the name *Wagamama* was quite meaningless to the public, being an entirely made-up word, imperfect recollection of the mark was very likely. Therefore, although seen side-by-side the marks were easily distinguishable, in normal use they would not be so seen. Moreover there was a real risk of indirect confusion – many of those who did not mistake *Rajamama* for *Wagamama* might think that *Rajamama* was run by the same concern that ran *Wagamama* – an Indian variant of the Japanese restaurant. There was a substantial likelihood of confusion on both counts and hence trade mark infringement.

The concept of confusion is sufficiently broad to include situations in which although the mark is used and causes initial confusion, a consumer would always know the truth by the time he or she came to make a purchase. So in *Och Ziff*, 2011, that so-called 'initial interest' confusion would count.

As far as the similarity of goods/services is concerned, there are a number of things to consider when making a comparison. The most important are their nature, their intended purpose, their method of use and whether they are in competition with each other or are complementary. Thus, buckles and shoes have been considered similar goods (*Zanella's Appn*, 2000), as have medical apparatus for placing a suture and hollow-fibre oxygenators (medical devices capable of oxygenating the blood during surgery) (*Boston Scientific*, 2008). Both cases were decided on the basis that the goods were complementary, and that when the similarity of marks was taken into account, the consumer could therefore think they came from the same undertaking.

(iii) Identical or Similar Marks and Identical, Similar or Dissimilar Goods/Services – 'Free Riding'

The final category of trade mark infringement case is primarily concerned with cases in which the defendant is attempting to free-ride on the reputation of the claimant's mark. Originally it was assumed, at least in the UK, that this type of case was limited to dissimilar goods. However, the ECJ has categorically stated that it also applies where the goods/services are identical or similar (see *Davidoff v Gofkid*, 2003, and *Adidas-Salomon v Fitnessworld*, 2003). Whatever the nature of the goods/services, there will only be trade mark infringement if the claimant can show that his trade mark has a reputation and that the defendant's use of the mark, 'being without due cause, takes unfair advantage of, or is detrimental to, the distinctive character or the repute of the trade mark'. The effect is to give the owner of a well-known trade mark a greater degree of protection – but precisely how much still remains rather uncertain, despite repeated references to the CJEU, in *L'Oréal*, 2009 and *Interflora*, 2011-12.

First, the requirement that the claimant's mark have a reputation is akin to that in passing off (as to which see Chapter 15). Customers must know the mark as the claimant's 'badge'. The degree of knowledge required is that the mark must be known by a significant part of the public concerned by the products or services covered by that trade mark in the territory in question. In deciding whether this condition is satisfied, the court must take into consideration all the relevant facts of the case, in particular the market share held by the trade mark, the intensity, geographical extent and duration of its use, and the size of the investment made by the undertaking in promoting it (*General Motors v Yplon*, 1999). For a UK mark, the territory in question would obviously be the UK and for a Community mark, the EU – although in the latter, the CJEU has held that a reputation enjoyed only in Austria still satisfied the requirement (*Pago*, 2009). Whether the same could be said for even smaller Member States remains to be seen.

The second part of the test is more complicated: the ECJ says a public perception of 'a link' will do – though precisely what amounts to 'a link' remains a mystery at present. Some examples may assist. The kinds of scenario which are likely to be caught are as follows.

Dilution

If a famous mark and, in particular, one known for exclusiveness and luxury, is used for all manner of goods, its identity and value will be undermined or diluted. So use of *Chanel* or *Gucci* on plastic toys, pizzas, disposable nappies or betting shops would be detrimental to the distinctive character or repute of those marks.

Tarnishing

Some goods or services are generally considered by the public to be unattractive in character. Tarnishing occurs when a mark with a reputation for something entirely different is used in connection with goods or services of this type. Classic instances of tarnishing are use of the mark VISA for condoms, *Sheimer's TM Appn*, 2000, and use of the mark *Klarein* for a liquid detergent when the mark *Claeryn* was well known for Dutch gin, *Lucas Bols v Colgate-Palmolive*, 1975, a famous Benelux case. Some think that this sort of decision can go too far – in the UK for instance, Jif lemon juice happily coexisted for many years with Jif detergent and even Jiffy condoms.

Exploitation

This has been described as 'free-riding on the coattails of a famous mark', *Adidas-Salomon*, 2003. In that case, it was suggested that use of the *Rolls-Royce* by a manufacturer of whisky in order to promote his brand would amount to taking advantage of the mark's distinctive character or repute. Again, to English eyes that is taking things a bit far. Nevertheless, it is clear that a comparison list that mapped famous perfumes onto smell-a-like doppelgangers would be caught by the provision – a position that one member of the Court of Appeal described as an example of 'trade mark law prevent[ing] the defendants from telling the truth' (*L'Oréal v Bellure*, 2010).

But note that the detriment or unfair advantage must be real and not fanciful. See, for example, *Premier Brands v Typhoon Europe*, 2000, in which the owner of the well-known mark *Typhoo* for tea, failed to prevent the defendant from using *Typhoon* for kitchen equipment. The claimant's argument that *Typhoon* would cause dilution and tarnishing, because of the association with the destructive power of tropical cyclones, was rejected. The fact that anyone even dared advance such an argument shows how far things have gone.

Use

What type of use of his mark may the owner of a registered trade mark prevent? The first thing to note is that the use made by the defendant must be in the course of trade, as opposed to for private or domestic purposes. But as long as the use is in trade, a very wide variety of acts may be prevented. The most obvious uses the claimant will be able to stop are putting the mark on goods or their packaging, offering goods or services for sale by reference to the mark, actually selling or supplying them by reference to the mark, importing and exporting them by reference to the mark, and using the mark on business papers (catalogues, invoices, headed note paper and the like) and in the advertising. The use does not have to be in writing; oral use of the mark (e.g. a radio or television advert) can also be prevented.

However, the mark must be used 'in relation to' the relevant goods or services. There is a quite complicated theoretical question about what use should be considered to be infringing and the case law is not wholly consistent on this issue. Nonetheless, in practice, the courts do not have much difficulty in differentiating cases where a mark is used in relation to the goods in question from cases where it is not. There are harder cases, such as ones where a keyword is used in an internet referencing service: that too can count as 'use' of a mark (*Google/Louis Vuitton* 2010). The courts are quite well used to distinguishing between cases where a sign can be found somewhere on goods and where it can genuinely be said to be used in relation to those goods so as to identify the trade origin.

There are also potentially difficult areas where marks are used on the internet and therefore visible worldwide, but directed more at one territory than another. In general, if it is clear (as it usually is) that the website is (for example) soliciting business from the UK, that will count as use in the UK, even though the server may be based very far away.

Who Should be Sued for Infringement?

Most prudent traders avoid the possibility of infringement by checking the Registers of trade marks in the UK and at OHIM before adopting a new mark. But if infringement does occur, an action to enforce the rights of the owner of the mark may be brought either against the person who applied the mark to the goods in the first place (or imported them, if they were marked abroad), or against anyone who has subsequently traded in them. Each subsequent trader, however, will usually have the right to bring into the action as a 'third party' the person who sold the goods to him, so that in the last resort whoever marked or imported the goods will usually be liable for the whole of the damages, and if he has the money to pay them there will often be commercial advantages in bringing the action against him only. Dealers lower down the line are less frequently sued, unless the owner of the mark cannot discover who made or imported the goods (suing the dealer may be one way of finding this out), or the dealers themselves have large stocks of falsely marked goods.

In this connection, trade marks for services marks are ordinarily quite different from trade marks for goods: trade marks go on goods, and stay with them as they pass from hand to hand. Marks for services are ordinarily used just by the one business that actually provides the services.

Threats

If the owner of a registered trade mark discovers that someone is carrying out activities which he believes infringe his trade mark, then one apparently obvious thing to do before suing is to write a warning letter to the potential defendant. If this course is taken (and in many cases it can be an extremely useful tactic, since it may avoid the need to issue proceedings altogether) some care must be taken. This is because the Trade Marks Act provides a person aggrieved by unjustified threats of proceedings for infringement of a registered trade mark with a cause of action against the person who makes such threats, in certain circumstances. If successful, the person aggrieved can obtain an injunction against the continuance of the threats and damages in respect of any loss sustained by the threats, for example, if he has lost customers as a result of the threats. The relief cannot be obtained, however, if the person who made the threats can show that the acts in respect of which proceedings were threatened do constitute a trade mark infringement.

The simplest way around the problem is to do nothing more than merely notify the potential defendant that the trade mark is registered, which does not constitute a threat. If any other type of letter is to be written, then the safest thing to do is to instruct a solicitor or trade mark agent. Sometimes the best thing to do is sue first and offer to settle at the same time – there is a difference between threatening to put the knife in, and negotiating terms for its removal.

Contested Actions

The defendant in an action for infringement of trade mark can (and if he fights the case at all usually does) claim by way of defence that the registration of the mark is invalid, and ask the court to cancel it. If this happens the case is likely to be made more lengthy, complicated and expensive. If the validity of the registration is disputed and is upheld by the court the owner of the mark may ask the court for a 'certificate of validity' for the registration (just as in a patent case, see Chapter 5). In practice, the certificate acts as a warning to the trade that this particular mark is too firmly established to be safely challenged.

11

Exceptions to Trade Mark Infringement

Introduction

It will have been seen from the previous chapter that the owner of a registered trade mark has the potential to prevent a wide range of activities by another trader on the ground that they constitute infringement of his trade mark. In order to ensure that other traders can nevertheless compete freely and fairly in the market place, trade mark law provides a number of defences to an infringement action. One possible defence is that the trade mark should never have been registered; this is dealt with in Chapter 12. This chapter deals with the specific exceptions to trade mark infringement, which apply even if the mark is validly registered.

Use of Own Name or Address

Honest use (strictly 'use in accordance with honest practices in industrial or commercial matters') by a person of his own name, even though that name is used in the course of trade, is not a trade mark infringement. The use will not be considered to be honest, however, if it causes deception of customers. So in practice, save in relation to unused registered marks (where there will be no confusion), this defence is seldom of value. For instance, a Mr William Asprey could not rely on this defence in respect of his use of the name 'William R. Asprey' for a shop selling luxury goods when there was evidence that customers of the claimant's well-known shop Asprey would be confused (*Asprey & Garrard v WRA*, 2002). The defence probably applies to company names as well as those of real people (see *Cipriani*, 2010), but there are moves afoot to limit the scope of the defence, at least in connection with CTMs. Otherwise, there would be an obvious way to avoid trade mark infringement.

Descriptive Use – 'Indications of the Characteristics of Goods or Services'

This is probably the most important exception, although also the most difficult to identify in practice. This is mainly because there are a number of different types of 'descriptive' use which may be covered by the exception. We use inverted commas because the exception covers uses which are not purely descriptive, in particular, use in a trade mark sense for the defendant's goods (*Premier Luggage*, 2002 and *Gerolsteiner v Putsch*, 2004). The latter case illustrates the point. The claimants' registered mark was 'Gerri' for mineral water. The defendants sold an Irish mineral water called 'Kerry Spring', imported into Germany from a company called Kerry Spring Water. The German court thought that Kerry was so close to the registered mark that there would be confusion (only aural – and note that German courts are more apt than most to find confusion). On a reference, the ECJ held that the descriptive use defence applied, even though the use had trade mark significance. Other, more obvious, cases are where the defendant is using the claimant's registered trade mark as a description, rather than as a trade mark. For example, use on the label of a jar of spread of the words 'Robertson's Toffee Treat' was held not to be an infringement of the claimant's mark Treat, on the ground that 'Treat' was being used by the defendant descriptively, in contrast with its name as maker, i.e. Robertson's (*British Sugar v James Robertson*, 1996). Similarly, 'spork' on a price list to describe a cross between a spoon and a fork was not an infringement of the registration of Spork, the term having been used generically in the trade and the defendant's price list clearly indicating the manufacturer of the product (*Green v Regalzone*, 2002). Likewise, 'Huggies will keep your baby dry' for nappies would not infringe the registered mark BABY DRY.

There are also cases where the defendant is using the claimant's registered mark to refer to the claimant's goods or services by way of comparison. For example, the use by Ryanair of the British Airways trade mark, BA, as part of the slogan 'EXPENSIVE BA . . . . DS!' (*British Airways v Ryanair*, 2001). The precise circumstances in which comparative advertising will be permitted are discussed below. Next, the defendant may be using the claimant's registered trade mark to refer to the claimant's goods or services, so as to indicate some characteristic of the defendant's goods or services. For example, 'These tights contain Lycra'. Finally, the defendant may be using the claimant's registered trade mark to refer to the claimant's goods or services because he is legitimately dealing in the claimant's goods or services.

The courts have tended to take rather a practical approach to this provision: where it is clear that the defendant is using a term in a descriptive manner and fairly, there will be no infringement. If not, there will be liability.

Descriptive Use and Spare Parts

Where a defendant needs to use the claimant's registered trade mark in order to indicate the intended purpose of a product or service, there is an exception to infringement. The most common examples are use by the defendant to refer to accessories and spare parts. This type of case often arises in the car industry. Thus, use of the phrase 'Ford spares sold here' would not be an infringement. However, the use made of the trade mark must be honest. In a case where the defendant had previously been an authorised Volvo dealer, had then had the dealership revoked and started using the phrase 'Independent Volvo Specialist', with the words 'Independent' and 'Specialist' appearing in much smaller lettering, the court found that the defendant could not take advantage of the defence. The court was clearly influenced by the fact that the defendant had previously been an authorised dealer and had written to customers in such a way as to give the misleading impression that it continued to be an authorised dealer (*Volvo v Heritage*, 2000). By way of contrast the ECJ held that 'BMW Specialist' written fairly was all right (*BMW v Deenik*, 1999). In trade marks, as in life, a lot depends not only on what you say, but how you say it.

But there Must be Honesty

In the case of all of the above exceptions, the defendant will only be able to take advantage of it if his use is in accordance with honest practices in industrial and commercial matters. There is a duty to act fairly with respect to the interests of the trade mark proprietor. The test is objective, and requires consideration of whether there would be unfair competition with the claimant and whether the use suggests a link to the trade mark proprietor (see *Celine*, 2007). In particular, use will not be considered honest if: it is done in such a manner as to give the impression that there is a commercial connection between the third party and the trade mark owner; it affects the value of the trade mark by taking unfair advantage of its distinctive character or repute; it entails the discrediting or denigration of that mark; or where the third party presents its product as an imitation or replica of the product bearing the trade mark of which it is not the owner (*Gillette Finland*, 2005).

Comparative Advertising

Comparative advertising is dealt with under its own special EU Directive – the aptly named Directive Concerning Misleading and Comparative Advertising

(CAD). The Directive contains a list of criteria that must be met before a comparison may be considered acceptable. This includes things like making sure that it compares goods or services meeting the same needs or intended for the same purpose; that the comparison is objective and verifiable; that it does not take unfair advantage of, discredit or denigrate the trade marks; and that it does not cause confusion. The CJEU has clarified that essentially what matters for the purposes of the CAD is whether the products are interchangeable (*Lidl*, 2011) – i.e. that the comparison is like-for-like. Furthermore, an advertisement can be misleading if the information in it (or omitted from it) was such that the decision to buy the goods was made in the mistaken belief that the selection of goods from the advertiser was representative of the general level of his prices or in the mistaken belief that all of the advertiser's products were cheaper than those of his competitor. Use which does not comply with the Comparative Advertising Directive would not be regarded as fair (*O2*, 2007).

Earlier Rights

Generally speaking, a registered trade mark cannot be used to stop someone who has used the mark continuously in a particular locality prior to the date on which the trade mark was registered from continuing to use the mark in that locality. However, if the trade mark was already in use at the date of application, then any prior use must have commenced before the date on which the trade mark owner first started using the trade mark. In such a case, the owner of the earlier right must show that at that date his use of the mark was protected in the relevant locality by the law of passing off. (For the requirements of a cause of action in passing off, see Chapter 15.) An example will illustrate: suppose, the claimant had registered a trade mark for domestic cleaning services, but prior to the date of his application, the defendant was already using the same mark for domestic cleaning services in the London area. If the defendant could prove that it had a reputation for cleaning services in the London area at the date of the claimant's application such that it could have prevented the claimant from using the mark in the London area by relying on its rights in passing off, the defendant will have a defence to an action for trade mark infringement.

Defendant Using his own Registered Mark

The Trade Marks Act states that if the defendant has himself registered a trade mark, the use of that registered trade mark for the goods or services for which it is registered will not amount to an infringement of the claimant's registered trade mark. This defence, available under the previous Trade Marks Act, was reintro-duced in the new Trade Marks Act 1994. However, this is one of the more blatant instances of the UK legislators going on a frolic of their own, since the defence has no basis in the European Trade Mark Directive from which the Act is supposed to be derived. Consequently, it is probably unsafe for a defendant to rely on it in relation to a UK mark. It does not appear in the Community Trade Mark Regulation and, therefore, does not apply to Community registered trade marks. Nor does it apply to a passing off claim (*Inter-Lotto v Camelot*, 2003).

12

Removal from the Register – Revocation and Invalidity

Introduction

Once registered, a mark is not immune from attack. Anyone can apply for its registration to be revoked (removed from the register) or declared invalid (treated as though the registration never was). Which procedure is used depends on the ground of attack. In general, a declaration of invalidity is used where the problem is that the mark should not have been registered in the first place. So, proof of one of the grounds for refusal of registration normally leads to a declaration of invalidity. In contrast, revocation is used where a problem has arisen with the mark since it was registered. If, for example, a mark has not been used for the required period, it will be liable for revocation. Either way, the mark is knocked out. However, the practical effects of revocation and invalidity do vary significantly. Invalidity rips the mark out at the roots, the effect being that it is treated as never having existed. Revocation, in contrast, only applies from the point at which the grounds are met: it therefore leaves a stump behind, with the consequence that past infringements may still be actionable.

Most applications for invalidity or revocation occur because the mark is (or is perceived to be) an obstacle to another's trade mark application or because the owner of the trade mark has sued for infringement and the defendant says, by way of defence, that the mark should not be on the Register at all. Sometimes applications are made to limit the scope of protection of a mark (partial invalidity or partial revocation) where the problem arises only in respect of some of the goods or services. For example, a mark might have been used for a narrow range of goods but registered for a much broader class.

For UK trade marks, applications are made to the Registrar or the High Court, although if proceedings concerning the mark are pending in court (as they will be in an infringement case), the application must be made to the court. The procedure in the case of Community trade marks is covered in Chapter 13. This chapter sets out the grounds on which a mark can be removed from the Register. Many of the grounds are the same as the grounds for refusing to register a mark which are dealt with in Chapter 9, and reference should be made to that chapter where indicated.

Grounds for Revocation

Non-Use

There is a general maxim in trade mark law: 'Use it or lose it', but in practice this is more qualified. The proprietor of a mark is given a period in which to put a mark into use before it will become vulnerable to cancellation on this ground. A mark which has not been used in the UK (or in the EU, in the case of a Community trade mark) for five years can be revoked. The rationale for this rule is to reduce the number of trade marks and, hence, conflicts between them. Time only begins to run from the date when the mark is actually put on the register. Since it can take a while for an application to be processed (about two months for an unopposed UK mark, six months for an unopposed Community mark – opposition in both cases will push the date back), in practice the owner has a long time from application to put it into use. When challenged for non-use, the burden is on the trade mark owner to show that the mark has been used within the relevant period. The use must satisfy a number of requirements. First, it must be by the owner or with her consent: so use only by a licensee will do.

Secondly, it must be in relation to the goods or services for which the trade mark was registered. If the goods or services are widely defined, it may be necessary to dig deeper into the specification to work out precisely what things the mark has been used for in order to arrive at a fair specification of goods or services having regard to the use made. For example, in *Thomson Holidays v Norwegian Cruise Lines*, 2003, FREESTYLE was registered for 'arrangement and booking of travel, tours and cruises; escorting travellers and arranging the escorting of travellers; providing tourist office services and booking and provision of accommodation and catering services for travellers'. The mark had actually only been used by the trade mark owner for package holidays of the 18–30 variety. The claimant sued the defendant for using FREESTYLE for cruise holidays (generally known for attracting older customers). At first instance, the judge limited the specification to exclude cruises on cruise ships on the ground that they formed a distinct category of holiday product which differed in kind and customer from land-based holiday products, such as those offered by the trade mark owner. The Court of Appeal rejected this limitation, saying that the specification should be limited to 'package holidays', since this would be how the average consumer would describe the services provided by the trade mark owner.

The precise scope of the limitation made by the court can be crucial in a trade mark infringement case. In *Thomson Holidays*, the trade mark owner lost on infringement at first instance, when its mark was limited to exclude cruise holidays, but won on appeal, when its mark was limited to package holidays. Cruise holidays were held to be a type of package holiday. It followed that the marks and services were identical and there was infringement of the same mark/services type.

So, if a mark has been on the register for more than five years, a trade mark owner cannot be sure that a widely drawn specification will enable him to prevent any use of the trade mark falling within the specification. If he has not used the mark across the whole width of the specification, it is vulnerable to being cut down. Nonetheless, in the real world he is likely to gain an advantage. People do not want to get into trade mark fights so, if a company is not committed to a mark, it is likely to use another rather than become involved in a protracted non-use fight.

Thirdly, the use must be use of the trade mark as registered, or of a form of the mark differing only in elements which do not alter its distinctive character. How different can the mark actually used be from that registered before it alters its the distinctive character? Some guidance can be obtained from the cases but it can often be a difficult question on which reasonable people can differ. Thus, '2nd Skin' was held not to be an alteration of the distinctive character of the registered mark 'Second Skin' (*Second Skin TM*, 2001). In the long-running beer wars between the US and Czech Budweisers, the Court of Appeal upheld the decision of the hearing officer in the Trade Mark Registry that use of the words '*Budweiser-Budweiser-Budvar-Budweiser-Budbräu-Bud-*' in block capitals around a circle enclosing a motif consisting of a shield with a lion on it, superimposed on a castle with towers, was use of the registered mark in a form which did not alter the distinctive character of the registered mark consisting of the words '*Budweiser Budbräu*' in stylised writing. The High Court had concluded differently. The Court of Appeal said that if there been a free choice between the hearing officer's decision and that of the judge in the High Court, it would have preferred the latter (there was no free choice because the appeal court is limited to correcting an error of principle) (*Bud and Budweiser Budbräu TMs*, 2003). The differing views expressed indicate the uncertainty where a trade mark owner uses his mark in a different form from that registered. The moral is clear: the mark should be used in the same form as registered to avoid the danger of revocation for non-use. And if the owner decides to vary the mark, he should at least attempt to register the variant, too.

Fourthly, the use must be 'genuine'. The meaning of 'genuine use' was considered by the ECJ in *Ansul v Ajax*, 2003. MINIMAX was registered for fire extinguishers and associated products. The owner had stopped selling fire extinguishers, but continued to sell parts for MINIMAX fire extinguishers and to maintain, check and repair them. The ECJ held that, where the trade mark owner sells parts which are integral to the structure of the goods previously sold and for this purpose makes actual use of the mark, the use may be genuine. More generally, it found that genuine use entails use of the mark on the market, not just internal use by the undertaking concerned. Therefore, use of the mark must relate to goods or services already marketed or about to be marketed for which preparations by the undertaking to secure customers are under way, particularly in the form of advertising campaigns. Further, use of the mark must be real, i.e. warranted in the economic sector concerned to maintain or create a share in the market for the goods or services protected by the mark. Use with the motive of maintaining the registration is not 'genuine' in this sense. Even a tiny amount of use (e.g. samples to test the market), with no intention other than trading under the mark, will do (*Laboratoires Goemar's TM*, 2004). However, free samples handed out when another product is purchased are not at all distributed with the aim of penetrating the market for goods, and so will not amount to genuine use (*Silberquelle*, 2009).

If the owner cannot show use of his registered trade mark, it may still be open to him to show that there are proper reasons for the non-use. If proper reasons can be shown, then the mark will not be revoked. 'Proper reasons' are limited in scope. Any obstacles must have a direct relationship with the use of the trade mark and which make that use impossible or unreasonable. The obstacles must be 'independent of the will' of the proprietor – and not just 'out of their control' once created (*Armin Häupl v Lidl*, 2007). They do not include ordinary commercial delays (*Philosophy di Alberta Ferretti TM*, 2003). Here the owner relied upon problems with a first licensee and delays due to the time taken to develop and market a fragrance. The Court of Appeal held that such ordinary commercial delays in producing a new product did not amount to proper reasons for non-use.

The Mark has Become a Common Name in the Trade

If an owner, through his acts or inactivity, permits his trade mark to become the common name in trade for a product or service for which it is registered, then it is also liable to be revoked. This is sometimes referred to as the mark becoming 'generic'. This may occur where the owner is the first on the market with a new product, the trade mark of which then becomes generally used in trade as the name of products of this type. There are numerous examples where trade marks have come to be generally used by consumers as the common name for a product. Sometimes the mark just turns completely into the generic word: 'gramophone' is an old example; 'aspirin' is another (though it is still a trade mark in Germany). There are other, subtler, cases: where the public know the word is a trade mark but nonetheless commonly use it in a generic context; 'Hoover' is the classic example, 'Yale' and 'Biro' are others. The latter sort of case is not strong enough for revocation. Revocation is limited to cases in which the mark has become a common name in the trade. Moreover, this must have come about due to the acts or inactivity of the owner. This means, in practice, that an owner must be careful to ensure that she polices use of her mark.

In the case of a Community trade mark, there is a specific provision which allows a trade mark owner to request that any publisher of a dictionary or the like who reproduces his mark in a way which gives the impression that it constitutes a generic name ensures that the reproduction of the trade mark in the next edition is accompanied by an indication that it is registered.

The Mark has Become Misleading

This is similar to the requirement for registration that a mark applied for must not be deceptive, as to which see Chapter 9. However, for revocation, the misleading nature of the mark must have arisen as a consequence of the use made of it by the owner or with his consent.

Partial Revocation

As noted, in relation to each of the grounds for revocation, if the grounds only exist in respect of some of the goods or services for which the trade mark is registered, then the mark will be revoked only for those goods and services. See, for example, the *Thomson Holidays* case, above.

Grounds for Invalidity

An application for invalidity of a trade mark may be made on the ground that the mark was registered in breach of one or more of the requirements for registration.

In other words, that the mark is not distinctive, is descriptive, contrary to public policy or morality, deceptive, a specially protected emblem, applied for in bad faith or, in the case of a shape mark, that it does not comply with the special requirements laid down for these. The difference in the case of an application for invalidity is that on the question of distinctiveness and descriptiveness, the facts will be considered as at the date of the application for invalidity. So, if as a result of use which has been made of the mark since the date of registration it has acquired a distinctive character, it will not be invalidated.

An application for invalidity may also be made on the ground that there are other earlier trade marks or earlier rights which should have prevented registration. In the case of a Community trade mark, an application for invalidity based on an earlier mark or right can only be made by the owner of the earlier mark or right. In the case of both UK and Community marks, if the owner of the earlier mark or right relied upon has acquiesced for a period of five years in the use of the registered trade mark, with knowledge of that use, he cannot apply for a declaration of invalidity based on that earlier mark or right. Nor can he prevent the use of the later trade mark in relation to goods or services in relation to which it has been used, based on the earlier right, except if the later mark was applied for in bad faith.

As with the grounds for revocation, if the grounds for invalidity exist in respect of only some of the goods or services, there may be partial revocation of the mark in relation to those goods or services only.

13

Community Marks, International Registration of Marks and Well-Known Marks

The Community Trade Mark

The crucial difference between a UK trade mark and a Community trade mark (CTM) is that a UK trade mark provides protection for the UK only, whilst a CTM covers the whole of the EU. Importantly, injunctions can be granted in court in one Member State of the EU which prevent use of a CTM throughout the EU in appropriate cases. The legislation that governs the CTM regime – the Community Trade Mark Regulation – is, to all intents and purposes (at least as far as this text is concerned), substantively identical to the Community Trade Mark Directive, upon which the UK Trade Marks Act 1994 is itself based. Accordingly, for the most part the substantive law relating to UK trade marks and CTMs is the same. But the procedure for applying for and, in certain respects, litigating, a CTM is rather different. The main differences are covered here.

The CTM system is administered by a body called OHIM (although there are proposals to change its cumbersome name). OHIM and its boards of appeal decide on whether CTMs should be registered in the first place and will also consider applications for their revocation and invalidity.

Applications for a Community Trade Mark

An application must be made in one of the official languages of the EU. In addition, a second language must be indicated which is one of the five languages of OHIM, namely English, French, German, Italian or Spanish. The application can be filed at OHIM or the UK Trade Marks Registry. OHIM has a useful website, at http://oami.europa.eu/ which contains detailed information about the application procedure, among other things. Natural or legal persons not having either their domicile or their principal place of business or a real and effective industrial or commercial establishment in the EU must be professionally represented before OHIM, although an application can be filed by anyone without specialist assistance. However, as with an application for a UK trade mark and, probably more so, the assistance of an experienced representative is likely to prevent problems from arising with the making of the application and any registration subsequently acquired. The cost of an application for a CTM is significantly higher than for a UK trade mark. The basic cost of filing an application is currently €1,050 (€900 if filing online) plus €150 for each class of goods or services in excess of three. The renewal fee is €1,500 every 10 years (€1,350 if done online), with an additional €400 for each class of goods or services in excess of three.

As with an application for a UK trade mark, a CTM must be applied for in specific classes for specific goods or services and these should be carefully chosen to reflect the use which the applicant intends to make. A recent case, *IP TRANSLATOR* (2012) has emphasised the importance of clarity and the headings of classes. The application should be made by the person, firm or company actually using or intending to use the mark. An agent or representative of the proprietor should not apply for registration of the mark in his own name without the proprietor's consent, otherwise the proprietor may be able to oppose the grant of the mark on this ground, apply to have the mark invalidated once registered and oppose use by the agent or representative, if such use is not authorised.

OHIM examines the mark to see whether any of the 'absolute' grounds for refusal of the mark apply, e.g. that the mark is not distinctive (as to which, see Chapter 9). OHIM cannot itself raise any objection based on earlier marks or rights: these must be raised by the proprietor of the earlier mark or right in opposition proceedings. The applicant will be given the opportunity to respond to any objections raised on the examination. If these are overcome, the application is published in the *Community Trade Marks Bulletin*. If they are not, and the application is refused, an applicant may appeal the refusal to the Board of Appeal. From the Board of Appeal, a further appeal lies to the General Court of the EU.

Upon publication of the application, any person can submit observations to OHIM as to why the mark should not be registered (again, based on the grounds for refusal in Chapter 9). These observations are sent to the applicant for comment.

The proprietors of earlier marks or rights identified in the search will be informed of the publication of the application. They have three months from the date of publication to give notice of opposition to the registration of the mark based on their earlier marks or rights.

During any opposition procedure both sides (the applicant and the opponent) are given the opportunity to file written observations. A decision is made on the opposition by the Opposition Division. An appeal from the Opposition Division can be made to the Board of Appeal. Again, any further appeal from the Board of Appeal lies to the General Court. If there is no opposition, or any opposition is unsuccessful, the application will proceed to registration.

Applications for Revocation or Invalidity

Applications for revocation or invalidity of a CTM may be made to OHIM, where they will be considered by the Cancellation Division (with appeal to the Board of Appeal and then the General Court). In the case of applications based on earlier marks or rights, they must be made by the proprietor of the relevant earlier mark or right.

Each country has to nominate a 'Community Trade Mark Court' where CTMs can be litigated. The UK has nominated the High Court (Chancery Division) and the Court of Session in Scotland. Applications for revocation or invalidity may be made by way of counterclaim in those courts.

Actions for Infringement

Actions for infringement of a CTM must be brought in a Community Trade Mark Court, ,and normally in the country where the defendant is domiciled or in which he has an establishment. In these circumstances, the court will have jurisdiction over acts of infringement in any country in the Community. An injunction may be granted so as to operate EU-wide, though certain, essentially administrative functions by way of registration, have to be gone through before it can be enforced in another EU country.

'International' Registration of Trade Marks

Companies with an international business may wish to obtain trade mark protection in other countries in the world. There now exists a centralised system which simplifies the procedure for obtaining trade mark registrations in other countries. This is provided by the 'Madrid Protocol', to which the UK, along with most other countries is a signatory.

Whilst a detailed explanation of the ins and outs of the procedure under the Madrid Protocol is outside the scope of this book, in essence what the procedure allows a trade mark applicant to do is apply for an 'international registration' designating the countries in which protection is sought. The application is made through the trade mark registry of one country, but is then subject to examination in each of the countries designated. The registration obtained as a result gives the same protection as a national mark in each country.

What is not obtained by a so-called 'international' registration is a true international registration – a single registration taking effect in a number of countries. You simply get a bunch of national registrations.

Well-Known Marks

Some foreign marks may be well-known in the UK, but not registered or even used here. Consider, for example, a recording studio situated in New York with an international reputation and clientele (as in *Pete Waterman v CBS*, 1993). Previously, whether or not such a business could bring proceedings to prevent the use of its name by a third party in the UK was somewhat uncertain. The Trade Marks Act 1994 now gives the foreign owner of a mark which is well-known in the UK the right to protection of his mark here whether or not he carries on business or has any goodwill in the territory.

The owner must show that his mark is well-known in the UK. Well-known probably means something less than famous, but something more that merely having a reputation, as would be required in a passing off case (as to which, see Chapter 15). The owner of a well-known mark can prevent the use of any mark which is identical or similar to his mark and is being used for identical or similar goods or services, if he can show that the use in question is likely to cause confusion. This is similar to the test for registered trade mark infringement, which is discussed in Chapter 11. It should be noted that although use of the mark can be prevented in these circumstances by the grant of an injunction, there is no right to damages.

Whether this right really adds anything to the law of passing off as now developed by the courts is doubtful. Since it came in in 1994, there has been no case where its existence made any real commercial difference; and it is difficult to think of one that might.

14

Collective and Certification Marks

Collective Marks

A collective mark is a special type of trade mark: one applied for and used by members of a trade or professional association to distinguish the goods or services of members of that association from other goods or services. The general provisions of the Trade Marks Act 1994 apply to collective marks, subject to certain qualifications. The main qualifications relating to collective marks are addressed here.

Application

The usual requirements for registration of a mark are adapted in the following way in relation to applications for registration of a collective mark. First, as already mentioned, the mark is applied for by an association and must be shown to be distinctive of the association. Secondly, although the mark must not be descriptive, unlike a standard trade mark application a collective mark may consist of something which designates the geographical origin of the goods or services. For example, the trade association of producers of San Daniele ham in Italy registered a mark comprising the words *Prosciutto di San Daniele Sd* for dry cured ham from the area geographically delimited by the current boundaries of the Municipality of San Daniele del Friuli. Thirdly, the mark must not be something which is liable to mislead the public as to the character or significance of the mark, in particular, by being taken as something other than a collective mark. Fourthly, an applicant for a collective mark must file with the Trade Mark Registry regulations governing use of the mark. These regulations should include the persons authorised to use the mark, the conditions of membership of the association and, where they exist, the conditions of use of the mark. The mark will not be registered unless the regulations meet these requirements and are not contrary to public policy or accepted principles of morality. The regulations are open to inspection by members of the public, and any amendments to the regulations must be accepted by the Registrar.

Infringement

The same tests for infringement apply to collective marks as to standard registered trade marks. In the case of collective marks consisting of signs or indications designating the geographical origin of the goods, the proprietor cannot prevent the use of such signs or indications by a third party where they are used in accordance with honest practices in industrial or commercial matters.

Revocation and Invalidity

A collective mark may be revoked or invalidated on the same grounds as a standard registered trade mark (see Chapter 12). In addition, the mark may be revoked if it has become misleading in the way outlined above in relation to applications, if the proprietor has failed to observe or secure the observance of the regulations governing use of the mark or if the regulations have been amended in such a way that they no longer comply with the requirements outlined above or are contrary to public policy or to accepted principles of morality. The mark may be invalidated if it was registered in breach of the requirement that it not be misleading in the way outlined above or the requirements outlined above relating to the regulations.

Community Collective Marks

A Community collective mark exists, which may be obtained from OHIM. It is very similar to a UK collective mark, but is subject to the Community Trade Mark Regulation. It takes EU-wide effect.

Certification Marks

A certification mark is unlike a trade mark (or even a collective mark), in that it does not indicate the origin of goods or services as such, but serves to indicate that the goods or services in connection with which it is used are certified by the proprietor of the mark in respect of origin, material, mode of manufacture of goods or performance of services, quality, accuracy or other characteristics. By way of example, the British Standards Institution has registered the 'kite' mark as a certification mark – goods are only permitted to carry the mark under licence from the BSI. The general provisions of the Trade Marks Act 1994 apply to certification marks, subject to certain qualifications. The main qualifications relating to certification marks are addressed here.

Application

The usual requirements for registration of a mark (which are covered in Chapter 9) are adapted in the following way in relation to applications for registration of a certification mark. First, the mark must be shown to distinguish goods or services which are certified from those which are not. Secondly, as with collective marks, a certification mark may consist of something which designates the geographical origin of the goods or services. Thirdly, the applicant for a certification mark must not actually carry on business involving the supply of the goods or services of the kind certified. In other words, the applicant will generally be a trade or professional association (e.g. the Stilton Cheese Makers' Association). Fourthly, the mark must not be something which is liable to mislead the public as to the character or significance of the mark, in particular, by being taken as something other than a certification mark. Fifthly, an applicant for a certification mark must file with the Registrar regulations governing use of the mark. (An example of the sort of thing is to be found in the report of *Stilton TM,* 1967.) Such regulations must not be contrary to public policy or morality and must comply with the following requirements. They must indicate who is authorised to use the mark, the characteristics certified by the mark, how the certifying body is to test those characteristics and to supervise use of the marks, the fees (if any) to be paid in connection with operation of the mark and the procedures for resolving disputes. As with collective marks, the regulations must be open to inspection and the Registrar must approve amendments to the regulations. Sixthly, an applicant for a certification mark must be competent to certify the goods or services for which the mark is to be registered.

Infringement

The same tests for infringement apply to certification marks as to standard registered trade marks. These are covered in Chapter 10. In the case of collective marks consisting of signs or indications designating the geographical origin of the goods, the proprietor cannot prevent the use of such signs or indications by a third party where they are used in accordance with honest practices in industrial or commercial matters.

Revocation and invalidity

A collective mark may be revoked or invalidated on the same grounds as a standard registered trade mark (see Chapter 12). In addition, it may be revoked if the proprietor starts to carry on business supplying goods or services of the kind certified, if it has become misleading in the way outlined above in relation to applications, if the proprietor has failed to observe or secure the observance of the regulations governing use of the mark, if the regulations have been amended in such a way that they no longer comply with the requirements outlined above or are contrary to public policy or to accepted principles of morality or if the proprietor is no longer competent to certify the goods or services for which the mark is registered. The mark may be invalidated if it was registered in breach of the requirement that the proprietor must not carry on business supplying goods or services of the kind certified, the requirement that the mark not be misleading in the way outlined above or the requirements outlined above relating to the regulations.

Geographical Indications and Designations of Origin

We should add that there are various complicated EU regulations relating to the registration and use of geographical indications and designations of origin for agricultural products, food and wine. An explanation of this legislation is outside the scope of this book. The whole subject of 'protected designations of origin' ('PDOs') has become of increasing importance not only within the EU but also internationally. Wine names, for instance, are now very well protected within the EU (the PDO system has taken over from various national law systems, for instance our own passing off law which protected 'Champagne', *Bollinger v Costa Brava Wine,* 1961). Cheese names are similarly protected – *Stilton* is the only British cheese PDO (and is a certification mark too). There have been major running battles to reclaim some 'stolen' names. *Feta* is a good example, made the subject of a PDO in 2002. The argument was between Greece, which wanted it as a PDO, and Germany, France and Holland, which did not (until the Greeks won this battle, most 'Feta' cheese in Europe was not Greek). Some names (Cheddar, for instance) are past recall. Even where PDOs are well established within the EU there is friction with other countries (often the USA). American wine-makers, for instance, are apt to use 'stolen' European names such as Chablis. These sorts of battles are often fought within the context of the WTO.

15

Passing Off

A General Rule

The general rule governing passing off is that no man may so conduct his business as to lead customers to mistake his goods, or his business, for the goods or business of someone else. There are lots of ways of doing this, but the heart of this wrong is telling lies to the public in such a way as to damage another trader's goodwill. If the court thinks that is going on, it is going to want to stop it – in reality this general rule is often more important than all the technical rules of the law of registered trade marks put together. Still, it is important to remember that the law of passing off is not simply a law that prevents the telling of lies. It is about the telling of specific kinds of lie in specific circumstances. The reason that discussion of this subject belongs in a book about intellectual property is that the lies that passing off law prevents are those which injure a kind of proprietary right built up through trading; it is therefore very closely allied to infringement of trade marks. Indeed some people talk of passing off as protecting a 'common law trade mark', but that terminology is a bit confusing. This chapter looks at the boundaries of this aspect of the law.

Varieties of Passing Off

Lumped together under the name 'passing off' is a considerable variety of activities, ranging from simple cases of dishonest trading – where someone puts someone else's brand on a product of theirs or where a garage-owner is asked for a particular brand of oil, or a doctor prescribes a particular manufacturer's drug, and the customer is simply given a different, cheaper brand – to cases that are almost cases of infringement of trade mark. In these days, the simple cases are less common; the trades mentioned are unusual in that customers still expect to get something not in the manufacturer's own package. In most shops, goods pretending to be of a national brand but supplied unmarked would be immediately suspect. The majority of passing off cases now are akin to trade mark infringement cases, in that a defendant has used the trade name or other badge of the claimant on a product not originating from the claimant. There are more sophisticated versions now and again, such as the manufacturer who declares, untruthfully, that his is the brand you find advertised on television. Or there is the practice of some large supermarket chains of getting up their 'own brand' to look like the brand leader's packaging, so that a significant number of people are deceived. Until the mid-1990s, a number of cases where the brand owner had tried to stop a looka-like, failed at the interlocutory stage. The brand owners tried to prove the public believed that he made the goods for the supermarket; the supermarkets said they used the lookalike get-up just to show that their goods were the same sort of thing as that of the brand owner. But then *United Biscuits v Asda,* 1997 went to a full hearing and the claimant showed (although only just, and then with a bit of a fair wind from the judge) that the public believed that a *Penguin* biscuit lookalike called a *Puffin* was made for the supermarket by him. After that trial, supermarket 'lookalikes' became a little rarer (or perhaps more subtle), although walking the supermarket aisles today one may be forgiven for thinking the change of tide was short-lived. There are odd cases of passing off too, that fit no general category, but where the court feels that some kind of deceptive conduct ought to be stopped. Whenever one trader manages to benefit from another's goodwill there is likely to be at least an arguable case of passing off.

'Badges' and Reputations

Most cases of passing off, then, are cases where a trader without in so many words saying that his goods are someone else's nevertheless indicates this by applying to his goods some badge or sign that people have come to regard as a mark of that other's goods. In the simplest case, this badge may be an ordinary trade mark – perhaps a trade mark that for one reason or another is not registered for the goods concerned. (If it is so registered, there will be trade mark infringement as well as passing off.) It may be the name of a business, or of someone associated with the business. It may be a special appearance or 'get-up' of the goods: a specially shaped package, for instance, such as a plastic lemon (see the *Jif* case). But all such cases have these essentials in common: the 'badge,' whatever it may be, must be one that has come by use in this country to distinguish the goods of a particular trader or group of traders; and it must have been imitated, whether deliberately or by accident, closely enough for people to be deceived, or at least to be confused. So the claimant in an action to stop the passing off must prove two things: that the mark or other 'badge' he is relying on has a sufficient reputation amongst custom-ers; and that there is a real risk that what the defendant is doing will lead to decep-tion or confusion of those customers. Actually there is also a third thing the claimant ought to prove: damage – usually that the deception causes the custom-ers to buy the wrong brand, though this is often assumed or overlooked.

The risk of deception

Judging the risk of deception in these cases is not unlike judging whether one of two trade marks infringes another (a matter we have already discussed). But in a passing off action, the question is not whether any fair use of the defendant's mark or other 'badge' would be likely to cause confusion to the average consumer, but whether what the defendant is actually doing is misleading, so that a court may have to look at all the circumstances to see whether they increase or decrease the risk. It may be important, for instance, whether and how the defendant puts his own name on his goods, and what, if anything, his name will mean to the customer. So, whereas in trade mark infringement the comparison is 'mark for sign' leaving out aspects of context likely to increase or diminish confusion, for passing off there is a more general assessment. The degree to which the customers already know where the goods come from may also be important. A business dealing direct with manufacturers probably knows very well whom it is buying from, and is unlikely to be confused by markings which would be misleading to the less experienced; it is when the goods get into shops before the general public, who often make purchasing decisions in a hurry, that misleading markings really matter most.

'Get-up'

It will be clear from what we have just said, that cases of passing off by 'get-up' are not very common. Very few manufacturers these days put the real emphasis of their advertising upon the mere look of their package. Even if packages did not change as often as they do, it would still be more sensible to put the real emphasis on a brand name. So the public is taught to look for the name, and they do; and people are not deceived by similar packages with a different brand name, or none at all. There was a case some time ago, *White, Hudson v Asian,* 1965, where the court held that merely to use a red-coloured wrapper for wrapping cough-sweets was passing off; but it happened in Singapore, where (at the time) many customers could not read the names printed in European lettering on the rival wrappers. The evidence was that the claimant's sweets were known and asked for simply by words meaning 'red paper cough sweets'. In *Reckitt & Colman v Borden,* 1990, the claimants, who sold *Jif* lemon juice in a plastic lemon carrying a loose neck label, were able to prove that the defendant's plastic lemon, although it also carried a loose but different label, would deceive customers. The case was exceptional, however. The claimants were able to prove that the customers not only did not bother to look at the label, but also that they cared about the make of lemon juice (an American judge with the improbable name of Learned Hand once put the point this way: 'What moves the customers to buy?'). The claimants were also able to prove actual deception by stationing solicitors behind refrigerators in supermarkets on Pancake Day, the solicitors asking people who had picked up the defendants' lemon what they thought they had. Despite some predictions to the effect that this plastic lemon case would spawn many more passing off actions, it remains the fact that get-up cases are rare precisely because most people do read the labels on most things. Since the 1994 Act, registered trade mark law has spawned a variety of attempts to protect by trade mark registration that which cannot be protected by passing off: for instance the three headed razor, (such as *Philips*, 1999 held no because only engineering features) and the shapes and colours of washing machine tablets (*Procter & Gamble* and *Henkel*, both 2004, also no – because not distinctive), or the shape of a torch (*Mag*, 2004, which was held non-distinctive as the public would not perceive the shape as a trade mark).

Business Names

Many passing off actions have been concerned with business names, just because, in the past, these could not be registered as trade marks. Actions about business names are much like actions about trade marks: the claimant has to show on the one hand that people have come to associate the name in dispute with him and, on the other, that the defendant's version of it is misleadingly similar to his. In judging similarity, it is particularly important to have in mind what sorts of customers are concerned, and this may depend on use of the name in advertising. If the claimant's or defendant's name is merely used as a company name, in dealings with other companies and so on, it may remain unknown. In *HFC Bank v Midland Bank*, 2000, HFC tried to stop the Midland Bank from changing its name to HSBC. It failed because it could not show that someone with whom HFC had achieved brand name recognition would be deceived by the use of HSBC.

Exceptional Cases where Confusion is Tolerated

In certain special cases, the law accepts as inevitable a certain amount of confusion, and the court will not interfere so long as the defendant does nothing dishonest and nothing to make matters worse. The following are examples.

Use of own name

People have a limited right to use their own name in business, even though they have a surname that is better known in the trade concerned as the name or mark of someone else. But a person who takes unfair advantage of the possession of such a name will be restrained from doing so; the books record far more cases where the courts have interfered with the use men were making of their own names, than cases where the court has let them go on. An established company may claim a right to trade under its name very much as an individual may; but if a new company is formed with a name that is confusingly similar to that of some other business, the court will usually order it to change that name. There is no special right to trade under one's surname alone; nor any special right to mark one's name on goods, where the general public may see it and be misled by it. Readers needing further warning of the dangers of assuming a right to trade under one's own name may care to look at *Wright's* case, 1949 (for soap), *Parker-Knoll v Knoll International*, 1962, *Dunhill v Sunoptic*, 1979, *Asprey & Garrard v WRA*, 2002 and *Cipriani*, 2010.

Descriptive Names and Marks

Those who choose to carry on business under a name which does little more than describe their activities cannot complain if others do the same, and must put up with quite small differences between their trading name and those of other people. Thus in a 1946 case between rival office-cleaning companies, it was held that the names 'Office Cleaning Services' and 'Office Cleaning Association' were not too close. In the same way, those who choose as trade marks words which virtually describe the goods should not complain if others describe their goods in similar terms: 'Oven Chips' is the sort of thing which the courts will not protect, *McCain v Country Fair*, 1981. But in all these cases, the court will intervene if the defendant is dishonest. A defendant who is trying to get his goods or business mistaken for someone else's will find the court very ready to believe that he has succeeded.

Marks that the Public Treats as Descriptions

Special difficulties arise with those very well known trade marks that the general public treats as merely the name of the article concerned. If a person goes into an ironmonger's shop and asks for a new 'Yale lock', he or she may be wanting one made by the Yale people themselves, but equally may just mean that he wants an ordinary pin-tumbler cylinder lock, without caring by whom it is made. There may be genuine confusion between the customer and the shop assistant as to which is meant; or a dishonest shop assistant may use the ambiguity as an excuse to supply a substitute. As one of the AERTEX cases illustrates (*Cellular Clothing Co v White*, 1953), this may make it very hard for the owner of such a mark to prevent its misuse. Here, the case hinged on a number of trap orders made by people in the pay of the claimant. They went into the defendant's shop and asked for AERTEX goods, but were sold those of another manufacturer. Unfortunately for the claimant, their counsel conceded that some members of the public used AERTEX as a description of a particular type of fabric. The judge observed that this was fatal to the case unless it was made clear that the 'customers' in question were not using the word in this sense.

It may be noted that the courts have held that, on the one hand, where a former trade mark had become descriptive, adding the word 'Genuine' to it did not make it into a trade mark again ('Genuine Staunton' for Staunton-pattern chessmen (*Jacques v Chess*, 1940), whilst on the other, use of someone else's trade mark is not made permissible by adding the word 'type'. A Scottish judge once described 'genuine' as almost as sinister in significance as 'type' (*Harris Tweed,* 1964).

'Extended' Passing Off

Geography, the Wine and 'Class' Cases

It may be as misleading to say, untruly, that goods come from a particular area (as with 'Scotch whisky' and 'Swiss chocolate') as to use the wrong trade mark on them. In such cases, any trader who has a legitimate claim to use the place name concerned for his goods may sue the trader who misuses it for passing off. (By way of example, see *Bollinger v Costa Brava Wine,* 1961; *Chocosuisse,* 1999, and *Greek Yoghurt,* 2013, where the courts effectively protected against misuse descriptions of a product (respectively, champagne, Swiss chocolate and Greek yoghurt).) But place names, and especially anglicised place names, may become merely descriptive of things made in a particular fashion (for example, Cheddar cheese).

Nevertheless, where the public expects goods bearing the description to possess certain qualities, or to be made in accordance with certain techniques or to a particular recipe, then whilst anyone who genuinely makes his product that way may use the mark, its use on the wrong sort of goods may still be passing off (*Erven Warnink v Townend,* 1979 (ADVOCAAT); *Diageo v Intercontinental Brands,* 2010 (VODKA)).

There may be intermediate cases in which the meaning of a geographical term or other description may depend on context. Thus it has been held that 'Champagne' necessarily connotes wine (of a particular sort) from the Champagne district of France, and that its use for similar wine made in Spain cannot be justified, even if it is expressly labelled 'Spanish champagne'. So also with 'Elderflower champagne'. 'Sherry' was for some years ambiguous. Following a decision on passing off, the position was that it could only be used alone for wine (of a particular sort) from the Xeres region of Spain, but 'British sherry' was allowed because it had been used for 100 years. Now, 'British sherry' is not allowed at all, Sherry having become a PDO. Many wine names now also have protection as PDOs (see the previous chapter).

In all these cases the class of people who genuinely use the mark lose trade to the person who falsely uses it. A logical extension of the rule includes cases where the claimant uses some official approval mark to indicate compliance by his product with certain regulations, and the defendant falsely uses such a mark to indicate he complies too. It seems probable that the courts will support such an action as passing off, though a case has yet to get to full trial. The nearest the trade mark system has to this sort of thing are collective and certification trade marks (see Chapter 14).

A different situation may arise in an endorsement, as opposed to a merchandising, case, where the defendant uses a celebrity's name or image in connection with the promotion of his product or service. In this type of case, particularly if the celebrity in question has already previously been involved in endorsement work and the manner in which the celebrity's name or image is used gives the impression that the celebrity recommends or approves the product or service, then the public may well be misled and the celebrity would be entitled to prevent such use on the basis of passing off. This was the case in *Irvine v Talksport*, 2002, in which the defendant radio station used a photograph of the well-known racing driver Eddie Irvine on the front of a brochure without his permission, in a move to promote advertising opportunities on the station. The photograph had been manipulated to show Mr Irvine listening to a radio, prominently marked with the radio station's name. The judge held that a significant proportion of recipients of the brochure would have thought that Mr Irvine had endorsed or recommended the radio station. The Court of Appeal agreed.

Other Odd Instances

The ordinary case of passing off concerns the sale of goods in such a way that purchasers will be deceived or confused as to whose goods they are. But there can be passing off where the goods come from the right manufacturer: by selling second-hand goods as new, or spoilt goods as sound, or lower-priced goods as superior ones. There can also be passing off where sellers are confused as to the identity of the buyer instead of the other way round. It might even be passing off where the defendant's name cannot be objected to and it is his address that is confusing. A single case illustrates these last two possibilities (*Pullman v Pullman,* 1919). The defendant, a former director of the family firm, had many years later set up on his own, under his own name (as he was entitled to do). He subsequently altered the name of his house to resemble that of one of the claimant's factories (in itself, probably legitimate: it is not passing off to call a private house by a name confusingly similar to that of someone else, so long as no business is involved). However, he then moved his business office to his house, and wrote from that address to people who had been supplying the claimants with materials, offering to buy from them. That was held to be passing off.

Another odd case is illustrated by the facts of *Bristol Conservatories v Conservatories Custom Built*, 1989. Here the defendants showed photographs of conservatories to potential customers, claiming falsely that they, the defendants had built them. In fact the photographs were of the claimants' work. This was also held to be a type of passing off (often known as 'reverse' passing off). Likewise in *Matthew Gloag v Welsh Distillers*, 1998, placing a lable which read 'Welsh whisky' on bottles containing Scotch whisky was found to be, arguably, passing off.

Odd and Unusual Instances

Where the Claimant does not Trade

There can be passing off, even though there is no trade or business in
sense concerned; thus the professional institutions can (and now an
to) sue both people who put letters after their names so as falsely to
professional qualification and people who form societies with simila
to give members something they can put after their names. There ha
ing off actions about *noms-de-plume* as well as about the titles of bo⟨
But there has to be some sort of business connection, in a wide sense
claimant and the sort of thing the defendant is doing, so that the
satisfied that there is a real likelihood of the claimant suffering dai
sort of business interest if the defendant goes on with what he is d⟨
Stringfellow, the owner of a famous nightclub, failed to stop a comp
long thin frozen chips 'Stringfellows' because the court thought th
really suffering damage (*Stringfellow v McCain*, 1984), and the four
political party called the Social Democrats could not stop the use ⟨
the later, more famous, party (*Kean v McGivan*, 1982).

Over the last 40 years there have been a number of cases coi
chandising rights in popular characters. They tend to arise in the ⟨
a manufacturing organisation takes a well-known television or ra⟨
– real, fictional or even mythical – and exploits the popularity of tl
the advertising and selling of his goods. The question arises: car
concerned (or in the case of fictional characters, their creators)
prevent such exploitation? Again, the answer turns on whether a r
son would think that there was any business connection betwee
and the defendant. Thus, in interlocutory proceedings the co
restrain a builders' skip hire business from using the name of fict⟨
creatures (*Wombles v Wombles Skips*, 1975). In another case *(Tav⟨*
Trexapalm, 1975) a lollipop manufacturer, who had taken a fi
'Kojak', the name of a television character associated with lollipo
self enjoined from using the name (pending a full trial) at the
manufacturer who had built up a reputation selling lollipops u
without taking a licence. In the case of Teenage Mutant Ninja ⟨
Studios v Counter-Feat, 1991) it was held arguable that a defer
T-shirts with pictures reminiscent (but not enough to infringe c⟨
turtles was passing off. The court said that most people expec
thing to be licensed, and so 'non-genuine' goods would deceive t⟨
may have been overlooked, however, is that the public were pro
ested in whether or not there was a licence, what they wanted wa
the T-shirt with the design in question.

Suing for Passing Off

Most ordinary actions for passing off follow one of three patterns. In the first, the claimant acts at once, on learning of the passing off. He starts the action and immediately applies for an interim injunction to stop the passing off temporarily, until the case can be brought to trial. It takes about a month for the parties to prepare written evidence from a few important witnesses and bring the case in front of a judge, who decides on the spot whether the case justifies a temporary injunction or not. By that time, both parties know enough of the strength of the other side's case to have quite a good idea of how the trial is likely to turn out, so there is generally no point in actually fighting the action any further.

In the second type of case, the claimant acts quickly, but either does not ask for, or perhaps cannot obtain, an interim injunction. Instead, the court may order a so-called speedy trial, that is a trial within a few months, rather than the more usual 12 to 18 months which most cases take to come to trial. The case will still require the considerable preparation involved in a full trial, as to which see below, and with less time to do it in, but the advantage for both sides is that the matter will be resolved quickly and, at least in theory, before the dispute has caused significant commercial damage.

The third type of case goes something like this. The claimant waits for months, or even years, before taking any action. It is of course too late to ask the court for an interim injunction or speedy trial; it is the claimant's own fault that the case was not tried long ago. There is no way the parties can accurately assess each other's cases, or see how the matter looks to a judge, without taking the dispute to trial. At the trial, the claimants must prove at length, by evidence from those concerned with the trade, how well known their business or their goods are and how confusing whatever the defendant is doing is. The defendant for his part produces witnesses who have never heard of the claimants; witnesses who by that time have got used to the two parties having similar names or similar trade marks (or whatever the dispute is about); witnesses who are too alert to be confused by any state of affairs worth arguing over at all. The trial will probably be long and expensive. The outcome will be uncertain, because of the difficulty of knowing how the evidence will turn out and what the judge will think of the witnesses. Furthermore, by the time the case comes to trial, the trade and public generally have got used to having these two businesses or trade marks about and have learnt to distinguish them; so that what was passing off when it started may have ceased to cause serious confusion by the time the case comes to trial.

The moral of this story should be clear, but if not: route three is rarely the sensible option.

Note: Trade Marks and the Internet

When the internet started to become popular among corporations, the practice of 'cybersquatting' sprang up. This involved registering domain names that it was thought large corporations would want to use, and would accordingly be prepared to pay for, and then approaching the corporations offering to sell these to them for large sums, usually with a thinly veiled threat that if the corporation did not pay, the name would or might fall into the hands of others.

Two mechanisms have been developed to deal with this practice. The first is reliance on ordinary registered trade mark rights (and possibly passing off). By these means Marks & Spencer (and a number of others) were able to stop a cybersquatter who had registered domain names with the words 'marksandspencer', and variants thereof, in them (*Marks and Spencer v One in a Million*, 1998). The advantages of bringing actions in this form are primarily that firm, readily enforceable, relief can be obtained and the claimant has all of the flexibility of court procedures to deploy. It is, however, not cheap.

The second procedure is much less expensive and can be quicker. ICANN and certain of the domestic domain name registration bodies (such as Nominet) have developed dispute resolution procedures by means of which it is possible to divest cybersquatters of domain names which have obviously been registered to take advantage of someone else. ICANN will (in broad terms) take action where a person has registered a domain name which is (i) identical or confusingly similar to a trade mark or service mark in which the complainant has rights; and (ii) the registrant has no rights or legitimate interests in respect of the domain name; and (iii) the registrant's domain name has been registered and is being used in bad faith. ICANN regards as bad faith the following (by way of example): (i) circumstances indicating that a person has registered or acquired the domain name primarily for the purpose of selling, renting, or otherwise transferring the domain name registration to the complainant who is the owner of the trademark or service mark or to a competitor of that complainant, for valuable consideration in excess of documented out-of-pocket costs directly related to the domain name; or (ii) the person has registered the domain name in order to prevent the owner of the trademark or service mark from reflecting the mark in a corresponding domain name, provided that he has engaged in a pattern of such conduct; or (iii) the person has registered the domain name primarily for the purpose of disrupting the business of a competitor; or (iv) by using the domain name, the person has intentionally attempted to attract, for commercial gain, Internet users to his website or other on-line location, by creating a likelihood of confusion with the complainant's mark as to the source, sponsorship, affiliation, or endorsement of his website or location or of a product or service on his website or location.

Nominet's approach is similar, except that it deals only with .uk registered domain names.

Both ICANN and Nominet have helpful websites which offer comprehensive guidance to the procedure: http://www.icann.org/ and http://www.nominet.org. uk/.

16

Malicious Falsehood

Introduction

This chapter deals with a different sort of unfair competition, known variously as trade libel, slander of goods, slander of title, or malicious or injurious falsehood. It consists of injuring someone else's business, by making, from some 'indirect or dishonest motive', a false statement to some third person. To prove dishonest motive is not always easy. Generally the statement must be so false that the defendant cannot have believed to be true. Real financial loss (or the real risk of it) must be shown by the claimant.

Because of the difficulty in proving the necessary dishonest motive, cases for slander of goods are relatively unusual. They have become even more so since the introduction of the Trade Marks Act 1994. This provides the alternative cause of action for trade mark infringement in cases where the statement made by the defendant makes use of the claimant's registered trade mark and causes detriment to it. In this situation, there is no need for the claimant to prove a dishonest motive on the part of the defendant. Cases of this type are discussed in Chapter 10. Accordingly, where a claimant can rely upon trade mark infringement it will usually be a waste of time and money to include a claim of malicious falsehood (as the court held in *Cable & Wireless v BT*, 1998).

The law of malicious falsehood will still be relevant in some cases, for example, where the claimant does not have a registered trade mark or the defendant has not referred to the claimant's registered trade mark. It is best seen by considering a few examples.

Examples

De Beers v General Electric, 1975

The claimants and the defendants were both manufacturers of abrasives made from diamonds. The defendants had circulated to prospective customers a pamphlet purporting to show by the results of scientific tests that the claimants' products were inferior to those of the defendants. On an application by the defendants to strike the action out as disclosing no reasonable cause of action, it was held that when 'puffing' of goods turns to denigration of the goods of a rival, there comes a point where this becomes actionable. In such a case, if a reasonable man might consider that an untrue claim was being made seriously, and with malice, then the claimant disclosed a reasonable cause of action.

Hayward & Co. v Hayward & Sons, 1887

The defendants, having brought a passing-off action against the claimants and lost, issued advertisements that made it look as if they had won. The claimants brought another action, successfully, to get these advertisements stopped.

Mentmore v Fomento, 1955

The defendants had sued a third party for infringement of patent and had won; but there was an appeal from the decision to the House of Lords still on foot. The claimants were (or so at least the defendants thought) infringing the same patent. The defendants' solicitor approached Selfridge's, just at a critical moment from the of view of the Christmas trade, and indicated to the buyer that if the claimants' goods were not withdrawn from sale at once, the defendants would get an injunction against the store. What he actually said was 'there will be a little court job again'. The defendants knew very well that, until the appeal had been decided, they would get no injunction against other infringers. The court granted an injunction to stop the defendants telling people about their successful patent action without disclosing the full facts.

Riding v Smith, 1876

The false statements concerned need not relate directly to the business. This was a case where the claimant's trade decreased, because of rumours that his wife, who served in his shop, had committed adultery. It was held that this was good ground for an action.

Compaq v Dell, 1992

Dell's advertisement showed pictures of computers in pairs, one of theirs and one of Compaq's. Under each was a price and the accompanying text said that the computers were 'basically and essentially the same'. The judge held they were not, and granted an injunction. Obviously this sort of comparison involves a question of degree (for instance in one pair the Compaq computer had 50 per cent more memory). Had the difference been less marked, the defendants might have succeeded with only a slightly unfair comparison.

DSG Retail v Comet Group, 2002

The claimant and defendant were electrical retailers. The claimant began a series of promotions, the first offering discounts of 10 per cent off ticketed prices for selected goods and the second offering to beat the defendant's price by £10 for any product over £300. The defendant retaliated by using posters at its stores stating: 'Today and everyday Comet prices will be lower than local competitors . . . We even beat competitors' 10% off and £10 off weekend promotions.' The judge held that read as a whole, the public would understand the defendant's posters to mean that the defendant's ticketed prices were invariably less than the claimant's promotional prices. This was false, since the defendant would only charge a lower price when challenged by a customer. The judge dismissed the defendant's argument that the public would understand the statements on the posters as a mere puff, and granted an injunction.

Conclusion

Enough examples have been given to show the scope of this sort of action. It must not be assumed that claimants would always win such actions; traders are apt to say that other people's goods are worse than theirs, and even where such statements are demonstrably false a judge will not necessarily decide that they are dishonest. There is this further difficulty that interim injunctions are very rarely granted in these cases if the defendant intends to try at the trial to show that what he said was true. The *Compaq* case was an exception: the judge found that no jury could reasonably conclude that the statement was true. A case the other way is *Bestobell v Bigg*, 1975. The defendant decorators had painted a house on the South Circular brown. The paint started to turn green, with hideous effect. The defendant said the paint was no good but the paint company said he had mixed and applied it wrongly. To make his point the defendant put up a large notice for all to see saying 'This house was painted with Carson's paint', clearly implying the paint was indeed no good. An interim injunction was refused, because the defendant intended to justify at trial.

Litigation is always uncertain, however, and it is wisest not to do anything that can result in an action reaching a court. The safe rule is not to make disparaging statements about a rival business or its products – especially not using a rival's trade marks. It should not be forgotten that if such statements hurt anybody's feelings, an expensive libel-type action may result – and these days, the feelings of limited companies are rather easily hurt.

There is another problem with cases of this kind. Usually a defendant has said something about a claimant's goods which the defendant regards as unfair. Such cases therefore provide a forum for inviting the court to compare rivals' products to determine whether the respective claims made for them are correct. Thus in *Electrolux v Dyson*, 1999, the court was essentially asked to rule in the course of a malicious falsehood case of this kind on the suction and dust pick-up characteristics of Dyson vacuum cleaners as compared with their Electrolux rivals – a kind of *Which!* magazine test by litigation. In that case, the court sent both companies home with fleas in their ears, having held that neither side had been quite fair about the other in their consumer advertising.

Part IV

Copyright and Related Rights

17

Introduction to Copyright

Introduction

Copyright was originally intended primarily for the protection of authors, artists and composers, and to provide a legal foundation for the innumerable transactions by which they are paid for their work. Copyright sits alongside other, so-called, related rights (such as moral rights and rights in performances – see Chapter 23). Conceptually, these should be kept separate as, despite often deriving from the same creative efforts, they are underpinned by different rationales as well as possessing very different terms and scopes of protection. Over time, copyright and related rights have expanded far beyond their original scope, both in terms of the subject matter protected and the extent of that protection. This chapter is concerned with the whole field of copyrights.

Immediately before the enactment of the current copyright legislation, the Copyright, Designs and Patents Act 1988, copyright had been stretched so far by the courts that it gave a very long period of protection (then life of the author plus 50 years) to industrial designs for even the simplest articles. The 1988 Act restricted copyright protection for industrial designs, replacing it with design right, such that 'full' copyright now only applies to prevent others making such articles in certain special cases – for example where the original work was a work of artistic craftsmanship. But while legislators in the UK were cutting back protection, legislators in the European Community (as the EU was then called) were busy extending it, in the name of harmonisation. These harmonisation Directives have had an important influence on UK copyright law, and have resulted in significant amendments being made to the governing legislation. That said, many of the underlying principles of copyright have remained largely undisturbed and the courts regularly refer to the old cases for help with new problems.

The Nature of Copyright

The primary function of copyright law is to protect from exploitation by other people the fruits of a person's effort, labour, skill or taste. As with the other forms of intellectual property, copyright provides negative rights – i.e. rights to prevent others from doing certain things that fall within the copyright owner's control. However, in contrast to patents, for example, copyright requires a derivative link between the copyright work and any infringement thereof. Accordingly, it is an 'infringement of copyright' to reproduce or copy, for example, any 'literary, dramatic, musical or artistic work' without the consent of the owner of the copyright in that work. However, as we shall see, even complete identity of works will not amount to infringement where there is independent creation and derivation is disproved.

It is works that are protected, not ideas; if ideas can be taken without copying a 'work', the copyright owner cannot interfere. This distinction is a difficult one to draw, both theoretically and practically, but here is an example. If a photograph is taken of a landscape, that photograph will be copyright: good or bad, it counts as an 'artistic work'. It will be an infringement of copyright (subject to exceptions dealt with in Chapter 21) if, without consent, that photograph is reproduced – either in the sense in which a newspaper would 'reproduce' it, by scanning it and using it for printing, or in the sense in which it could be said to be copied, if an artist were to sit down with the photograph in front of him and make a painting out of it. Nevertheless, in the latter case there are evidently questions of degree – whilst a cubist interpretation of the photograph might in some respects be considered a copy, there are prickly questions over whether this should be seen as a reproduction (and thereby infringement) for copyright purposes. Furthermore, as a general rule, it would not be an infringement for another photographer to take a similar photograph of the same landscape: the landscape is not copyright, for the photographer did not make it (the position might be different if he had), and the second photograph, though using the idea of the first, would not be a reproduction of the first. The distinction between taking an idea (allowed under copyright law) and taking the expression of that idea (generally prohibited) is, even in the field of photography, a difficult one to draw and sometimes even with the best of intentions, the courts have simply got it wrong: see, e.g. *Temple Island Teas v New English Teas*, 2012.

An extension of this point, and a further wrinkle of copyright law, is that 'reproduction' has rather different meanings in different contexts – a difficulty that runs right through the law. Accordingly, while the Act does differentiate between different categories of 'works' in some respects, for other purposes it lumps them all together. If we speak of one book being copied from another, this is not the same sort of 'copying' as occurs when (for example) a painting is made into a plate to illustrate a book. In fact the 'copyright' in a work of literature and the 'copyright' in a painting are not quite the same sort of thing: the 'copyright' in a song is again something rather different. Nor is the legal protection needed by the author, or by the publisher of a novel, really the same as that needed by the author of a song (who is mainly concerned to stop its being sung or recorded without payment) or by an architect (who is mainly concerned to ensure that anyone wanting a house such as he would design will employ him as architect, rather than a competitor). A sculptor, furthermore, will get her main protection from the general law of property; her copyright will usually be, at best, of secondary concern.

Copyright, Reputations and Competition

It is not the function of copyright to protect personal or business reputations, or to prevent business or professional competition: it can sometimes be useful for such purposes, but these uses are in a sense accidental. Thus it is no infringement of copyright to imitate an author's literary style, or to take the title of one of his books, or, probably, even to write a book including characters he has invented – though any of these things may be unlawful for other reasons, e.g. if people are misled into thinking that the original author is responsible for the imitation. Thus also it is normally no infringement of copyright to copy another firm's brand name or one of their advertising slogans. (Here again, such acts are likely to be unlawful for reasons discussed elsewhere in this book.) It may or may not be an infringement of copyright to use a photograph of a respectable actress to adorn the cover of a disreputable magazine: it depends on who owns the copyright in that photograph, and whether it is a publicity photograph issued for general use. The actress's remedy for that sort of thing may be an action for libel, or for breach of confidence (if her privacy has been invaded), or (if the photograph was taken for private or domestic purposes) for infringement of her moral rights (see Chapter 23). On the other hand, if in such a case the actress does happen to control the copyright in her photograph, an action for infringement of copyright is likely to provide the simplest way of dealing with the matter. So too, though an advertising slogan will probably not have a copyright, a complete advertising brochure is likely to be copyright as a 'literary work', while any photograph or drawing in it is likely to be copyright as an 'artistic work'. Such works may be trivial from an artistic or literary point of view, but for copyright purposes they have to be very trivial indeed before they lose protection altogether, and commercially they may have great value. A trade mark may consist of a picture and the copyright in the picture or logo might be of great value in supplementing ordinary trade mark protection.

Types of Copyright Dispute

Copyright disputes (other than disputes about industrial designs) tend consequently to fall into three groups. There are the rare straightforward cases where a substantial work such as a computer program or a film has been pirated for its own sake. There are also many cases where the original work has little intrinsic value or has not been reproduced in any ordinary sense, and where copyright is invoked for ulterior reasons, usually of a commercial character. In between come those cases where the work copied is a substantial one embodying a great deal of skill or labour – a fixture-list or a timetable or something of that sort perhaps – but nevertheless its value derives more from such things as goodwill than from the labour put into it. In cases in these last two groups there is apt to be a lot of argument as to whether copyright law applies to the case at all.

Copyright in Practice

Although reported copyright disputes tend to fall mainly into these last two groups, the practical and commercial importance of the copyright system lies elsewhere. The main function of the copyright system is to provide a legal foundation for transactions in 'rights': to provide a legal sanction behind the customary arrangements by which, for instance, a composer is remunerated when some of his music is used on radio or in a film. It is very rare for such matters to give rise to litigation, and very rare for people outside the particular industry to be concerned with them or to find out much about them.

Copyright and Confidence

It is not the function of copyright to prevent betrayal of confidence, whether personal or commercial. But the conditions under which English law protects confidences as such are somewhat limited (they are discussed in Chapter 25), and copyright may be a valuable additional weapon. For instance, an ordinary business letter may be indiscreet without being confidential, and may fall into the hands of competitors without any illegality that will allow the courts to intervene. But even a business letter is a 'literary work' and so copyright. There may be no way to stop a competitor into whose hands it falls from showing it to customers, but he can be stopped from making copies of it for circulation.

A Short History of Copyright Law

As we have said, copyright was originally intended to protect authors, artists and composers, not industrial designers or engineers. In the beginning, the Crown assumed a royal prerogative of granting licences to printers. These licences were highly profitable for the King, and gave him an opportunity to keep printers of seditious material in line. In the sixteenth century, decrees of the Star Chamber were used to keep printers in check. There were common law rights which gave authors (and of course the Crown, which never turned down an opportunity for profit) a limited right to share damages from book pirates.

The first real Copyright Act, the Statute of Anne 1709, gave authors of books the sole right and liberty of printing them for a term of 14 years. 'Books and other writings' were held to include musical compositions (*Bach v Longman,* 1777) and dramatic compositions (*Storace v Longman,* 1788). In the former case JC Bach sued the publishers for reproducing harpsichord and viol di gamba sonatas. Lord Mansfield said: 'A person may use the copy by playing it; but he has no right to rob the author of the profit by multiplying copies and disposing of them to his own use.' This is an early instance of a recurring theme in copyright law: if something is worth copying, it is worth protecting. That principle has heavily influenced the courts and Parliament for the last 200 years.

There were further Copyright Acts in 1814, 1842, 1911 and 1956, as well as Acts dealing with specific aspects of copyright, such as the Engraving Copyright Act 1734 (the introduction of which was largely influenced by Hogarth), the Sculpture Copyright Act 1814 and the Dramatic Copyright Act 1833. The period and scope of protection was extended with each passing Copyright Act, since the lobbying power of persons with most to gain from extended copyright protection usually outweighed that of consumers who had most to lose from it. The Berne Convention – one of the main international treaties on copyright – accordingly now provides for a minimum period of life of the author plus 50 years. The current period in the UK (in the main, life of the author plus 70 years) derives from an EU Directive.

The current Copyright Act, the Copyright, Designs and Patents Act 1988, mainly came into force on 1 August 1989. The Act is long and (unnecessarily) complex, but the basic principles of copyright embodied within it have remained unchanged for the last 200 years. The previous (1956) Act is also still of major importance, since a large number of copyright works were created when it was in force. By and large, if a work had copyright under the 1956 Act, it will keep it under the 1988 Act.

One of the original aims of the 1988 Act was to simplify copyright law. That was not realised in practice. In fairness, it is probably impossible to make a simple statutory code which deals with something as complex as creativity and its commercial exploitation; nevertheless, the 1988 Act takes statutory obfuscation to new levels. The Act was also intended to serve as the law for the twenty-first century. That too has not proved possible – the 1988 Act has been amended in several major ways, including to deal with extensions to copyright term, and to cope with the problems of reverse engineering in computer software as well as to implement the various other requirements of EU Directives. The Act as now exists resembles a somewhat tattered cardigan; with holes, new buttons and patches strewn across its previously pristine knit.

Old Copyrights

As has been noted, copyright lasts a very long time. There are still many works in existence that have copyright, although they were created well before the present Act (or even its predecessor) came into force. For most purposes, any copyright that such works enjoy is governed by the present law; nevertheless, questions of whether the works have lost copyright protection (or whether they had it in the first place, and if so, who owns it) may have to be answered by considering the law applicable when they were created. Such cases are not of sufficient practical importance to justify detailed discussion of the old law in a book such as the present one. It is usually sufficient to remember that if a work had copyright before 1 August 1989, its copyright continues after that date.

18

Works the Subject of Copyright

'Works'

Copyright extends to almost everything, published or unpublished, that can be called 'a work'. The governing legislation (the Copyright, Designs and Patents Act 1988 – 'CDPA') provides an exhaustive list, and limited definition, of such things in ss 3–8 inclusive. These categories of 'works' include: novels; lectures, addresses, speeches and sermons and other 'literary works'; tables, compilations and computer programs, which are also deemed 'literary works'; plays, scripts for cinema films, dance and mime all of which count as 'dramatic works' (the 'film' itself is also a work, but of a different category); paintings, drawings, engravings, photographs and similar things (such as photo-lithographs and holograms), sculptures, works of 'artistic craftsmanship', and works of architecture – all counting as 'artistic works'; scores, tunes and melodies – all 'musical works'; gramophone records, tapes, CDs, MP3s, perforated rolls and other devices for reproducing sounds – 'sound recordings'; sound and television broadcasts; and the typography of books – 'typographical arrangement of published editions'. The primary function of this final type of copyright work is to protect publishers of new editions of works which are no longer in copyright from those wishing to make facsimile copies.

It is of some importance to which category a work belongs since – see Chapter 20 – the rights of the copyright owner depend on it. Distinction is also drawn between so-called 'authorial works' (literary, dramatic, musical and artistic works) and 'entrepreneurial works' (sound recordings, films, broadcasts and the typographical arrangement of published editions) for certain purposes, as elaborated below.

Foreign 'Works'

Foreign works are protected if they are first published, or their author is a citizen, resident, or person domiciled in a country with which the United Kingdom has made a treaty to that effect. This covers practically the whole world. The foreign countries concerned likewise protect British works more or less as they protect local ones.

Merit, Originality, and Substance

In general, works are protected regardless of merit. A play is not deprived of copyright because it is a bad play, or a painting because the artist is completely lacking in skill or taste. Furthermore, things as mundane as television programme listings have been given protection as 'literary works' *(Independent Television Publications v Time Out,* 1984), a tune made up of four notes is a 'musical work' *(Lawson v Dundas,* 1985), and drawings of simple machine parts have been held to be 'artistic works' *(British Northrop v Texteam,* 1974). Authorial works ('literary', 'dramatic', 'musical' and 'artistic' works) must, however, must be 'original', in the sense of not being entirely copies of another similar work – in other words, they must 'originate' from their authors. So, for example, one would not get a new copyright in a tracing of an old drawing *(Interlego v Tyco,* 1989). For certain works, the nexus between the author (and their aspirations for the creative project) and their ultimate creation is stronger still – when considering sculptures (artistic works), for example, the intention of the creator is of paramount importance in determination of the fact of sculpture itself *(Lucasfilm v Ainsworth,* 2010). For entrepreneurial works ('sound recordings', 'films', 'broadcasts' and the 'typographical arrangement of published editions') the standard is subtly different: copyright is said not to subsist to the extent that they are a copy of a previous work of the same type.

'Works' must also be substantial enough to deserve the name, though here again the standard is not high. They must also not be too ephemeral: accordingly, whilst spoken words may fall within the definition of 'literary work', copyright will not subsist until they are recorded in some material form.

Triviality

In copyright disputes of a commercial character, the main issue in the case is sometimes whether a work which has been copied embodies enough 'skill, labour and effort' to be called an original work. It is not easy to lay down any clear rules as to this, for it is essentially a matter of opinion – of the opinion, that is to say, of whatever court tries the dispute. The opinions of judges are never very easy to forecast, necessarily depending a great deal on the precise circumstances of the case in which the issue concerned arises. For instance, few judges can avoid giving some weight to their opinion of the relative merits and morals of the parties to the dispute. Nevertheless, it is possible to give some idea of the probability that a particular 'work' will be held to have copyright.

'Anything Worth Copying is Worth Protecting'

One way of approaching the problem of where to draw the line between that which amounts to an original 'work' and that which does not, is to say that anything worth copying is prima facie worthy of protection against copying. In many cases, this rule is a useful guide. But the line must still be drawn somewhere, and the difficulty of drawing it tends to be most acute just in the sort of case where the rule is not applicable, in those commercial cases where something has been copied, not so much to avoid the trouble of producing something similar, as for extraneous reasons. The most that can be said with certainty is that any sort of drawing may be held to have copyright; that even a few bars of music may have copyright; and that short literary works, such as limericks or haiku, will not be deprived protection on the mere count of simplicity. Nevertheless, the dividing line between original works and those that do not attract copyright because the author's input is below the de minimis level, is fiendishly difficult to divine. Accordingly, whilst the title of a song has been held not to enjoy protection as a literary work (*Francis Day & Hunter v 20th Century Fox*, 1940), more recently the court has stated that newspaper headlines may (*Meltwater Holdings v Newspaper Licensing Agency*, 2011). Nevertheless, it would appear that where a single word is concerned, literary copyright is not the appropriate form of protection – no matter how novel the word may be (see *Exxon*, 1982).

Merit is not necessary, but a composition that is striking – 'original' in the ordinary, as distinct from the copyright, sense – is more likely to be protected by the courts than a commonplace composition of the same size or length. Even so, short business letters have been held to be copyright, notwithstanding a characteristic absence of signs of literary skill. So have advertisements in newspapers.

Updated Works

The first question that arises is how much of the 'work' derives from any particular author: for it is only the part for which an author is responsible that can be considered in deciding whether she has produced an original work. Suppose for instance that a textbook has run, as legal textbooks often do, into a large number of editions in the course of a great many years. The first edition was no doubt copyright; perhaps it still is, perhaps that copyright has lapsed. Each subsequent edition may or may not give rise to a new copyright in the whole book, depending on whether the amount of work done by the editor in producing the new edition is sufficient to be called the creation of a new work. (It does not matter for this purpose whether the new edition is edited by the original author or by someone else; the test is the same in either case.) In connection with a textbook this question is usually not very hard to answer, though the answer is hard to put into words; one can 'feel' the difference between making minor or routine alterations in the book and making a more substantial contribution to the book as a whole. In other cases the distinction may be very hard to draw, and when this is the case, courts may reach seemingly illogical decisions that confuse matters still further. On one side of the line, copying from memory the drawings for 'Lego' bricks (adding a few manufacturing directions) has been held not to give rise to a new copyright (*Interlego v Tyco*, 1989). On the other, a learned musicologist who stitched together surviving fragments of the music of a seventeenth-century composer, filling in the gaps to create a performing score, was held entitled to copyright in the whole. The court held that the process of editing undertaken here combined the scholarship and knowledge derived from a long and detailed study of the composer's music with a certain amount of artistic inventiveness. A claim against a record company which had issued recordings of music performed according to the claimant's score accordingly succeeded (*Sawkins v Hyperion Records*, 2005).

Compilations, Databases, and a Different Standard of Originality

It is particularly difficult to lay down rules for determining whether there is copyright in a compilation or arrangement of facts or of non-copyright material. Traditionally, there would clearly have been copyright in such things as *Who's Who*, railway timetables or mathematical tables, if they were 'original' in the copyright sense. Messages sent out by news agencies have accordingly been held copyright, even where literary form was not involved – as with stock-exchange prices; so have a week's radio programmes; so have the starting prices for a race (which took some skill in sorting out), but not a list of starting positions (which were merely written down as they were determined by ballot); so has an anthology of poems, not themselves copyright; but not an edition of an out-of-copyright book shortened by cutting out about half of it. (In the last case, there were critical notes published with the new edition and these were held copyright.) Copyright has been refused to a local timetable, made by selecting and rearranging entries from a larger timetable relating to a particular town, and it has been refused to a selection of seven non-copyright tables of conventional type for inclusion in a diary (*Cramp v Smythson*, 1944). About all that can be said in general is that mere industry counts less than knowledge, skill or taste in such matters; that the amount of labour that goes into a particular compilation is of great importance; and that anything published in permanent form – a book, for instance – has a better chance of protection than such ephemeral productions as a notice on a notice board. The rest is a matter of how the court feels about it. In the case of the diary, for instance, the Court of Appeal decided one way, the judge who tried the case at the first instance and the House of Lords the other; a sure sign of the sort of case where anything can happen.

An ordinary book of non-fiction may well be copyright on two separate grounds: both from the literary skill that went into writing it, and from the skill and labour that went into selecting the facts set out in it. Historical facts alone are not copyright in themselves, but a selection of them may have copyright as a compilation. Here again the line is difficult to draw: a compilation of facts will have copyright, but mere ideas will not.

Since the enactment of the Database Directive in 1996 if anything things have got even murkier. Now a collection of information which may previously have been considered a table or compilation could find itself labelled a 'database'. The distinction is important. While sharing many aspects, databases differ from tables and compilations in that the materials that make them up are arranged in a systematic or methodical way and are individually accessible. Databases are also held to a different, and possibly stricter, standard of originality. For, in line with an essentially European Unionised notion of what the word 'original' means, the CDPA was amended to require that databases would only be original to the extent that, by reason of the selection or arrangement of their contents, the database constitutes the 'author's own intellectual creation'. This standard of originality has been advanced in other areas as well: accordingly photographs and computer programs are held hostage to the same fortune (the latter by the Computer Programs Directive, and the former (somewhat bizarrely) by the Copyright Term Directive). More recently the Court of Justice of the EU has extended this notion to other works under the Information Society Directive (*Infopaq International v Danske Dagblades Forening*, 2009). It remains to be seen what practical difference (if any) this makes to English law. Early indications from the Court of Appeal suggest that it does not alter the traditional requirement of skill, labour and effort (*Meltwater Holdings v Newspaper Licensing Agency*, 2011). However, this nevertheless begs the question of why the CDPA was amended to take into account the revised standard under the Database Directive if the two are in fact the same. On a purely linguistic level, 'skill, labour and effort' would seem to encompass exertions that would not be described by anyone as 'intellectual creation'.

Photographs and Sound-Recordings

Photographs are not restricted as to merit or subject matter, but like any other works they cannot be copyright unless they are 'original', and this needs some consideration. In a sense, no photograph is original: for the camera only records what is presented to it. But there is more to making a photograph than that, and the skill of the photographer will found copyright just as will the skill of the artist who makes an engraving from a painting. It is the change of form of the work and the skill involved that in these cases justifies copyright. Where there is no change of form, copyright must be justified in some other way; a mere re-photographing of a photographic print, for instance, would not give the second photograph a copyright of its own. For this there would have to be sufficient alteration combined with the re-photographing to make the second a different 'work'. But it may be assumed that, in any practical case, whoever did the re-photographing could show that enough additional skill and originality was put into to give the new photograph a new copyright.

A similar issue applies in the field of sound-recording. Whilst not technically subject to a requirement of originality, copyright in a sound recording is deemed to subsist only to the extent that it is not a copy taken from a previous sound recording. Accordingly, the same sound recorded by two independent people could form the basis for two separate copyrights in those records. However, a 'mere' re-recording would give no additional protection. Nevertheless, in practical cases, such as transfer of a 'historic' recording from wax cylinders into digital format, there may be arguments at the fringes that a recording company has done enough work improving the recording quality to make it effectively a new recording and so give it a new copyright.

Copyright Can Exist only in 'Works'

It is worth emphasising that apart from questions of amount – of whether there is enough of a product for it to count as a 'work' for copyright purposes – nothing can attract copyright unless it is the sort of thing that is called a 'work'. For instance, it will be an infringement of copyright to film a play without consent, but not to film a dog-show or a boxing match: the one is a 'dramatic work', the others are not, for nobody has composed or arranged precisely what happens at them. If the promoters of such spectacles want to prevent photography, they must do it in some other way – such as by only selling tickets to people who agree not to take photographs. So also, a card-index system is not copyright: nor is a game, though the written-out rules of the game will be, and so may any board on which it is played. Thus the inventor of a new game may be able to prevent other people copying his board or his book of rules. A collection of five-letter code-words was held copyright as a 'literary work' (skill was needed in selecting the words so as to guard against errors in transmission), but not a system for coding the wholesale prices in a catalogue: however ingenious a system, and however successful in concealing the retail profit from customers, it was a mere scheme and not a 'work'. The instructions for decoding the prices could have been copyright: but that copyright would not be infringed by a competitor who wrote his own instructions, quite independently. Similar issues arise in respect of the question whether copyright can attach to the spectacle that evolves as one plays a computer game. The general view is that it cannot, certainly not as a dramatic work: the court having held in one case that as the sequence of images varied greatly from game to game, there was no sufficient unity for it to be capable of being performed before an audience (*Nova v Mazooma*, 2006).

Illegal and Immoral Works

By way of exception from the general rules, it has been said that the courts will not protect a work that is illegal, immoral, indecent or similarly undeserving of protection. Accordingly, it is open to question whether a libellous poem can claim copyright; so too an obscene picture or photograph. Inevitably, a great deal will depend on the attitude of the judge trying the case. Late in 1939, for example, copyright protection was refused to a would-be humorous document entitled 'The Last Will and Testament of Adolf Hitler'; while not obscene, it was in the view of the judge vulgar and indecent. Presumably however some people thought it funny, or it would not have been worth publishing, let alone worth copying too. The judge concerned was evidently not blessed with the same sense of humour, but if he had been, the case would probably have gone the other way. Cases of this sort being rare, the limits of this exception have never been very clearly laid down, and it is perhaps questionable whether in this day and age the 'exception' still remains except for all but the most scandalous or scurrilous publications.

Overlapping Copyrights

It is in general irrelevant to the question of whether copyright subsists in a work to consider whether it is covered by some other copyright too. In the case for instance of what are called 'collective works' – symposia, magazines, encyclopedias and so on – there must necessarily be a whole series of copyrights in the separate articles or stories, as well as a copyright in the work as a whole: in the general plan and arrangement thereof.

Furthermore, it is also generally irrelevant, at least as far as copyright subsistence is concerned, that a given work contains within it something that is an infringement of (or perhaps merely copy of) another, earlier, work. The key aspect, in much the same way as the example of the new edition of a book discussed above, is the contribution made by the author of the later work. Accordingly, in Chapter 17, it was pointed out that a painting can be a reproduction of a photograph for copyright purposes. In such a case there will be a copyright in the painting separate from that in the original photograph: the painting is an 'artistic work' in its own right, requiring skill and labour for its execution, notwithstanding that the scene depicted is, in one sense, taken from a photograph. In such a case it will be unlawful to reproduce the painting unless the owners of both copyrights consent. Similar cases are common in other arts too: in a record of music, both the music itself and the recording will be copyright, unless the music is quite old. The point is important in dealing in copyright, for it will be ambiguous to refer to 'the copyright in the painting,' if more than one copyright exists in the painting, and an agreement using such language may have rather unexpected effects.

Translations

A translation will have copyright, independently of the work from which it is translated. The classic example of this was a case where the court had to decide upon the ownership of the copyright, if any, in a book said to have been dictated to a 'medium' by the spirit of a biblical character who had died some 2,000 years before. The court noted that the book was written, not in any language current in those days, but in somewhat archaic English, and decided that the translation from one language to the other must have been done by the medium – who consequently had a translator's copyright. The case is *Cummins v Bond*, 1926; the full report ([1927] 1 Ch 167) is well worth reading itself as a 'literary work'. It must not be supposed that the judge necessarily believed the book to have been dictated by any spirit; but a judge has to decide an ordinary civil case on such evidence as the parties choose to put before him. Since both parties accepted that the book had a ghostly origin, it was proper for the judge to decide the case on that basis.

It should be noted that the matter translated need not be anything that is capable of sustaining a copyright; the test to be applied is whether the translator has expended a substantial amount of labour, skill and knowledge upon making their translation. If they have, copyright will subsist.

Other Cases

In much the same way, it has been held that a shorthand report of a speech has its own copyright (as a literary work), separate to that of the person who spoke the words themselves (*Walter v Lane*, 1900). In such a case, it is the shorthand-writer's skill and labour from which the copyright derives. The speech will in itself probably also be copyright, again as literary work. A photograph of a painting, or a painting made from a photograph; a film made from a book or play and the 'book of the film' – and all similar instances will share a comparable approach. In these cases there are two copyrights (at least): one, in the original work, covers both works; the other covers the transformed work only. So again an architect's plans will be copyright as drawings (an artistic work) – unless of course they are merely copied from other plans. If a building is built from the plans, it will attract architectural copyright; also an artistic work, but one which is quite distinct from the copyright in the plans themselves. Finally, there is a copyright in the typographical arrangement of a published edition of a work, which is separate from the copyright in the work itself.

19

Ownership of Copyright

Introduction

Copyright comes into existence automatically (if it arises at all), without need for formalities or any form of application. As a person writes or paints an 'original' work, so a copyright work is created. Copyright is quite unlike patents in this respect. The result is that it is possible for the question of subsistence and ownership never to arise at all, until the copyright is the subject of some dispute. It will then be necessary to work out who is the owner, with no assistance from registers or formal documents. The rules of law governing ownership are therefore important: fortunately, they are simple too.

This chapter deals with the question of who owns a copyright in the first place; what may happen to it afterwards is a different question and will be considered in subsequent chapters.

The Basic Rule – Copyright Belongs to the Author

Except for the situations mentioned below, the first owner of the copyright in a given work is its author. The author, for this purpose, is the person who actually expends the effort, labour, knowledge, skill or taste in creating the work. In the case of a book for instance, the 'author' of the work will be whosoever composes the sentences of which it is made up. This is not necessarily the same person that writes it down. Accordingly, if a person dictates a book to her secretary, she will be the author – not the secretary. If, on the other hand, she merely provides the ideas, and the secretary writes the book, the secretary is the author – whether or not the book is published in her name (however, see exception (i) below). If a book is illustrated by drawings, the 'author' of the drawings will be whoever drew them, notwithstanding that the idea for each illustration was taken from the book itself. There may of course be books where, although one person wrote the whole text, another provided and selected the material for the book and determined its arrangement to a sufficient extent to be considered a joint author of it. In general, however, the person who chooses the actual words used will be the sole author: for instance, where a 'ghostwriter' composes a person's autobiography, the 'ghost' will be held to be the sole author, even though the subject of the autobiography supplies such facts as may be included. It has even been held that the compiler of a work such as *Who's Who* is the 'author' of each of the entries, although the material for the entry is supplied by the person concerned in response to a questionnaire.

In the case of a photograph, the 'author', for the purpose of copyright, is the person who creates the photograph.

Sound recordings are considered to have been authored by their producer – defined within the Act as the person by whom arrangements necessary for the making of the work have been made. The author of a film is the producer and principal director. If these are different people, then the copyright will be held between them as joint authors. For broadcasts, the author is the person making the broadcast, and for the typographical arrangement of a published edition it is the publisher.

Where two people have made a significant and original contribution to a work and share responsibility for the form of expression, they may be entitled to claim joint authorship – provided, that is, their contributions are not distinct. Contributors of separate chapters to an edited collection, for example, will not gain joint authorship of the whole, but will remain individual authors of their own contributions. However, a musician who contributes a distinctive part to a musical track may well be considered to be a joint author of the resultant musical work (see e.g. *Fisher v Brooker*, 2009).

Exception (i) – Works by Employees

Where a literary, dramatic, musical or artistic work or a film (note the works missing from this list) is made by an employee in the course of his employment, the copyright belongs to the employer (subject to any agreement to the contrary). This does not include cases where the author can be loosely said to be 'employed to produce the work', but is not employed in the ordinary sense. Thus the editor or publisher who commissions a book or article gets the copyright only if the author's contract says so; the publisher who employs an author (by a 'contract of service') gets the copyright automatically: in the same way, if a man were hired to make boots – there would be no need for a contract saying that the boots would belong to the owner of the factory. Similarly an architect who is 'employed' to design a house does not lose the copyright in his design to the building owner; but the architect's draughtsman, who works for a salary, will be an employee, and the copyright in the plans he is paid to draw will belong to the architect who employs him. The exact limits of the phrase 'in the course of his employment' are not very easy to define, and the phrase has given rise to much litigation. For most purposes, however, it means simply that he was an employee (rather than an independent contractor) and it was part of his job to produce that work. One example is the architectural draughtsman already mentioned. On the other side of the line, there was a case where a translation had been made by a man for his employers, but in his spare time and for extra payment (as distinct from an overtime payment). It was held that the translator, not his employer, was the first owner of the copyright in the translation (*Byrne v Statist*, 1914). (It may be that the employer could have demanded that the copyright be handed over to him; but this question did not arise, for it was not his employer that the translator was suing.) It is not quite clear to whom works of a secretly moon-lighting employee belong.

Exception (ii) – 'Commissioned Works'

There *used to be* an important exception to the general rule that the author was the first owner of copyright (it has now been abolished). This related to commis-sioned works of certain kinds. If someone commissioned the taking of a photo-graph or an engraving or painting a portrait, and paid or agreed to pay for it, the commissioner would get copyright automatically in the work made in pursuance of the commission. There were quite a few cases about this – several turning on whether there was payment or an obligation to pay, since, if the sitting was free, the photographer or engraver or portraitist would own the copyright. As noted, this rule has now been abolished, but the exception still applies to works made before the Copyright Designs and Patents Act 1988 (CDPA) came into force (of which, because of the long duration of copyright – see further below – there are still many) and can therefore be important, particularly for old photographs. One case concerned the photographs for use on the Beatles' 'Sgt Pepper's Lonely Heart's Club Band' album. These photographs were taken in 1967 by Michael Cooper, a fashionable sixties photographer. He and his assistant had taken several rolls of film of the Beatles on the famous set and of them wandering about the studio. The photographs included the one actually used for the cover and several other similar ones – 'outtakes'. Michael Cooper's son wanted to exploit some of these outtakes. The Beatles wanted to stop this, and one of the questions raised was who owned the copyright in them? This depended on whether they had been taken pursuant to a commission from the Beatles (or people acting for them), and whether they had paid or agreed to pay for them. The judge held that there was not enough evidence to show that there was a commission prior to the taking of the photographs, or that the person doing the commissioning had paid or agreed to pay for them. So the Beatles lost.

There are many situations in which a person commissions another person to do some creative work. Under the current law the question of ownership might be thought simple: given that the commissioning exception has been abolished, we revert to the general rule – the author is the first owner of copyright. While this is generally true, it can still cause problems. For example, if an engineering company asks an advertising consultant to design a campaign poster, and nothing is said about copyright, then surely it is the consultant who owns it. Similarly, if a partner in a firm does a drawing in her work hours and for company purposes – she is not an employee but a partner, so the first of the employees' exceptions does not apply – then she must now own the copyright.

In strict law, both of these conclusions are true. Nevertheless, the courts are not especially comfortable with such solutions, since they can lead to results which no one really intended at the time. So they occasionally fudge the issue a bit. Some judges take the view that if commercial people and organisations do not make proper provision to regulate their affairs, then that is tough luck: the courts won't spring to their aid. But others will say one of two things: either the engineering company has an implied licence to use the poster design for its campaign or, more rarely, that the company is the 'equitable owner' of the copyright. The same will apply in the second example – the company may be held to have an equitable right to the copyright. Being the equitable owner means that you have a right to have the legal title to the copyright transferred into your name. Accordingly, in a case in which a designer who had been commissioned to create a logo for a client purported to transfer the copyright in the design to one of his client's competitors, the court of appeal considered equitable ownership to vest in the client notwithstanding the provisions of the CDPA (*Griggs v Evans*, 2005). This solution is evidently a way of getting around the problem that the legislation principally gives rights to the creators of the work, but this can sometimes result in the creators holding the people for whom they do the work to ransom when this was never intended by either party at the time.

Crown Copyright

Where a work is either made by Her Majesty or by an officer or servant of the Crown in the course of his duties, the copyright belongs to the Crown. There is a separate Parliamentary copyright. The Crown does not always enforce its copyrights and allows such things as Acts of Parliament to be freely reproduced from the official editions published by the Stationery Office; but the copyright is there, and it is enforced in relation to things like Ordnance Survey maps, or directions from Ministries to local authorities. Crown copyright lasts for 125 years from the end of the calendar year in which the work was made or, if the work was published within 75 years of it being made, 50 years from commercial publication. This provision has the merit that it is possible to find out whether the copyright in Crown works has expired without having first to find out who the author was: an almost impossible task in the case of, say, an Ordnance Survey map.

Where Authorship is Uncertain

If a work appears to be signed, or to bear an author's name, the courts will assume, unless it is proved otherwise, that the person whose name or signature the work bears is the owner of the copyright in it; if not, the first publisher will be presumed to own the copyright. These are however merely rules of evidence: they do not alter rights, but sometimes make it easier for the plaintiff in a copyright action to prove his case. In particular, they make it possible to sue for infringement of the copyright in an anonymous work without disclosing the author's name.

Duration and the Importance of Identifying the Author and the 'Work'

Obviously, determining the category of work that a particular creative endeavour falls within is important from the perspective of subsistence – as there are often subtle differences between the different groups in the criteria required for copyright to exist. However, the classification of a work has more importance than this. Duration of copyright, for example, will vary depending on the type of work under consideration – this, again, reveals another significant distinction between the authorial and entrepreneurial works.

Authorial Works

For authorial works (literary, musical, dramatic and artistic works) not covered by crown copyright, the general rule is that copyright expires at the end of the period of 70 years from the end of the calendar year in which the author dies (which, even considering the economic incentives provided by copyright, is an awfully long time – and which defies rational explanation). For works where two or more people are joint authors, the clock only starts to run when the last of them dies. Evidently, given the importance of the author in this equation, there are supplementary rules that will apply where the work is of unknown authorship, or has been created by a computer. In the former case, the right expires 70 years from the end of the calendar year in which the work was made or, if made available to the public within this period, 70 years from the end of the calendar year in which it was first made available. In the case of the latter, the term of protection is 50 years from the end of the calendar year in which the work was first made.

Entrepreneurial Works

For entrepreneurial works, duration varies somewhat from category to category – gone is the comfort of a general rule. Sound recordings are, at the time of writing, currently protected for 50 years from the end of the calendar year in which the recording was first made or, if published or otherwise (legitimately) made available to the public within this period, 50 years from first publication. Authors from non-EEA states, however, only get this term of protection provided their national laws entitle them to the same (or longer). However, this 50-year term is soon set to change, as, following successful lobbying by a series of aging musicians (for whom the word 'pension fund' apparently has no meaning), the EU has recently legislated to extend the duration of protection for sound recordings (and performance rights) to 70 years from making/publication.

Films are something of an anomaly as far as duration is concerned. In contrast to most other works, their term of protection is determined based on the demise of a collection of people, only one of whom is considered an author of the cinematographic work itself. Accordingly, protection is again pegged at life plus 70 years, but the clock only starts ticking once the last to perish of a set list-macabre has shuffled off this mortal coil. The list includes: the principal director; the author of the screenplay; the author of the dialogue; and the composer of music specifically created for and used in the film. Only the first in this list is actually considered an author of the 'film' for copyright purposes.

Copyright in a broadcast lasts for 50 years from the end of the calendar year in which the broadcast was made, with copyright in any repeat broadcast expiring at the same time as that in the original.

The typographical arrangement of published editions gain copyright for a period of 25 years from the end of the calendar year in which the work was published.

20

What is Infringement of Copyright?

Introduction

It was pointed out in Chapter 17 that copyright is essentially just a right to stop other people doing certain things (the 'acts restricted by the copyright'). The definition of infringement is consequently of very great importance. The present chapter sets out to explain just what activities an owner of a copyright is entitled to stop; the rules stated in this chapter are however subject to certain exceptions, discussed in the chapter following.

Primary and Secondary Infringement

When classifying the acts of infringement, a fundamental distinction must be drawn between those deemed 'primary' and those labelled 'secondary'. The basic distinction is twofold. Primary infringement requires no mental element – an unconsciously or accidentally made copy is just as much an infringement as if duplication were intentional. It can also occur in private settings: there is no requirement for any of the acts of primary infringement to be carried out in the course of trade. Liability for secondary infringement, by contrast, concerns commercial acts (such as importation or dealing in the course of business), and rests on the person accused knowing or having reason to believe that she is working with an infringing copy. The majority of the remainder of this chapter concerns the acts of primary infringement, however, we return to briefly consider secondary infringement at the end.

The Importance of a Derivative Link

The most important point to note about copyright infringement is the fact that it will only prevent people doing things with material that has some causal link with a copyright work. In contrast, therefore, to patents, independent creation will always be a defence – in fact, if a work is independently created, then there is no infringement in the first place, irrespective of what restricted act is alleged to have been committed. It has been said, for example, that six monkeys, operating typewriters at random, would sooner or later reproduce all the books in the British Library; among them, works that were copyright. But there would be no infringement of the copyright, for there would be no copying: the work would have been reproduced quite accidentally, without reference to the original. Accordingly, even complete identity of works may not be sufficient to found a claim for copyright infringement if there was no opportunity for copying to have taken place.

Proving Derivation

The difficulty of proof is often a serious one. It will very seldom be possible to prove directly that copying, for example, has taken place: for only the alleged infringer knows how the work came into existence. The result is that in practice, the only thing to do is to point to the resemblances between the two works and to say that these resemblances are too many and too close to be due to coincidence. Where there is also some proof that the alleged copyist had access to the original work, the court can then be asked to infer that some sort of copying must have taken place. If the court accepts this argument it will then be up to the alleged infringer to explain the resemblances away if possible. That is to say, a reasonable explanation of how those resemblances could have come into existence without any copying must be produced. Not every explanation will do, for judges are not exactly credulous people; if the explanation is that X thought the whole thing up without ever having seen or heard of the earlier work, the judge will want to see X (or hear some good reason why he cannot see X) and find out whether to believe the story or not. But if the explanation is reasonable, the copyright owner must find some other way of proving the case, and as we have said, there is usually no other way available. An illustration of this is *Francis Day & Hunter v Bron* (1963) where the court held that although there were very great similarities between the claimants' tune 'In a Little Spanish Town' and the defendant's pop song 'Why', this was not enough to prove infringement where the composer of 'Why' (whose story was believed) said he could not remember ever hearing the claimants' tune, although he was prepared to admit that he might have heard it on the radio when he was young.

Derivation need not be direct – one work may, for example, be a window into another such that when a restricted act is carried out in relation to it, the copyright in both is infringed. Suppose, for the sake of argument, that a short poem written by X is incorporated by Y as one verse of a song. If Z then performs the entire song in public without consent of the others she may well infringe the copyright in both Y's literary work (in the lyrics) and X's poem (also a literary work) even though she has never seen X's work or perceived it to have an independent existence. Moreover, infringement need not be conscious or deliberate – it is just as much a derivative copy if made carelessly as if duplication were intentional. All that is necessary for an infringement (so long as a substantial part of the earlier work is taken – discussed below), is that the work in respect of which the restricted act has been performed should somehow, through some channels, be derived from the earlier.

Infringement by Reproduction

Whilst there are a number of acts of primary infringement, the one that first comes to mind when most people think of copyright is that embodied by the name itself: the right to copy a work. This right is infringed if the work is reproduced in any material form without the consent of the owner of the copyright. To give a simple example, consider an article in a magazine. In the ordinary course, it will have been sent in by the author (or by her literary agent): sending it in will mean that she owns the copyright and she wants it published so long as she gets the proper fee – and the only possibility of argument lies in the size of the fee. It is only when something goes wrong that a dispute about copyright can arise. Suppose she sends in illustrations with her manuscript and they are not hers to offer for publication; then each copy of the magazine 'reproduces' them without the consent of the copyright owner, and that is infringement. (The person who sent the article in would usually end up paying the damages, if she has the money, but the magazine would be primarily liable for copying). Or the whole article may be very like one that appeared earlier in some other magazine, but not quite the same. This may or may not constitute an infringement of the copyright in the earlier story according to circumstances; and it is necessary to consider in some detail just where the line is to be drawn.

Copying

The Copyright Designs & Patents Act 1988 ('CDPA') uses the word 'copy' in this connection. To copy is an act restricted in all descriptions of copyright work and, for authorial works, refers to the reproduction of the work in any material form – including storing the work in any medium by electronic means. For artistic works, this also includes making a two-dimensional copy (perhaps a photograph) of a three-dimensional work (say a sculpture), and vice versa. Copying of the other forms of work shares a similar definition. However, for broadcasts and films this is extended to include the making of a photograph of the whole or any substantial part of any image forming part of that broadcast or film. For the typographical arrangement of published editions, copying is, in contrast, restricted to facsimile reproduction. In all cases, a reproduction is still a copy irrespective of whether it is transient or incidental to some other use of the work.

A Substantial Part Must be Copied

As for all restricted acts, copying is only actionable as infringement when it is carried out in relation to the whole or a substantial part of the work. This require-ment – sometimes called 'substantial taking' when discussed in the context of copying – has the potential to pose fiendishly difficult questions: the precise divid-ing line between a substantial and insubstantial part of a work being essentially a question of fact, impression and degree.

Where Some Part (But Only a Small Part) Part is Copied Exactly

While the principle 'what is worth copying is worth protecting' is not always a good guide, in this case it is. Once a court is satisfied that there is a copyright work, and that the defendant in the case before it has thought it worthwhile copy-ing out word for word some part of that work, it will be very hard to persuade that court that the part copied was not substantial. Thus where four lines of a short poem of Kipling were reproduced in an advertisement, the court found no diffi-culty in holding that this was a substantial enough part of the poem for there to be infringement (*Kipling v Genatosan*, 1923). As usual however, a lot depends on how the court feels about the case. Where for instance the title of a short story was taken from the refrain of a popular song, and four lines from the song were printed below the title (as of course quotations often are), the court held that this was not an infringement of the copyright in the song (*Chappell & Co v DC Thompson & Co*, 1935). The line must be drawn somewhere: the owner of the copyright in the song was not really deprived of his property or of an opportunity to draw profits from his property; and regarded as a literary work, the song was not quite in the same class as a poem of Kipling.

This question of merit is rather a difficult one. Strictly speaking, it is not easy to see how the merit of a work should affect the matter at all. Yet in practice, it is always easier to found a successful action for infringement of copyright upon a work that has merit than upon a work that has not. The law is never absolutely rigid, and the court will give a common-sense decision where it can. It is fortunate that this is so; but it is sometimes in consequence a little difficult to forecast what a court's decision will be in any particular case. The imponderable influence of merit (or the lack of it) in copyright actions is one of the things that make predic-tion difficult.

An instructive case as to what is a substantial part of a work arose from the inclusion, in a newsreel of a military parade, of a sequence taken while the band was playing the copyright march, 'Colonel Bogey'. The sequence lasted less than a minute, and other things were happening at the same time, but the principal air of the march was clearly recognisable. This was held to amount to taking a sub-stantial part of the march; the more so, because the soundtrack of the film could have been used by itself as a record of the march – to provide incidental music during an interval for instance (*Hawkes v Paramount*, 1934). While the defence of incidental inclusion (discussed in Chapter 21 below) could now be used to excuse this infringement, the principle remains.

Divination of what constitutes a substantial part of any given work is undoubtedly tricky. The absolute quantity that is taken is clearly not a sound guide by itself – four lines from a limerick may well cross the threshold, but four lines from *War and Peace* may not. Equally, reliance upon the proportion of a work taken would again unfairly prejudice longer, and arguably more creative, endeavours. The courts have therefore often stated that substance is not a question of quantity, but is rather one of quality. In this respect, we revert to what it is that makes a work original in the first place – the skill, effort and labour of the author.

Remember always that we are considering substantial *taking*, and therefore our focus is not on the contribution that the material taken makes to the defendant's work. Rather we consider the contribution that the part reproduced makes to the work from which it was derived – i.e. the claimant's copyright work. The link between originality, the authorial contribution of the creator of the work, and the concept of infringement is therefore critical.

Where There is Merely a Similarity of Form or General Idea

In discussing this question, it must first of all be remembered that there is no copyright in ideas. The mere concept of a story about star-crossed lovers, or a school for young wizards, cannot be claimed as anyone's property under copyright. Equally, mere factual information, such as the length of a river or the height of a mountain cannot be the subject of ownership by any one person. Nevertheless, the dividing line between idea and expression is often a difficult one to draw. It is clear that the protected element of a literary work, for example, goes deeper than just the precise words used by the author to describe their scene. It is also apparent that the 'part' to which we refer when considering substantiality need not be discrete; it can be feature or combination of features of the work abstracted from it. Accordingly, even where there is no textual reproduction, elements of the underlying architecture of a work (plot, characters, storyline, etc) may be sufficiently expressed in the text as a whole for them to gain protection from copyists.

However, determining where 'idea' ends and 'expression' begins is so fraught with difficulty as to be impossible to predict with any degree of precision – which makes for wonderful arguments over the substance of any given work where there is no textual copying. A recent example of such delights may be found in the *Da Vinci Code* case (*Baigent & Leigh v Random House*, 2007). Here the American author, Dan Brown, was accused of copying the central plot and theme of the claimants' book *Holy Blood and the Holy Grail*. The plot itself, which the claimants described as one of 'historical conjecture', revolved around the idea that that the bloodline of Jesus survived in France after his crucifixion, merging with the Merovingian bloodline around the fifth century and carrying on. The Court of Appeal considered that whilst it was evident that inspiration had been taken from the claimants' work, and that reproduction of the underlying architecture of a text could found a claim to copyright infringement, on the facts before it there was not enough to find substantial taking. The parts reproduced were of too generalised and abstract a nature to be considered a substantial part of the claimants' work.

It must also be remembered that every competent worker in any field must be expected to be familiar with any important work that has gone before; and it is just these important and successful works, that everyone ought to know and that will inevitably influence works that come after them, that are likely to attract infringers. In fiction it is indeed often the poor and unknown author whose unexpectedly brilliant work is stolen, but in real life that sort of thing seems not to be a commercial proposition. The inevitable influence of one work on those that follow it does not involve infringement of copyright. The difficulty is to distinguish between drawing on the common stock of experience, and making improper use of other people's work. It is often difficult to determine whether a defendant has got sufficiently close to the claimant's work to infringe. A good rule of thumb is that if a defendant has reproduced enough for it to be clear that he has copied, that amount of reproduction will be sufficiently substantial to infringe (see *Designers Guild*, 2000). The key question is again, however, whether the defendant's work incorporates a substantial part of the elements that made the claimant's work original in the first place – whether this be the skill, labour and effort expended by the creator or, as the circumstances dictate, the elements that made the work the author's own intellectual creation).

Judges have sometimes tried to express the way the line is to be drawn, by saying that for there to be infringement, one work must produce the 'same effect' as the other but this is not always a reliable guide. To put it slightly differently, there must be something that might make people encountering the two works in succession feel, 'I have read this story – or seen this play – or heard this music – before.' But the mere fact that one work reminds a reader or viewer of another work is not enough – it is not an infringement of copyright to try to reproduce someone's style of writing (or composing). Some examples may help to explain how such tests work out in practice.

Example 1:

Many years ago, one Austin composed a new arrangement of the music of a work that had long ago lost any copyright it had ever possessed: the 'Beggar's Opera'. The new arrangement was of course copyright; it was also a popular success. A manufacturer of gramophone records, wishing to take advantage of Austin's success, brought out a recording of extracts from the 'Beggar's Opera'. Since the tunes were all old, this was not in itself any infringement of Austin's copyright. But the recording went further: although the actual notes were not copied from the Austin arrangement, the tunes were 'dressed up in the same way', as the judge put it. That was infringement: a record is a 'reproduction'. The case in fact raised in a different context the same question as the example discussed in earlier chapters, of the photographer who sees a successful photograph of a landscape and goes and takes another like it. He may photograph the same view, for there is no more copyright in a view than there was in the tunes of the 'Beggar's Opera'. But he must not go further and imitate to any substantial extent the tricks by which the first photographer has converted the view into a successful photograph.

The Austin case illustrates also the way in which the circumstances of a case influence the court's findings. The defendants there had advertised their records in a way that emphasised the relation with Austin's successful arrangement, and in fact in this connection lay the whole reason for bringing out those records at that time at all. This made it by no means easy for the defendants to argue that they had really taken nothing from Austin: the defence was in effect merely that, as a technical legal matter, what they had done was not reproduction of a substantial part of that which was the subject of copyright. Purely technical defences are always dangerous. If such a question arises on a comparison of two apparently independent works, the case is not prejudiced by any admissions that the one work is connected with the other, and such a defence takes on a rather different aspect. The defendant can, and does, argue that there has been no copying at all in any ordinary sense; that the resemblances between the two works if not pure coincidence – any two works being indeed much more alike than perhaps their authors would admit – are the result of the sort of unconscious influence mentioned above as inevitable and legitimate; and that these resemblances are trivial, not substantial. (He may even argue that the resemblances are due to legitimate 'quotation' of phrases that the hearer will be expected to recognise as coming from earlier works.) Only then does he argue that in any case, what is common to the two works is not the sort of thing that the law calls 'reproduction'. If there is real doubt as to the copying, the technical defence will have a much more favourable reception.

Example 2:

Bauman was a photographer of high repute who took pictures for the *Picture Post* magazine. One of them was of two fighting cocks, which he took in Cuba. Fussell was a painter. He saw Bauman's photograph in the *Picture Post*, cut it out, pinned it to his studio wall and from it painted a picture of two fighting cocks in the same position and attitude as the birds in the photograph. In the painting, the colouring was different, as was the general effect of the painting, which was not at all photographic. Experts were lined up on each side, including the Arts Director of the Arts Council and Professor Moyniham, a well-known painter from the Royal College of Art. The Court of Appeal judges (who were divided 2:1) spoke of the 'feeling and artistic character' of the respective works. These were different and so, somewhat surprisingly, the plaintiff lost. Moral: when courts get into the realms of the 'feeling and artistic character' of a work, anything can happen (*Bauman v Fussell*, 1953).

Changes in material form

A rather similar sort of question can arise where there is a change in the material form taken by a work; for instance, to take examples that have come before the courts, where it is suggested that a dress infringes a drawing of a dress, or a shop-front an architect's sketch of a shop-front. Clearly the two cannot be identical, in either case, but there is still a sense in which it can be said that there can be reproduction of one work by the other. Whether there is reproduction or not in any particular case is a question on which opinions are likely to differ, with the result that it is likely to be very hard to forecast what view the judge who decides the case will take.

Other Forms of Infringement

In most cases, reproduction (in a material form) is the chief type of infringement. However, the legislation also contains a list of other primary acts of infringement. Some are applicable to all forms of works and others to defined subsets. As for copying, in each case the following acts are only infringing if carried out without consent in relation to the whole or a substantial part of someone else's copyright work.

Issuing Copies to the Public

Issuing copies to the public (without consent) is an act restricted in all types of copyright work. It essentially involves putting into circulation a physical copy not previously put into circulation (posting things on the internet is covered by another restricted act: communication, discussed below). This sort of infringement very seldom occurs alone, unless one is dealing with imported works. That is because publication is impossible unless copies of the work are in existence and the making of the necessary copies in this country will normally itself constitute infringement. Nevertheless, it can apply even where the copies that have been made are legitimate, providing, that is, that their issuance has not been explicitly or impliedly consented to. An example may assist: suppose that a recording artist gives his manager permission to make and sell copies of the artist's work only during the course of their management contract. During the course of the contract the manager exercises this right and makes 100 copies, but only sells 50. Despite their legitimacy as copies, it will be an act of infringement for the manager to sell his stockpile once the contract is over (*Nelson v Rye*, 1996)

The right is not aimed at curtailing a second-hand market in copyright goods: there are exceptions in respect of copies of works which have already been put on the market in the EU. Nevertheless, putting a copy of a work on the market for the first time in the UK which has not previously been put on the market in the EU will, without the consent of the copyright owner, be an infringement.

Publishing an Unpublished Work

It is also impermissible to publish a previously unpublished work without consent. This can be important, for large damages may flow from it: in particular, the author's own chance of a successful launch may be completely spoilt by an anticipatory publication.

Renting/Lending a Work

Deriving from an EU Directive, the public rental or lending of a copy of a work is an act restricted by copyright in: literary, dramatic and musical works; in sound recordings and films; and in artistic works other that works of architecture and applied art. A copyright owner is, in essence, given the right to take a reasonable royalty every time any of these works is rented to the public. While evidently not applicable to private lending between friends, of a book or DVD for example, the right does enable the copyright owner to an extra stream of income (particularly lucrative in the film industry) that is not exhausted by the first sale of the copy in question. This is of considerable commercial importance and, to avoid abuse of monopoly, the Copyright Tribunal can set an appropriate royalty.

Performing/Showing a Work in Public

It is an infringement of copyright to perform a literary, dramatic or musical work in public without consent, or to play or show a sound recording, film or broadcast (again in public and without consent). (The same applies to public performance of anything close enough to a work for its reproduction to infringe copyright.) 'In public' has here a rather special meaning. It refers, not to the sort of place where the performance takes place, but to the sort of audience that is present. Nor does it mean that the performance is one that anyone can attend who likes, still less that a charge must be made for admission. For this purpose, any performance is 'in public' that is not restricted to members of the home circle of whoever is responsible for the performance. Guests can be present of course; there can be a very large party to see or hear the performance: but it must be a genuinely domestic affair, or it will be public for copyright purposes. An amateur dramatic show by members of a Women's Institute for fellow members only; 'Music While You Work' in a factory; music played so that it could be heard in the public parts of a restaurant – all these have been held to infringe copyright as 'performances in public'. For the showing/playing of a broadcast in public there is a specific defence that operates where the audience has not paid for admission to the place in which the broadcast is to be seen or heard – see Chapter 21, below.

'Performance' for this purpose includes 'delivery' (i.e. by a human performer) and any mode of visual or acoustic presentation. Accordingly, showing a film in public is both 'playing or showing' the film itself, and a performance in public of any play or music embodied in the film; similarly with sound recordings.

Communicating a Work to the Public

Following the implementation of the Information Society Directive, the CDPA was amended to add a new form of infringement: communication to the public. The act applies to literary, dramatic, musical and artistic works, to sound recordings and films, and to broadcasts. 'Communication' may be distinguished from 'issuing copies to the public': whereas the former is concerned with prohibiting the distribution of intangible copies of the work, the latter is concerned with tangible copies. It also differs from 'performance in public' and 'playing or showing in public' (at least under the UK's legislative understanding of the terms) in that the public does not *need* to be present at the point of communication in order for there to be an infringement (although it may be – see below). Accordingly, a person who plays a tune on a saxophone in the street would be performing the (musical) work in public, whereas someone recording themselves playing the same and then uploading it to the internet would be committing an act of copying (making the recording) followed by an act of communication to the public (uploading it). The Court of Justice of the EU has recently confirmed that the act of communication is to be broadly construed. Accordingly, it covers the transmission of broadcast works, via a television screen and speakers, to those present in a pub (*FAPL v QC Leisure*, 2011). Evidently there is overlap between this and the UK's understanding of 'playing or showing' in public.

Communication to the public has particular relevance in the context of online piracy. Merely connecting a computer running p2p software to the internet where music files containing copies of a claimant's copyright works are placed in a shared directory falls within the infringing act (*Polydor v Brown*, 2005).

Adaptation

It is an infringement of the copyright in a literary, dramatic or musical work to make or reproduce an 'adaptation' of it. Adaptation includes translation, and conversion into a strip-cartoon, as well as conversion of a literary into a dramatic work, and vice versa. Cases about conversions and other adaptations are often very difficult, for they raise in acute form the same sort of difficulty as has already been discussed in connection with the phrase 'reproduction of a substantial part of a work'. Such a conversion need involve no detailed copying: a novel could be converted into a silent film, for instance (which would be 'reproduction' of a dramatic adaptation, if not 'reproduction' of the original work) without taking a single word – there would indeed be no words, apart from occasional captions. This would be an infringement, if done without consent. If instead a non-silent film were produced, it could still be an infringement, notwithstanding that the dialogue was independently written without any copying from the novel. In the same way, it has been held that a ballet infringed the copyright in a short story; there could be no question of using the same words, but the ballet nevertheless 'told the same story.'

There is obviously a question of degree here – substantial taking will apply in the same manner for adaptations as it will for other forms of infringement – and therefore taking a bare plot may not be sufficient to constitute infringement; incidents of the story must be taken too. However, the nature of the act itself would suggest that it is not necessary for two works to resemble one another to the extent needed for one novel to infringe the copyright in another novel, or one play in another play. Nevertheless, the exact boundaries of substantial taking for the purposes of adaptation are probably incapable of exact definition.

Getting Others to Infringe and Similar Cases

In accordance with ordinary rules of law, it is as much an infringement to get someone else to do an infringing act as to do it oneself. In particular, an employer is responsible for acts of infringement committed by employees 'in the course of their employment'.

But copyright law goes further, and makes it an infringement to 'authorise' another to perform any of the infringing acts. What constitutes authorisation is not always clear in practice. In essence it involves granting or purporting to grant the right to do one of the restricted acts. It can include commissioning another person to produce an article to an infringing design or selling a work such as a computer program, where loading and running it on a computer involves making an electronic copy.

In addition, an author who offers a manuscript to a publisher to publish authorises the publisher to do so; and if the publisher sends it to a printer, he authorises the printer to reproduce it. (It is usual for publishing agreements to make the author warrant to the publisher that the book infringes no copyright; but even without this warranty, the ordinary law would enable the printer to recover from the publisher, and the publisher from the author, any loss they had suffered as a result of copyright trouble.)

'Authorising' covers other things too: any case where someone who does not control a copyright accepts a royalty for its use would be authorising the use, even though the initiative came entirely from the user. So, when photocopiers became popular, those who allowed the public to utilise these services unaccompanied, for example libraries, needed to take special care to avoid being taken to authorise the use of those facilities for the purposes of infringement *(Moorhouse v University of New South Wales,* 1976) – usually by the deployment of prominent warning signs.

It should be noticed, however, that merely knowing that someone else is going to infringe copyright is not authorising an infringement: to sell a person a copy of a play, for instance, with a warning that it must not be publicly performed, can never be an infringement unless it is a copy of a pirated edition. What the buyer intends to do with it when she gets it is not the seller's affair. Such a sale without a warning is also probably safe, since a purchaser ought not to assume that she has any right to perform the play: with films, however, the position is different. Similarly, to hire out records or CDs to the public who will obviously frequently use them for home duplication is not an infringement *(CBS v Ames,* 1981); so also the sale of high-speed dual-deck tape recorders (cutting edge at the time – imagine being able to record a tape not just at normal speed, but *twice* as fast as usual!) is not an infringement in itself, though the accompanying advertising must obviously not go so far as to authorise infringement *(CBS v Amstrad,* 1988).

Secondary Infringement

The acts of secondary infringement are, as noted, dependent upon possession of the relevant mens rea – knowing or having reason to believe, for example, that one is dealing with an 'infringing copy', or that apparatus is likely to be used so as to infringe copyright. Self-evidently, an 'infringing copy' includes one whose making constituted a primary infringement of copyright, but the definition also encompasses works which are imported and which if made in the UK would have constituted an infringement or a breach of an exclusive licence agreement relating to that work. A copy which was lawfully made abroad can, therefore, still infringe in the UK, since the copyrights in different countries are separable.

Accordingly, it is an act of infringement in respect of all types of work to import an infringing copy, to provide means for making an infringing copy or to possess or deal with an infringing copy where the importer/dealer etc is in possession of the relevant knowledge. Generally speaking, 'dealing' covers any sort of commercial dealing (including, for instance, free distribution on any appreciable scale as well as sale). Infringing copies that are imported may be seized by Customs & Excise on entering the country if the copyright owner has taken the trouble to ask them to. (The traveller who brings home a book for 'private and domestic' use infringes no copyright, and the seizure provisions do not apply to her; but if she later sells the book she may infringe.)

It is also secondary infringement of a literary, dramatic or musical work merely to permit a place of public entertainment to be used for an infringing performance – 'permit' in this context simply meaning that the person in question has the authority to stop the performance but does not do so. There will, however, be no infringement where the person giving permission believed at that time, and upon reasonable grounds, that performance would not infringe copyright. The point of this provision is that the actual performers may well not be worth suing, whereas the owner of the venue may have deeper pockets.

Criminal Offences

As well as being actionable as a civil wrong, copyright infringement may also be a criminal offence. Directors of companies can be liable if the infringement was done with their consent or connivance just as easily as may seasoned pirates selling dodgy DVDs from the back of a battered van in a pub car park. Although people do not often go to prison for copyright infringement, the punishment can be severe and there are quite often stiff fines. In one case, a video pirate with no previous convictions had copied 219 video cassettes. She pleaded that she was 'only trying to earn a living'. The court was unmoved and, saying that it was an offence of dishonesty, gave her two nine-month suspended sentences. This is typical of the approach of the courts.

There are also provisions for Customs officials to seize infringing goods imported into the United Kingdom upon receiving suitable notice from the copyright owner.

21

What is not Infringement?

The Owner of the Copyright Cannot Control Legitimate Copies

The copyright owner, although given large powers of control over infringement by copying and over dealings with infringing copies, has no control within a single country over the re-sale of legitimate copies once they have left her hands. Such a copy enters free circulation and all the copyright owner can do is to ensure that such copies are not used for the purpose of other sorts of infringement. Accordingly, provided she commits no further infringing act, the purchaser of an authorised copy can deal with it as she pleases. Some examples illustrate the distinction: an ordinary business letter gains copyright as a literary work. Therefore the competitor who gets hold of an indiscreet letter and distributes copies of it will infringe that copyright. However, provided they get hold of the letter lawfully and properly, there is nothing to stop them showing the original to customers: a more troublesome proceeding perhaps, but probably just as effective. So also, the purchaser of a painting will probably not own the copyright in it, but that only matters if he wants to copy it: he can sell or exhibit the original without troubling about copyright. It is only 'infringing copies' of works that are dangerous in normal handling.

No formalities are needed for 'consent' to commit any of the acts that would, without it, constitute infringement; however, unless the consent takes the form of a proper licence (such as is considered in Chapter 22), it can be withdrawn at any time. Consent must be obtained before the acts to which it applies are done: in particular, a copy made without consent is an infringing copy, and a subsequent agreement with the owner of the copyright may not alter the fact. The flipside of this coin is that if, at the time when a copy was made, the making had consent, then that copy is generally considered to be an authorised copy and the copyright owner has no more control over it – unless, once again, additional infringing acts are committed.

This general rule is subject to some modification in relation to copies of works coming from outside the EU. If a copyright owner has sold copies of a work in (say) the US but has not given consent for them to be re-sold in the EU, he can stop re-sale in the United Kingdom on the basis that this would constitute issue to the public of the work in question.

Specific Exceptions to the Rules for Infringement

The Copyright, Designs and Patents Act lays down a number of specific exceptions to the rules for infringement. It will be observed that several of them apply only to particular categories of 'works'. This limitation to particular categories is important, for a court will pay strict attention to it. Some are too special to call for detailed discussion here: these include things like the use of typefaces (artistic works) in the ordinary course of printing; the public reading or recitation by one person of a reasonable extract from a published literary or dramatic work; and the recording of folk songs for archival purposes. Some, however, are general in application.

Temporary Copies

It was noted in Chapter 20, that the making of a copy that is transient or incidental to some other use of the work would still be an act of infringement. Whilst sensible in itself, the extension of liability to such copies has the potential to wreak havoc in the modern computerised world – every time an email is opened, or a web page displayed, for example, a copy of the content is made in the RAM of the device on which it is viewed (not to mention the parts cached on the hard disc or in FLASH memory). If all of these copies required consent from the owner of the copyright in the work, then either the Internet would grind to a halt, or else we would have to engage in ungainly debate about implied licences. Happily, consent is not required, as specific exception is made for such transient or incidental copies which have no independent economic significance, and which are created as an integral and essential part of a technological process for certain purposes (including to enable lawful use of the work). The defence applies to all works other than computer programs and databases (for obvious reasons), and broadcasts.

Fair Dealing for Non-Commercial Research and Private Study

First, copyright will not be infringed by 'fair dealing' with any literary, dramatic, musical or artistic work for purposes of non-commercial research or private study. 'Fair' here means little more than that the treatment must be genuinely and reasonably for the purpose. For instance, an examination paper will be copyright: it will be an infringement for anyone to publish or copy and distribute the paper either before or after the examination concerned; but for a student to make a copy for his own purposes will not be an infringement. He will clearly be acting for the purpose of private study, and to take a single copy of such a work is probably 'fair' in the sense of the Act. This in fact is a type of activity that copyright law is not, in any case, well adapted to prevent. On the other hand, to copy a large part of a library-bound textbook for 'private study', when the work is on sale and a copy could have been bought, probably would not be 'fair' and so would be infringement. 'Research' in this context will include both research in the traditional sense – for example to prepare for a scholarly essay on a subject – and also things like printing out product reviews from the internet when researching a potential purchase.

Fair Dealing for Criticism or Review and Reporting Current Events

In a similar fashion, fair dealing with any work for purposes of criticism or review does not infringe, provided: the work has already been made available to the public; the review/criticism contains an acknowledgment of the title and author of the work; and it is 'fair'. Here again, it is the dealing with the work that has to be fair – not, for instance, the criticism of it. Any extract may be published if its publication is genuinely intended to enable the reviewer to make his comments. However, the courts are alive to the prospect of infringement being dressed up as criticism/review where the purpose of the reproduction is, in reality, something different. Accordingly, students' study notes that abridged copyright works, reproducing substantial portions of them with critical commentary, were not protected by these provisions (*Sillitoe v McGraw Hill*, 1983). The court held in this case that the dealing was not fair: the real motive of the copyist was simply to enable the reader of the notes to enjoy the work concerned without buying it. This said, valid criticism, for example of a literary work, is not limited to commenting on the literary style, and evidently extends to the underlying ideas and thoughts expressed by the work (*Hubbard v Vosper*, 1972), and the doctrine and philosophy behind a work or its creation (*Pro Sieben v Carlton*, 1999). Whether the whole of the work can fairly be published in a review or criticism will depend upon circumstances: a whole short story could probably not be, but the decision in any case will inevitably be very fact-specific.

Again, there is no infringement in fair dealing with any work (other than a photograph) for the purpose of reporting current events in any media format. Sufficient acknowledgement – i.e. identification of the title and author of the work – is required to accompany the report unless, in respect of reporting by means of sound recording, film or broadcast, this would be impossible for reasons of practicality or otherwise. What is 'fair' for this purpose is less clear. Evidently, the amount reproduced, and the purpose and necessity of that use, as well as the motives of the copier will all be relevant considerations.

'Criticism or review' and 'reporting current events' are terms of wide and indefinite scope which should be interpreted liberally but the subjective intentions of the defendant are of limited importance in assessing whether the use of the work was for those purposes. The provisions are intended to protect the role of the media in informing the public about matters of current concern to the public. The upshot is that provided the use is reasonable and is genuinely directed to the purpose of criticism, review or reporting current events it is unlikely to be actionable as an infringement.

Incidental Inclusion

There is a rather narrow exception for incidental inclusion of copyright material in an artistic work, sound recording, film or broadcast. The defence covers situations like that in which an outside broadcast picks up a song being played over a loudspeaker on a pleasure boat as it sails by (which would ordinarily be infringement by communication), or where a photograph of a public monument catches an advert on the side of a bus as it drives past. The application of the defence requires consideration of whether the inclusion really is 'incidental'. Obviously where material is specifically chosen for inclusion in the work, it cannot fall within the defence, regardless of whether it appears somewhere in the background. Accordingly, where a publisher producing cards featuring pictures of famous footballers in their team strip was sued by the FA (which owned the copyright in a logo displayed on the shirts), the Court of Appeal held that this was not incidental (*FA v Panini*, 2004). The whole point of the photo was to show them in their strip, and the logo was integral to this.

An Artist Re-Using Sketches, Etc

It is not an infringement for the author of an artistic work who has parted with the copyright in it to make use again of preliminary sketches, models, etc, so long as he does not imitate the main design of the first work. That is to say, he may use details again, provided he does not actually copy them off the work whose copyright he has sold, but only separate details. It is, of course, never easy to show that an artist has infringed his own copyright, for if his style is at all individual, one picture of his is likely to be much like any other of a similar subject.

Representation of Artistic Works in Public Places

To paint, draw or photograph a building, or a piece of sculpture or suchlike work that is permanently displayed in public, is not infringement; nor is the publication or communication of the picture. Neither is it infringement to include such a work in a film or television broadcast. There are of course restrictions on photography in many public places, but they are not copyright restrictions. The pictures themselves are of course copyright, and their reproduction would need the consent of the owner of that copyright.

Broadcasts

For the showing/playing of a broadcast in public there is a specific defence that operates where the audience has not paid for admission to the place in which the broadcast is to be seen or heard. This defence extends to films and certain (but not all) sound recordings contained within the broadcast, but does not apply to other works. Accordingly a free public showing of a broadcast containing a recording of a speech (a literary work) will benefit from the defence as far as the copyright in the broadcast is concerned, but will still infringe the copyright in the literary work (subject, of course, to any other defence that may be applicable in the circumstances).

Time-Shifting

It is specifically provided that recordings made for the purpose of time-shifting are not infringements. But the recording must be made '*solely* for the purpose of enabling it to be viewed or listened to at a more convenient time'. So there is nothing wrong in building up a personal film library of films shown on television, provided that convenience is the motivation. However, dealing with any copies so made (by, for example, sale or hire (or the offer thereof) or by communication to the public) will render the copy 'infringing' for that purpose – and therefore invoke the secondary infringement provisions. There is a range of other detailed fair-dealing provisions dealing with broadcast programmes and provision of sub-titled copies.

Computer Programs

Computer programs present a special problem. There has to be a balance between the desire of creators of programs to earn revenues and the wishes of users to make back-up copies and the opportunity for other developers to create new programs which are compatible with existing ones. The result is that it is not an infringement (for a lawful user of a program) to make back-up copies where they are necessary for the purposes of her lawful use. Nor is it an infringement to convert a program from a low-level language into a high-level language (i.e. decompile it) or copy it by doing so, provided it is necessary to decompile it to create an independent program which can be operated with the existing one and the information so obtained is not used for any other purpose. Also, it is not an infringement to do things necessary to use the program such as correcting errors in programs unless that is specifically forbidden by contract. These exceptions derive from an EU Directive.

Other Cases

There are various provisions permitting reproduction and performance of works in the course of school lessons, and a rather limited provision permitting the publication of anthologies for school use. There are also special provisions allowing the supply by libraries of copied extracts from books and periodicals, and a provision allowing general copying, from archives, of unpublished works whose authors have been dead for more than 70 years. It is not an infringement of copyright to do any act for the purpose of parliamentary or judicial proceedings. Of course it is also not an infringement to do an act under specific statutory authority.

Problematic Situations

Parody

It is not usually fair dealing to make a parody of a work. There is no statutory exception for parody, and the sole test is therefore: has there been a reproduction of a substantial part of the original work?

This was graphically illustrated by a case involving a label very similar to the 'SCHWEPPES' Indian tonic water label (an artistic work), but with 'SCHLURPPES' on it instead. It was intended as a joke for use on bubble bath. Schweppes did not find it funny; they sued. History does not relate whether the court was amused – in any event, it granted Schweppes summary judgment.

The Public Interest – Control of Information and the Human Rights Act

Copyright can give its owner very great control over aspects of the information recorded in a work – for example, it can be a very effective instrument for stopping publication of embarrassing things, and interim injunctions are often available to restrain copyright infringement. However, as has been noted, copyright protects expression and not ideas (or facts) themselves. In contrast, therefore, to actions for breach of confidence (see Chapter 25, below), which will provide protection over information per se, copyright is not often troubled by questions of balancing its proprietary interests with the human right of freedom of expression. In most cases there is no need to reproduce someone else's expression in order to disseminate the information a work contains – and so arguments that the 'public should know about this' will rarely assist a copyist's defence: the information can usually be presented in a different manner and so not infringe in the first place. To the extent that reproduction is a necessity then there is always fair dealing – verbatim extracts of published works for the purpose of criticism or review or for news reporting will evidently be acceptable provided that the dealing is fair and that sufficient acknowledgement is given.

However, there are potentially situations in which this might not be enough, and where the public interest can only be fulfilled by more excessive reproduction. Where freedom of expression really is in the balance, there are two alternative solutions: first, the court may simply refuse to grant an injunction – it is, after all, a discretionary remedy; second, it may prevail upon the public interest defence. The Court of Appeal has noted that the circumstances in which public interest may override copyright are not capable of precise categorisation or definition (*Ashdown v Telegraph*, 2001). Nevertheless, the Human Rights Act 1998 would suggest that there is a clear public interest in protecting freedom of expression – giving a third party a right to perform a restricted act with the copyright work verbatim – in those rare cases where this right trumps the rights conferred by the copyright itself. Nevertheless, the circumstances in which public interest will be probably be few and far between, and the court in any such circumstance will inevitably proceed with an intense focus on the facts.

22

Dealings in Copyright

Introduction

The right given to an author by the Copyright, Designs and Patents Act of preventing other people from reproducing her works is of very little value in itself: for the main problem in almost every case is to get herself into a position where anyone wants to reproduce the works at all – a problem outside the scope of this book. Once it has been solved however, a whole group of legal questions arise: not only formal problems of transfer of copyright, but various other questions, as to the terms on which reproduction shall take place, what money is to be paid to the author and to the Inland Revenue, and so on. It is with questions of this type that the present chapter is concerned.

Formal Problems

On Transfers of Copyright

Copyright can be freely transferred, either as a whole or for a particular field: thus the film rights in a novel, for instance, or the performing rights in a play, can be transferred separately from the right of printing and publishing. Any such rights can also be transferred for the entirety of the copyright term or for a more limited term. In fact, copyright can be carved up pretty much as the parties please. Nevertheless, formalities must be satisfied: the transfer, whether whole or partial, must be in writing signed by, or on behalf of, the assignor.

Assignment may also be prospective: under the CDPA it is perfectly possible to assign copyright in a work that has yet to be created – there is no need for a subsequent assignment upon the work coming into existence. This said, it is worth remembering that a transfer (even one that is prospective) is not the same as a mere agreement to transfer. Consider for instance the common case of a book or article commissioned by a publisher for a lump sum, on the terms that the publisher is to get the copyright. Even if there is a written agreement to that effect, the agreement will not then and there transfer the copyright: for it will be entered into before the work is created, and so there will be no copyright then in existence for it to transfer. If the agreement purports to assign the copyright, and there is nothing else wrong, and the agreement is signed on behalf of the prospective owner of the copyright, the effect will be that the copyright belongs to the publisher when it comes into existence. If not, the position will be that the author owns the copyright, but he has agreed that the publisher shall have it. Some publishers do, some do not, demand an actual assignment in such cases, though all could do so if they wished. For most purposes, the position is of course the same as if the copyright had been transferred; but if any sort of dispute arises, the difference will become important. If the copyright is infringed, for instance, and the publisher wishes to sue the infringer, either the publisher must get a written assignment of the copyright, together with the right to sue for past infringements, or the action will have to be brought in the author's name, though the publisher must pay for it and will be entitled to any damages that may be recovered. Or again, suppose there is a dispute as to who is going to have the copyright, and the author (thinking herself entitled to do so, or even acting dishonestly) sends to a second publisher who knows nothing of the agreement with the first, the second sale will be effective: the author as actual owner of the copyright could validly sell it, and the only remedy of the first publisher is to sue her for breaking her contract. (If the second publisher knew of the agreement, or even if circumstances were such that he ought to have found out about it, then he will be bound by it.)

This distinction between selling and agreeing to sell runs right through the English law of property; confusing as it is, there are many problems that cannot be understood unless it is borne in mind. In connection with the sale of a house, or something like that, few people forget that until the house has been formally conveyed to its new owner, it is not theirs; but with intangible property like copyright this is not so easy to remember. There is a reported case for instance of the reconstruction of a company, where the old company's assets included a copyright of great value that was never actually transferred to the new company, the omission being discovered only after the old company had been dissolved. The difficulty could be, and was, overcome with the aid of the High Court; but that sort of thing costs time and money. Few companies would wind themselves up without for instance handing over the land on which their factory was built.

Foreign Formalities

The copyright in any country outside the United Kingdom can – so far as English law is concerned – be dealt with separately from the United Kingdom rights. However, where foreign copyrights are concerned, any transfer must conform to the legal requirements of the country concerned; some countries demand more and some less in the way of formalities when property is transferred, and although an assignment valid by English law will usually suffice if it is made in England, it is seldom wise to rely on this. In some countries, copyright protection may involve certain formalities, and failure to register may involve inconvenience. In countries like the United States of America, which have legislation regulating monopolies (as well as having copyright laws differing in some respects from ours), it is always unwise to try to attempt transfer without local advice. Of course, those who are much involved in copyright matters (film companies and music publishers, for instance) have rule-of-thumb methods for handling foreign copyright problems, which seem usually to work well enough.

On Licensing

An owner of copyright who does not want to transfer it outright may license it: that is to say, may grant to someone else the right to do acts that would normally infringe that copyright. There are no formalities required for the creation of a licence – the grant may be made orally just as well as in writing – however, a more permanent record obviously carries with it certain evidential benefits. There is also a distinction that must be watched – that between a licence and a mere consent to the doing of certain acts.

In the strict sense, a licence simply provides permission, perhaps within specific parameters and for a certain period of time, to perform an act that would otherwise infringe copyright. It does not convey a proprietary interest, and therefore in its general form does not provide standing for the licensee to bring an action in her own name or a right to transfer the licence to others (although this latter permission may be included in the licence itself expressly or by implication): as such, it may appear to offer little that a mere consent does not. However, the CDPA does provide for licences to enjoy certain proprietary elements. Thus a licence can give rights enforceable against the owner himself (in case he should change his mind), or against anyone to whom he transfers the copyright (except a purchaser in good faith for valuable consideration and without knowledge (actual or constructive) of the licence, or a person deriving title therefrom). A mere consent on the other hand can be withdrawn by the copyright owner, or overridden by a sale of the copyright, leaving the other party with nothing except (possibly) a right to sue for breach of contract. An exclusive licence, moreover – i.e. a licence authorising the licensee to do certain acts to the exclusion of all other persons, including the person granting the licence – carries even more rights, as it provides the licensee with standing to bring an action for infringement on her own account.

Contracts Relating to Copyrights

Apart from the points already mentioned in this chapter, dealings in copyright are entirely a matter for contract – that is to say, those concerned may make what rules they please. What has happened in relation to any particular copyright must consequently be deduced from such agreements, formal or informal, as the parties have made; this may be a matter of very great difficulty. It should in particular be assumed that any agreement drawn up by business people will prove difficult for lawyers (including judges) to sort out; for lawyers and business people have quite different ideas both as to the way they use language and as to the sort of things that agreements ought to provide for. It is however possible to lay down a few general rules as to what the position is likely to be, if the parties have said nothing definite to the contrary.

Implied Terms

In all cases it has to be remembered that the law is very wary of reading into agreements terms that the parties have not actually stated. The rule is: such terms will only be implied if the agreement cannot be effective without them, so that there can be no doubt that if when the contract was made the parties had been asked whether this was what they wanted, they would both have said, 'Yes, of course.' For example, if there is a sale of a copyright work of art, such as a picture, the copyright will not be transferred with the work unless the parties agree that it shall. This is obvious in the case of a work with many copies, like a coloured print; it is not so obvious in the case of something like a painting of which only the original exists. But if the parties are silent as to the copyright, the law will not assume that they meant to transfer it unless it is clear that this must have been so. In the case, say, of a sale of a painting to a maker of Christmas cards, if both parties knew that he meant to make a Christmas card of it, it will be clear that they must have meant that he should have some right to reproduce the painting; but even then, it does not necessarily follow that he must have the ownership of the copyright, rather than a licence to reproduce. In any event, unless there is something in writing, he will get merely a contractual right to have the copyright assigned to him or a licence granted to him, as the case may be.

Where Works are Made to Order

Commissioned works present a special problem (see Chapter 19). It will often be clear (if not expressly stated) that the parties meant the copyright to be transferred to the person giving the order; a term in their agreement to that effect will then be implied. For instance, where a publisher commissions a book for a lump sum payment, even if nothing is said about copyright, it will normally be assumed that the publisher is meant to have it. The author is not an employee, so as to make the publisher the first owner of the copyright: this is shown by the fact that the publisher cannot tell her how to write the book, but must take it as the author thinks it should be written. Nevertheless, for a lump sum payment the publisher presumably expected to get the whole thing, copyright and all. (But remember that there will only be an agreement to transfer the copyright to the publisher, not an actual transfer, unless a signed agreement says it is a transfer.) On the other hand if payment is to be by royalty there will be no reason to suppose that the publisher is necessarily to have more than a licence to publish; and in the case of an architectural work for instance, even if specially commissioned, the only term as to copyright which will be implied into the contract is a licence to the architect's client to erect the buildings contracted for in accordance with the drawings. The architect will therefore keep his copyright. A clear case the other way was of a man who was commissioned to do the choreography for a ballet (a dramatic work): clearly the copyright must have been intended to be transferred to the man who commissioned the work, for without that copyright he would not have a complete ballet. More recently, Robin Ray was asked by Classic FM to compile a list of suitable works for playing on its radio station in the UK. When Classic FM sought to use the list for other purposes, Ray sued, arguing that there was no licence to do so. Classic FM retorted that they owned the copyright in Ray's compilation – and that even if they didn't, then they were licensed. However, these arguments were rejected: the court held that the work was Ray's and that Classic FM did not enjoy a licence to do any more than was contemplated at the time of the agreement (*Ray v Classic FM,* 1998).

Where a Publisher Agrees to Publish an Author's Work

There are cases however where it is clear that the parties must have intended to provide for quite a number of matters they have said nothing about. For instance, an author may send the manuscript of a book to a publisher and the publisher agree to publish it, and nothing else is said at all. In that case the law will imply, grudgingly, the bare minimum of terms to complete the contract. The publisher has a licence to publish an edition of the book, but that is all: the author of course keeps the ownership of the copyright. The publisher must pay the author a reasonable royalty: not necessarily the royalty he usually pays, rather the sort of royalty an ordinary publisher would normally pay for that sort of book. The publisher must publish an edition of the book, of reasonable size having regard to all the circumstances, within a reasonable time. A reasonable time for publishing a book in these days will be many months, and there would certainly be no obligation upon the publisher to hurry unduly; but he must not deliberately delay. He must not for instance, as a publisher once did, deliberately delay publication so as to enable a rival to scoop the Christmas market with a book on the same subject – in return of course for a share of the profits on the rival's book. Finally he is not entitled to publish the book under someone else's name as author: the position would however be different if he had bought the copyright outright, then he could probably deal with the work as he pleased, subject to any moral rights that might apply (see Chapter 23).

In the same way, if a manuscript is sent to the editor of a periodical, the editor may publish it, and must pay at reasonable rates. His usual rates will usually do, and will certainly do if the author has taken them before: but a periodical which usually pays unusually low rates should tell new authors about them before publication, or it may find that the court considers them unreasonable. The editor of a periodical is not entitled to publish in book form manuscripts sent to him for periodical publication, without the author's consent.

Bequests of Copyright Works

In one case the CDPA itself creates a presumption that copyright goes with the property in the actual work: where an original document or other material thing recording or embodying an unpublished literary, dramatic, musical or artistic work, or a sound recording or film, is bequeathed by a will which does not mention the copyright. (Of course, this only applies so far as the testator owned the copyright when he died.)

Sales of Part of a Copyright

The same sort of considerations arise when a copyright is partially sold (or otherwise assigned); but here the position tends to be clearer, for the parties must have said something about what they intend shall happen; and all the lawyers have to decide is what the parties' words mean. (The answer may surprise the parties, but that often happens to those who are insufficiently explicit in the first place.) Thus the sale of the performing rights in a play or a song will not pass the right to make films or records of the work, unless there is some special reason why the parties must have meant this to be so; but it will pass the right to prevent any film or record of the work being shown or played in public. This will be vital in the case of a play to be made into a film, which is almost certainly intended for public exhibition (unless perhaps it is meant solely for export to a country where either there is no copyright or the performing right has not been sold); but it will be less important to the maker of a record. Records and CDs (or indeed MP3s) as normally sold are in fact not licensed for a public performance, and every UK record at least bears a notice to that effect – a similar notice is also buried in the terms and conditions of all the leading digital download services.

Collective Licensing – The PRS and PPL

What actually happens with musical copyrights is that the performing rights in published music are handed over to a licensing and royalty collection body called the Performing Right Society (PRS). The broadcasting, performing and diffusion rights in sound recordings go likewise to a collecting body called Phonographic Performance Ltd (PPL), set up by the recording companies. In the case of film, including previously published music, the film company buys a licence to include the music in the film (there are standard arrangements for this), but does not have authority to license public performance of it. The cinema has a standard Performing Right Society licence which covers that.

The film distributor, in effect, warrants that an exhibitor will have no copyright trouble, provided his cinemas have Performing Right Society licences (that is to say, the film company is expected to look after performing rights in any book or play the film is made from, but not performing rights in music except music especially written for the film). The actual agreements used in the film industry tend to be rather incomprehensible, but custom has established what they are supposed to mean.

People wanting to use records, tapes, CDs or digital sound recordings for public performance (e.g. for use in village halls) go to the two societies and obtain standard licences: one covering the copyright in music, one covering that in the recording. There is a Copyright Tribunal with power to see that the standard licences are not unreasonable.

It should be noted that the control of licensing by the Copyright Tribunal is of great importance, especially in the entertainment industry where collective licensing bodies are commonplace. In 1988, the Monopolies and Mergers Commission (as it was then called) said that collective licensing bodies were by their nature monopolistic and 'it is widely accepted that appropriate controls are needed to ensure that they do not abuse their market power'. There have been such controls for some time; prior to the 1988 Act there was the Performing Right Tribunal, which exercised similar powers. The 1988 Act changed its name and widened its jurisdiction considerably. As well as setting terms for collective licensing schemes, the Tribunal can, for example, determine royalties for the rental right, grant certain consents on behalf of performers in certain circumstances, and settle the terms of licences of right. It can also take remedial action following a determination by the Competition Commission that the copyright owner is engaging in anti-competitive practices contrary to the public interest.

Where the Ownership of the Manuscript and Copyright is in Different Hands

A case similar to overlapping copyrights arises where the owner of an unpublished manuscript does not own the copyright in it. He cannot publish it without the copyright owner's consent, but then the copyright owner cannot get at the manuscript without his consent: so that again an intending publisher must come to terms with both.

Publishing Agreements

Two odd points relating to publishing agreements deserve mention. Such agreements often contain a clause requiring the author to offer her next book (or next so many books) to the same publisher. This is a perfectly legitimate clause for a contract to contain, and can be enforced: a court will grant an injunction not only to prevent the author disposing of those books elsewhere, but also to prevent another publisher, who took those books although he knew about the agreement, from publishing them. On the other hand, an agreement to write a number of further books would not be enforceable by injunction: injunctions are not given to compel the performance of personal services.

The second point is more difficult. Suppose the author, not being under any obligation to offer his next book to the same publisher, writes another on the same subject and offers to a second publisher, who publishes it and so spoils the market for the first: has the first publisher any remedy? Or suppose the publisher puts out a second book on the same subject at the same time, and so spoils the first author's sales: has the author any remedy? The answer will of course depend on what the publishing agreement says, and since the publisher will very likely have drawn it up, it will probably protect him against the author but not the author against him. If the agreement is altogether silent on the subject, it seems fairly clear that in an ordinary case the author would have no remedy; probably the publisher would have none either, but this is not quite so clear.

Literary Agents

It is usual for established authors at least to employ literary agents to place their books and deal with the various forms of copyright arising from them. Here again, the rights of the author and his agent as against each other are what they have agreed them to be when the agent took the job. It should be remembered however that as against the outside world, the agent's powers to deal on behalf of his principal will in effect be those that such agents usually have. The author can, if she likes and the agent is willing, make special terms and place special restrictions on the agent's authority; but the special terms and restrictions will have no effect against third parties who do not know of them.

Manuscripts Sent for Advice

It is not unusual for authors who are not established to send their works to their more successful colleagues for comment, advice, and assistance in placing with publishers or producers. The rights of the author in such a case are clear. The person she sends her manuscript to must not of course publish it (though he may be expected to show to one or two colleagues), nor may he copy from it: but he is under no obligation to take any particular care of it, and if it gets lost or damaged, the author should not complain.

Taxation and Authors

The question of tax upon authors' earnings, important as it is, can be dealt with here only very briefly. The position is broadly this. Any author who makes a business or profession of writing or composing, or anyone who makes a business of dealing in copyrights, must pay income tax on the whole profits of that business, whether they are received in the form of royalties or as lump-sum payments.

Those who do not make a business of it, like casual authors or people who happen to have come into possession of an odd copyright, must pay income tax on receipts if they are income but not if they are capital. It does not necessarily follow that royalties are income, though they usually are; still less does it follow that lump-sum payments are capital. The test is more or less this: was there a valuable asset, and has it been converted into money (in which case the proceeds of conversion will be capital) or has it been used as a source of profit – as an income-bearing investment, so to speak? If it has, that profit will be income. A sale of an existing copyright, by someone who has never written a book before, whether for a single payment or an annual payments, may be capital, and not taxable by income tax; on the other hand, a royalty of so much a copy on the sales of a book is almost certainly income, even if it is paid as a lump sum when the agreement is made. If a work is commissioned, the payment is almost certain to be received as income whatever form it takes: for essentially it is payment for services, not the sale of any asset. It will be seen that the author of a really successful work will find some difficulty in arranging her affairs so as to avoid paying out in one or two years of extremely high income, most of what she gets for it. However, such an author can, to a reasonable extent, 'spread' out (for tax purposes) payments she receives, over a longer period.

23

Moral Rights

Moral rights have nothing to do with morals. They are special rights conferred by the Copyright Designs and Patents Act 1988 and are intended to give creative people a sense of artistic control over their copyright works. The name comes from the French ('droit moral') – the French and Germans have traditionally been much more interested in these kinds of rights. The main moral rights are unlike a lot of the rest of intellectual property: they are about creativity and art (and above all, reputations) not economics – or so the orthodox theory goes.

Artists and writers are often (and rightly) concerned about two things: fame and the 'artistic integrity' of their works. Of course, both of these can be of commercial importance too; fame is usually swiftly followed by profit. Much of the popular appeal of intellectual property is derived from images of the starving (balding and bearded?) inventor in a garret or impecunious artists eking out a living from a bare paint-splashed studio. Moral rights are inspired by a slightly different popular image: the artist whose creative genius goes unrecognised while his or her works are sold on every street corner; or the writer whose creative abilities are brought into disrepute by distasteful alteration. They are principally concerned with protecting the reputation of the artist or author. As such, they are independent of, and separate from, any copyright that may vest in a work.

There are four kinds of moral right that pertain to copyright works – although there are also moral rights in performances (discussed briefly below). First, there is the right to be identified as the author of a work. Secondly, there is the right to object to derogatory treatment of a work. Thirdly, there is the right not to have works falsely attributed to you. Finally, and in a slightly different class, there is a right to privacy of certain kinds of photographs and films.

Right to be Identified as the Author

This applies to literary, dramatic, musical or artistic works and films. There are certain exceptions, such as computer programs (which as we have seen are treated as literary works under the CDPA). This right is sometimes called the 'paternity right', probably also from the French (it may be thought that this is a physiologically and psychologically implausible term, as well as being sexist. Indeed, this is so).

An author (or director, in the case of a film) has the right to be identified as such, broadly speaking, whenever the work in question is exposed to the public. So in the case of a literary work, for example, whenever the work is published commercially, the author can insist that his or her name appears as the author. Or in the case of a film, when, for example, it is shown in public, it is communicated to the public, or copies are issued thereto, the director can insist that he or she is credited. Architects can insist that they are identified on the buildings they have designed.

But before anyone can insist on such identification, they have to assert their right. This can be done in various ways – either by a simple written document, signed by the author or the director, or upon an assignment of copyright (say when an author hands over the copyright in a manuscript to a publisher). Nowadays, one commonly sees at the beginning of books (including this one) a recognition of the assertion by the author of their rights to be identified as the author.

If the right is infringed, a person has the right to claim damages or an injunction: infringement of the right being actionable as breach of statutory duty.

Right to Object to Derogatory Treatment

This is arguably the most troublesome of the moral rights. The CDPA says that a treatment is derogatory 'if it amounts to distortion or mutilation of the work or is otherwise prejudicial to the honour or reputation of the author or director'. There is no real guidance as to what this means. The florid terminology 'honour or reputation' sounds like something out of another age, and the precious few cases that have discussed the term have (perhaps wisely) resisted the temptation to assess this standard purely through the eyes of the aggrieved author themselves. Instead, the courts have generally adopted a pragmatic view. Accordingly, in one case, colour variations and other 'trivial' alterations that could have been the 'subject of a Spot The Difference competition in a child's comic' were not considered objectively sufficient to comprise derogatory treatment (*Pasterfield v Denham*, 1999). In another, an objection to the overlaying of a musical track with a rap vocal that was claimed to contain references to violence and drugs was defeated on grounds that there was no evidence before the court concerning the claimant's honour or reputation or indeed of any prejudice to either (*Confetti Records v Warner Music*, 2003 – although the case is arguably more noteworthy for the judge's comments that 'the words of the rap, although in a form of English, were for practical purposes a foreign language'.)

Since the law is intended to protect the reputation of the artist or author, it is not an infringement if the author or director is not identified or has not previously been identified with the work or if there is sufficient disclaimer. There is no general right to prevent mutilation – the right is mainly there to prevent people thinking that the artist was responsible for it. Also, for example, making an adaptation or arrangement cannot per se amount to derogatory treatment – it must actually affect the author's honour or reputation.

This moral right does not apply to works made for reporting current events or in relation to the publication in newspapers of works made for that purpose. Nor does it apply to works where copyright is owned by someone's employer (when the person has made the work in the course of her employment pursuant to a contract of service).

There are certain other exceptions – for example, the BBC (and only the BBC) can chop works around with impunity in order 'to avoid the inclusion in a programme broadcast by them of anything which offends against good taste or decency or which is likely to encourage or incite to crime or to lead to disorder or be offensive to public feeling'. This exception was probably procured by the BBC as a result of its experience (pre-moral rights) in contract law. A playwright who had sold it a radio play successfully objected to its being broadcast yet omitting the vital line: 'My friend Sylv told me it was safe standing up' (*Frisby v BBC*, 1967).

As with the right to be identified as the author, the right to object to derogatory treatment is infringed, essentially, by people who put the mutilated or distorted work before the public. So, the right is infringed, for example, by someone who publishes commercially a derogatory treatment of a work or issues copies to the public. In the case of a film, the right would be infringed by someone who issued copies to the public, showed the film in public, or communicated it thereto.

The right to object to derogatory treatment is also infringed (essentially) by people who deal in works which have been subjected to derogatory treatment knowing or having reason to believe that they have been subjected to derogatory treatment.

False Attribution of Authorship

The law of defamation is designed to provide a remedy if people say untrue and unfortunate things about people. The right to object to false attribution of a work is similar in intent. Few things are as likely to bring a reputable author into disrepute as it being said: 'So and so wrote X', where X is some especially unmeritorious work. Accordingly, an individual is given the right by the CDPA not to have a literary, dramatic, musical or artistic work falsely attributed to him or her as author. It gives a similar right to directors in relation to films.

Again, it is an infringement to put a work before the public in or on which there is a false attribution (for example, by exhibiting it if it is an artistic work or by issuing copies to the public, if it is a literary work). It is also infringed by someone who deals in works on which there is a false attribution knowing or having reason to believe that there is an attribution thereon and it is false. There are various other restricted acts.

The right not only protects authors and directors. It is potentially valuable in the hands of interviewees of newspapers.

Examples:

The *News of the World* published an article with the headline 'How My Love For The Saint Went Sour by Dorothy Squires talking to Weston Taylor'. ('The Saint' was a well-known TV series, with the main hero played by Roger Moore.) Dorothy Squires sued for libel and for false attribution of authorship. The jury awarded her £4,300 for the libel and an extra £100 for false attribution of authorship. In the Court of Appeal Lord Denning said, with characteristic pithiness: 'The article purports to be written by Dorothy Squires. It says "By Dorothy Squires." That was untrue. She did not write it.' She won (*Moore v News of the World*, 1972).

Alan Clark, a colourful Conservative MP, also relied on this provision to stop a spoof of his diaries written by a satirist which appeared in the *Evening Standard*. Many readers thought it was the real thing. He had not written it, and he won as well (*Clark v Associated Newspapers*, 1998).

Right to Privacy of Certain Photographs and Films

If, for private and domestic purposes, a person commissions a photograph or the making of a film, if copyright subsists in the resulting work, he or she has the right not to have copies of it issued to the public, the work exhibited or shown in public or the work broadcast or included in a cable programme service. Commissioned wedding photographs should therefore be safe to some extent from media exposure.

Duration of Moral Rights and Waiver

Moral rights generally last so long as copyright subsists in the work; the exception being the right to object to false attribution, which continues to subsist until 20 years after a person's death. None of the rights are assignable, but all (apart, once again, from the right to object to false attribution) can be disposed of by will – the anomalous right is exercisable post mortem by the former holder's personal representative(s). Any of the moral rights may be waived by an instrument signed in writing by the person giving up the right, and people who commission works often insist that authors do this.

Other Related Rights

Performers

Performers' Rights and Recording Rights

Bootlegging has long been a problem in the entertainment business. Until the CDPA there was a kind of legal fudge which gave performers some rights to prevent these. There were also criminal provisions. However, the effect of the fudge was to give performers rights that were too extensive, and to give recording companies (who cared most about bootlegging) no real rights at all. The CDPA attempted to sort this out.

In essence, the new law gives a performer economic rights to control the exploitation of his or her performances, and (since 2006) separate moral rights to be identified and to object to derogatory treatment of a performance. It also gives a person with exclusive recording rights in connection with such a performance the right to prevent exploitation of illicit recordings (either by dealing in copies of them or by broadcasting the performance). Various criminal offences are also created.

There are certain qualifying requirements (mainly nationality or residence of the performer or the place where the performance took place). These are very liberal, and the likelihood is that if the person performing could get an English copyright, he or she would be entitled to a performers' right as well.

As regards recording rights, in order to be entitled to these, a person must have an exclusive recording contract (i.e. a contract entitling that person, to the exclusion of all other persons including the performer, to make recordings with a view to their commercial exploitation). Similar rights to performers' rights are given – essentially to prevent exploiting illicit recordings.

Performers' rights and recording rights subsist for 50 years from the year in which the performance took place or, if during that period a recording of the performance is released (in the sense of being consensually published, played or communicated to the public), 50 years from the year in which it was released. Performers' moral rights last for as long as that performer's rights subsist in relation to the performance.

Copy Protection – Anti-Circumvention

Companies, particularly in the entertainment and software industries, increasingly try to ensure that their works cannot be copied, by using copy protection technology. This prevents copies from being made from (say) a CD, DVD or Blu-Ray, or stops them being made in an unauthorised way. In 2003, the UK strengthened its anti-circumvention legislation by implementing an EU Directive to stop people selling (and using) devices intended to circumvent copy protection. This legislation (part of the CDPA) has been invoked by Sony to stop a trader selling chips which included a mechanism for circumventing games software copy protection. The chip could be fitted into a games console to trick the console into believing that the disc being played had the necessary embedded codes. So the console could be made to play not only authentic games designed for the geographical area for which the console was intended, but also unauthorised copies and games from foreign regions. Sony obtained summary judgment (*Sony v Ball*, 2004). Nintendo also got in on the action in respect of the sale of cards designed to get around the copy protection in its DS and DSi handheld games consoles. It also obtained summary judgment (*Nintendo v Playables*, 2010; *Nintendo v Console PC Com*, 2011).

Part V

Miscellaneous Matters

24

The Criminal Law

Introduction

Some types of IP infringement are so objectionable that they have been made crimes. There are laws directed at very specific targets (e.g. offences under the Hallmarking Act 1973, or more recently, under the London Olympic Games and Paralympic Games Act 2006), for which we have no space. More general are offences under the trade marks and copyright legislation. We talk about these here, along with something about more general rules of criminal law which overlap with or are akin to IP infringement. Note that patent infringement is not an offence (some say it should be, but the mind boggles at the idea of an Old Bailey jury deciding issues of infringement or validity).

The Trade Marks Act 1994

It is a crime to make unauthorised use of a registered trade mark under certain circumstances. For example, if a person applies to goods or their packaging a sign identical to, or likely to be mistaken for, a registered trade mark, or sells goods which bear (or the packaging of which bears) such a sign, or has such goods in his possession in the course of business for the purpose of selling them, an offence may be committed. The defendant must have acted with a view to gain for himself or another or with intent to cause loss to another and, obviously, without the consent of the proprietor of the trade mark. In addition, the goods in question must be goods in respect of which the trade mark is registered, or the trade mark has a reputation in the UK and the use of the sign takes unfair advantage of, or is or would be detrimental to the distinctive character or repute of the trade mark. This is similar to one of the tests for civil trade mark infringement. But, unlike the civil wrong, it is a defence to show that the defendant believed on reasonable grounds that the use of the sign in the manner in which it was used was not an infringement of the trade mark.

The House of Lords in *Johnstone* (2003) considered this offence. We have discussed its facts (bootleg Bon Jovi CDs) and the problem of whether non-trade mark use can count as infringement, above in connection with the *Arsenal* case.

Here we add the following points. Their Lordships held first that the criminal offence was no wider than the civil offence of infringement – any other conclusion would have been astonishing, though the criminal trial judge (who would have no experience of trade mark law) got it wrong. Second, whether a sign was being used descriptively is a question of fact. Third, that a defendant would have a defence where he reasonably believed that no relevant trade mark was registered. However, on this point, their Lordships confirmed that the burden of proof rests on the defendant to show that he reasonably believed that use of the sign was not an infringement. In reality this means the offence is one of near absolute liability. It is no use, for instance, for the defendant to say: 'but my customer knew it was a fake' (*Morgan*, 2006), or that 'this was such obvious rubbish that no one could think it was genuine' (*Boulter*, 2008).

The Copyright, Designs and Patents Act 1988

It is a crime for anyone, without the licence of the copyright owner, to make for sale or hire, or import (otherwise than for private or domestic use) any article which is, and which he knows, or has reason to believe, is an infringing copy of a copyright work. This provision has come into greater play in recent years, especially with the increase in penalties and in powers of police searches and seizure powers brought about by the Copyright etc and Trade Marks (Offences and Enforcement) Act 2002. There have also been a number of private prosecutions. Some of these collapsed because of technicalities – which matter much more in the context of a criminal charge with a person's liberty at stake, than they do in a civil case where the problem is usually cured by an amendment. Also there have been a number of public prosecutions – especially in the context of pirate videos/ DVDs and computer-related offences. For instance, before most people knew the Internet existed, a man was given a year in prison for supplying copyright games over it (*Lewis*, 1997). Illicit dealings in recordings which breach rights in performances ('bootlegs'), fitting games consoles with devices to overcome a technological measure aimed at preventing the playing of pirate games, and dealing in unauthorised decoders for satellite TV are also punishable criminally.

The Consumer Protection from Unfair Trading Regulations 2008

Until these Regulations were passed, the general criminal law about unfair trading with the public was governed by the Trade Descriptions Act 1968. Although bits of the Act are still in force, the key legal features of this area are now prescribed by the Regulations, often known as the CPR (not to be confused with the other CPR, the Civil Procedure Rules, which (as one might have guessed) govern civil procedure in the UK). The Regulations were made as a result of EU requirements for harmonisation of laws about protection of consumers. They set out a general code primarily aimed at consumer protection. But they also have the significant incidental effect of protecting IP owners

The Regulations say generally that 'unfair commercial practices are prohibited'. They then provide six categories of such practices. Each has a detailed definition. Here we just set out those most relevant to IP rights. First it is an offence for a trader to engage in a commercial practice which concerns any marketing of a product (including comparative advertising) which creates confusion with any products, trade marks, trade names or other distinguishing marks of a competitor. This conduct is actionable provided it causes, or is likely to cause, the average consumer to take a transactional decision he would not have taken otherwise. In deciding whether this will occur, account must be taken of the factual context and of all its features and circumstances. Secondly, it is an offence for a trader to engage in a commercial practice of promoting a product similar to a product made by a particular manufacturer in such a manner as deliberately to mislead the consumer into believing that the product is made by that same manufacturer when it is not. Broadly therefore the criminal law covers the same ground as that covered by the civil action for passing off. That is hardly surprising, since the heart of passing off lies in misrepresentation to consumers.

Other Criminal Laws

There are a number of other laws which can be employed to tackle counterfeiting and piracy:

(a) Serious collaborations to infringe by way of deceptive conduct – such as in *Pain* (1986) concerning counterfeit Chanel perfume – can be prosecuted for criminal conspiracy under the Criminal Law Act 1977 or as a breach of the common law (conspiracy to defraud).
(b) The Fraud Act 2006 makes it an offence for a person to have in his possession or under his control any article for use in the course of or in connection with any fraud. Under the previous law it was a crime to an article for use in the course of a cheat (*McAngus*, 1994).
(c) The money laundering provisions of the Proceeds of Crime Act 2002 (POCA) were used in an attempt to take action against a market operator and its two directors in *Wendy Fair Markets*, 2008. The company had 'turned a blind eye' to the fact that as many as a fifth of its stallholders were selling fake goods. In the end it was acquitted by the Court of Appeal, but only because the case was aimed at the management style, rather than the specific offences for which they were charged.

(d) A person who is convicted of one of the principal counterfeiting or piracy offences in the Copyright etc Act 1988 or the Trade Marks Act 1994 will be deemed to have 'a criminal lifestyle' under POCA and may be subject to a confiscation order – see e.g. *Priestley* (2004) (confiscation order for £2.29 million).
(e) Injunctive action under the Enterprise Act 2002 may be considered when breaches of 'criminal lifestyle' IP legislation harm the collective interests of consumers.

The Practical Working of the Criminal Law

As an Alternative to Civil Action

Although a criminal IP offence may have been committed, civil proceedings by a trader affected by their breach are often preferable if, as is almost always the case, there is also a civil wrong. This is for a number of reasons. First, the civil court has power to grant an injunction to restrain further acts of the type complained of and, in most cases, an injunction can be obtained very quickly. Secondly, the court can award damages (including additional damages in the case of a flagrant copyright infringement). Thirdly, the award of costs in a civil court is much higher than in a criminal court. Fourthly, the standard of proof required is lower (balance of probabilities for civil and beyond reasonable doubt for criminal). Finally, the procedure in a civil court is, generally speaking, much easier than in a criminal court, and is essentially under the control of the plaintiff.

Next, there is the fact that IP law is apt to have tricky points. Prosecuting authorities are, with a few notable exceptions, not experts in IP law and it has lots of little pitfalls – for instance, in *Higgs* (2008) the defendant had been converting games consoles so they could play pirate games. He was charged with the crime of selling a device designed for circumvention of effective technological measures. But over a three-day trial the prosecution failed to prove a simple necessary element of the crime, namely that illicit, albeit temporary, copies would be made within the computers of the users. So he got off, though he knew that he would not be so lucky a second time. Again in *Gilham* (2009) the prosecution made a complex meal of a case about pirate games, trying to say that the temporary copying of bits of a program was an infringement, when it had missed the straightforward case of infringement by copying whole images. It took the Court of Appeal to point that out. And of course there was *Johnstone,* which failed in trade marks but which would have succeeded if a copyright or performance right offence been charged.

It follows that in practice, the criminal provisions have their main application where the IP rights are clear, the real question being whether the defendant was responsible and how much he did. That alone can itself involve complex issues of fact. Nowadays in cases of large-scale counterfeiting, prosecuting authorities are much more prepared to act than they once were. Thus, for instance a large-scale counterfeiter of golf-clubs who sold them via eBay and who acted in a large global conspiracy was found guilty after an 11-week trial (*Bellchambers*, 2010). He got four years and co-conspirators lesser sentences. And in another case (*Braha*, 2011), a major dealer in fake Burberry shoes was subject to a confiscation order of £11 million, with 10 years' imprisonment if he defaulted. It remains the case, however, that prosecutors primarily concentrate on protection of the public at large – 'consumer protection', rather than enforcing IP for the benefit of the IP owner. Of course the two concerns overlap: thus trading standards officers do take action against blatant pirates, such as traders in markets or car boot sales selling pirate jeans or counterfeit DVDs.

Enforcement Provisions

The Trade Marks Act and the Copyright, Designs and Patents Act make local trading standards authorities responsible for the enforcement of the main offences. Trading standards authorities are empowered (actually by the Local Government Act 1972) to take proceedings. Authorised officers can make test purchases, enter premises (subject to certain conditions), and seize goods for the purpose of ascertaining whether an offence has been committed. It is also possible for a private prosecution to be brought, and they are (though rarely). Recently, trading standard officers gave evidence for the claimant, a vodka maker, who was complaining in a civil action that 'Vodkat' (a product which was not vodka) was passing off (*Diageo v Intercontinental Brands*, 2010).

In most cases, officers only act in cases of plain infringement and are more likely to do so if they receive a number of complaints from the public. Increasingly, at least in the case of counterfeits, the right-owners also complain and assist in the prosecutions. There is certainly nothing to prevent anyone who feels injured by another's passing off or infringement of a mark from reporting the matter to a local officer: this will generally produce some result, if only a warning letter to the culprit. However, officers are unlikely to do anything until they have checked the complaint out for themselves. In *Fage v Chobani* (2013), use of the phrase 'Greek Yoghurt' for what was, in fact, American yoghurt, was passing off, but a complaint to trading standards, even with some inaccuracy, was not considered to be a malicious falsehood, because damage was unlikely. The court was satisfied that trading standards were not likely to take action on a mere complaint without making an independent check to ensure that there was sufficient case for action.

Penalties

These have been made more severe over recent years – a response to the increase in counterfeiting and piracy. The current levels of penalty are provided by the

Copyright etc and Trade Marks (Offences and Enforcement) Act 2002 and the Digital Economy Act 2010. Broadly, the maximum penalty for serious cases is now 10 years' imprisonment plus fines. Those who run companies involved in pirating can also be disqualified from acting as company directors for up to 15 years. Large confiscation orders can also be made.

25

Confidence and Privacy

Introduction

Thus far we have generally been discussing matters that have revolved around the acquisition of, or dealings in, property rights: turning certain, essentially non-proprietary, elements – technical or creative ideas, for example – into something that the law will recognise and protect, and which thereafter form the personal property of the rights-holder. This chapter is different. Its subject matter is information itself – secrets and confidences, things unknown by the public at large – and information is not something traditionally treated as property: it is too slippery for that.

Nevertheless, the subject matter of this chapter does, to some extent, overlap with many of the things already discussed – indeed confidence and secrecy are essential before a patent is applied for, as any disclosure of the invention before the priority date may be grounds for refusal (or invalidation) of the grant. Accordingly, protection and enforcement of that secrecy is paramount. This chapter also straddles some of the same material as copyright: although not the right to stop others from reproducing a work as such, but rather to stop them making use of the information contained in it. This is a job which the ownership of copyright will seldom do. Thus it will be recalled that a purchaser of a book is entitled to read it and let anyone else read it, and even to recite snippets of it in public to anyone who will listen. No limitation by way of limited licence can be imposed by the owner of the copyright if the copy is an authorised copy; even if the copy is not authorised, all the copyright owner can do is to insist upon the handing over of the book to him – what he cannot do by virtue of his ownership of the copyright is to prevent readers of the book making use of what they learnt by reading it. However, if the work is unpublished and unknown and is given to another under conditions of secrecy, then the matter could be very different: the law may intervene to maintain the secret and restrain its use.

The sort of problems dealt with under breach of confidence will generally, although not always, arise in commercial matters: with the inventor who shows the invention to others before patents have been granted or even (inventors are not always cautious people) before he has applied for patents at all; the manufacturer who supplies manufacturing drawings and specifications to a subcontractor; the merchant who gives the names and addresses of customers to the manufacturer so that they can be supplied direct. In all cases of this sort, what the person who supplied the information really wants is to stop the recipient of the information from using it except for the purpose for which it was given. A mere right to stop the recipient from making copies, which is given by copyright, is useful but is not enough.

Rights to Privacy

In recent years, the action for breach of confidence has also seen use in a less commercial context, as the vehicle to prevent (or gain compensation for) invasions of privacy. The most well-known cases concern celebrities. There have been a number of actions, usually brought by famous people, to stop the press from disclosing things about them that they would either prefer the world not to know, or would prefer to disclose in a particular way. These actions have been given additional impetus by the 'right to private life' provisions incorporated into English law by the Human Rights Act 1998. This chapter looks first at the traditional law of confidence and then at the developing law of privacy.

The Action for Breach of Confidence

The General Rule

The law of breach of confidence is essentially concerned with the promotion of conscionable behaviour – if a person undertakes to keep a secret, then they should be held to this: there is a public interest in enforcing such pledges. Nevertheless, the rights to prevent unauthorised dissemination or use of the imparted information only arise in certain circumstances, and are subject to certain exceptions.

The general rule has been put in the following way, namely that a recipient of confidential information may not use that information without the consent of the person from whom he got it *(Saltman v Campbell,* 1948). Another way in which the rule has been expressed is that a claimant who sues for breach of confidence must show three things: first, that the information has the necessary quality of confidence about it; secondly, that the information was imparted in circumstances importing an obligation of confidence; and thirdly, that there was an unauthorised use made of that information *(Coco v Clark,* 1969). There is a degree of overlap between the elements of this test: fundamentally, one has to know the extent of the obligation before one can consider if the use is unauthorised; equally, the quality of confidence may be provided by the circumstances in which it was imparted. Nevertheless, it provides a useful manner of structuring an inquiry, and is often used for this purpose.

When is Information Confidential?

Circumstances Giving Rise to a Relationship of Confidence

These can be shortly stated: a person can be prevented from misusing information given to him if, when he receives it, he has agreed, expressly or impliedly, to treat it as confidential. This does not mean that there has to be a formal agreement, although, of course, having such an agreement helps to make the position clear to everyone (which is why the cases which are fought are mostly concerned with situations where the parties did not make it clear that their relationship was confidential from the outset).

What the judges do in cases where there is no express agreement is to look at all the circumstances surrounding the relationship between the parties. If it appears that the parties cannot have intended the information to be given freely – often considered through the eyes of a reasonable person in the shoes of the recipient of that information – then it was given in confidence. A lot may depend upon how the judge feels about the way the defendant behaved. If information is given for a particular purpose, it is easily inferred that the parties intended the information to be used only for that purpose. A few examples from cases, some of them quite old but which are still regularly referred to, will make the point clearer.

Example 1   In *Seager v Copydex* (1967) an inventor had discussed an invention of his with the defendant company with a view to their taking it up. In the course of the discussion, he mentioned the idea behind another invention he had in mind. Although the company did not take up the first invention, they later came out with a version of the second, even using the name which the inventor had given it. The Court of Appeal thought the defendant must have taken the inventor's idea, albeit subconsciously, and that the relationship between the parties must have been confidential since the inventor could not be supposed to have been giving the information freely; it was given merely for the purpose of interesting the defendant in his ideas.

Example 2   Again, in *Ackroyds v Islington Plastics* (1962) the defendants had been under contract to manufacture plastic 'swizzle sticks' (things for getting those nasty bubbles out of champagne) for the plaintiffs. The plaintiffs had supplied the defendants for this purpose with information and with a special tool. It was held that the defendants could not use either the information or the tool for the purpose of manufacturing swizzle sticks for themselves: both had been handed over only for the purpose of helping them manufacture for the plaintiffs.

Example 3   Another example shows that the law of confidence, although mostly finding its application in the commercial field, is perfectly general. In *Argyll v Argyll* (1965) the then Duchess of Argyll sued to prevent the Duke from supplying to a Sunday newspaper (and to prevent the Sunday newspaper from publishing) what the Duke had said to her in confidence during their marriage – the marriage had ended in divorce a little earlier. The judge said that the relationship was in its nature confidential and that the obligations of confidence continued after the marriage had ended. See also the 'privacy' cases, below.

Example 4   Similarly in *Fraser v Thames TV* (1982), three actresses had given to a television company, the idea of a soap opera relating the adventures of an all-girl rock band. They contemplated that they would take the starring roles, but the TV company stole the idea and had to pay heavy damages for breach of confidence.

Example 5   The interim injunctions against publication of the *Spycatcher* diaries in the United Kingdom were based on breach of confidence by Peter Wright, although the House of Lords said that the Crown might also be entitled to copyright in them (*Att Gen v Guardian Newspapers,* 1990).

Example 6   Similarly, in *HRH Prince of Wales v Associated Newspapers* (2006), Prince Charles succeeded in an action to restrain publication of extracts from a handwritten travel journal in which he recorded his experience of, and thoughts about, the handover of Hong Kong to China in 1997. One of the Prince's private office staff had taken a copy of the journal (and seven others from different trips) and given it to a newspaper. The Court of Appeal considered that the information had been disclosed in breach of a 'well recognised relationship of confidence, that which exists between master and servant'; the newspaper was aware of this and accordingly the Prince's case was 'overwhelming'.

The Effect of Marking Things 'Confidential'

We have said that the test of confidentiality is the express or implied intention of the parties. It follows that marking a document 'confidential' will not necessarily make it so, if the person who receives it does not know, and has no reason to believe or expect, that it is to be confidential. Accordingly, emblazoning a copy of today's newspaper with a handwritten banner proclaiming it 'Top Secret' will not bind any subsequent readers with an obligation of confidence in relation to it. Nevertheless, there are situations in which precisely such a marking may tip the balance.

Confidence and Contract

Where parties are in a contractual relationship, they often provide for obligations of confidence in express terms. Thus, normally no scientist will be employed by the research department of a company unless she agrees to keep the company information secret even after she leaves the company. But even where there is no such express obligation, the relationship between the parties may of its nature give rise to obligations of confidence: as in the 'swizzlestick' case mentioned above, or in *Robb v Green* (1895), where an ex-employee was restrained from using a list of his old employer's customers for his own benefit. The point is that the law of confidence exists apart from the law of contract, but when obligations of confidence exist there is often some contractual relationship between the parties.

What Happens where the Information Becomes Public Knowledge?

Suppose that by the time the action comes to trial, the information concerned has been either wholly or partly made available to the public – what then?

At first sight it would seem absurd that a defendant should be under any restriction in using information which is public knowledge. But things are not so simple: a defendant may obtain a considerable advantage from information which, when it was supplied to him, was confidential but which has now become public knowledge – one judge expressed this sort of situation vividly by saying that such a defendant was using the information as a 'springboard for activities detrimental to the plaintiff.' The exact scope of this notion is difficult to ascertain. At one extreme, it is clear that a man who lets all the information be disclosed by publication of his patent specification can no longer prevent ex-employees from revealing that information. On the other hand, it is also clear that the courts are willing to give some relief to a plaintiff who shows that the defendant has obtained an unfair advantage by using the plaintiff's confidential information as a 'springboard', even when the information has later become public. The courts say that, in such cases, although it is true that the information was available from public sources, the defendant did not get it from them, but got it from the 'tainted source' of the plaintiff's confidential disclosure to him. Once a defendant falls under suspicion of having used a 'tainted source', he may find himself in difficulty. It may then be no use his saying: 'Look, I know I had dealings with the plaintiff in the past which were confidential, but I developed this machine by myself and here are my plans to prove it.' The court may still feel he got the idea from the plaintiff and find a breach of confidence. *Seager v Copydex* is just such a case.

Accordingly, information may have a limited degree of confidentiality even though it can be ascertained by reverse engineering or through compilation of public domain sources. Additionally, an injunction may be granted to prevent a defendant from benefiting from a past misuse of confidential information even if the information had subsequently ceased to be confidential. However, in such cases any injunction will be limited so as to simply remove the defendant's head start: once information has become public, it cannot be a breach of confidence to gather it from public sources and to use it for one's own gain.

Remedies

The remedies for a breach of confidence are much the same as those granted for the infringement of the other rights discussed in this book (see Chapter 2). Thus injunctions can be, and often are, awarded, together with damages or accounts of profits. In some cases the court will not award an injunction but will award damages only. This occurred in *Seager v Copydex* where, since the information was, at the time of the action, publicly known and the plaintiff's information was only a part of the information being used by the defendants, an injunction was thought to be inappropriate and damages enough to compensate Mr Seager. In fact there followed a dispute as to the way in which damages should be calculated, and the matter had to go to the Court of Appeal again upon this question *(Seager v Copydex,* 1969). The Court held that damages should be paid upon the market value of the information, which depended upon how important it was: whether, for example, it was inventive enough to support a patent, or was merely the sort of information which could have been supplied by any expert. In any case, a court may be swayed by considerations of financial damage suffered by virtue of the defendant's unlawful use (and thereby calculate on the basis of lost profits), or perhaps by the claimant's propensity and willingness to licence (and hence calculate on the basis of a reasonable royalty).

Interim Injunctions

If the claimant acts quickly enough, he will in a suitable case be granted an interim injunction: where the information concerned is not yet public, for instance, to preserve the status quo while the case is fought. But in 'springboard' cases it seems that the courts are unwilling to grant such injunctions, partly because the questions of fact as to exactly how much of the information used by the defendant was taken from the plaintiff and how much the defendants got for themselves are too difficult to resolve without hearing all the evidence, and partly because, in such cases, the claimant may in the end, if he wins, receive only damages. *Coco v Clark* (1969) is an example of such a refusal. (But note that the judge, whilst refusing the interim injunction, thought that the defendants ought, pending the trial, to pay a potential royalty into a bank account so that if the plaintiff eventually won the action, he would be safeguarded, and an undertaking to this effect was given to the court.)

Suing Third Parties

If the owner of the information is able to act before it has been disclosed to any third party, then an injunction preventing disclosure should be all he needs to protect it. If it has already been passed on to a third party, an injunction will not be much good unless it binds the third party too. Anyone who receives information that he knows (or ought to know) reached him through a breach of confidence has a duty not to use or disclose it, and the court will in a proper case grant an injunction to enforce that duty. Thus in the *Argyll* case mentioned above, not only the Duke was placed under an injunction but also the Sunday newspaper which was going to print the information. There were similar results in *Spycatcher* and in the *Prince of Wales* case too.

The exact limits to the circumstances in which third parties can be sued are not yet fully worked out because there have not been many cases on the subject.

However, the law is probably that where someone pays for the information in good faith then he cannot be stopped from using it. It would be different if he acted in bad faith (for example, where a company has bought information from someone it knew to be an industrial spy or an employee of another company) and it may be different if he does not pay for it.

Problems of Proof

From what has been said, it might be thought that the law gave enough protection to confidential information to make dealing with it perfectly safe. Any such idea would be entirely wrong. As always, neither the general law nor even a carefully drawn contract is any real protection against dishonesty. The function of these things – of a proper contract, especially – is to make it clear, amongst honest parties to a transaction, just what they may and may not do.

If a would-be claimant does come up against a rogue, then she will find it difficult to prove her case. The burden will lie on her to show she gave the rogue confidential information in circumstances giving rise to a bond of confidence and that the rogue is using such information. In some cases the would-be claimant will not even know that the rogue is using the information. For example, suppose a company learns from an employee of another company that a particular line of research has been tried, and found useless. This will save the first company from trying that line, but the company from whom the information was 'taken' will have very little chance of proving that the other company acted in breach of confidence. When it comes to information passed on to third parties, the problems of proof become even harder.

Where the Action will not Lie

'No Confidence in Iniquity'

Since the action for breach of confidence is founded originally upon what is conscionable – it is a creature of equity – the courts will not grant a remedy if the information which the defendant threatens to reveal or use is something which ought not, in conscience, to be protected. There are many examples in the cases.

Example 1　In *Initial Towel Services v Putterill* (1967) the plaintiffs failed to obtain interim injunctions against an ex-employee and a daily newspaper when the ex-employee alleged that the information he was giving to the newspaper showed that the plaintiffs had been a party to a secret illegal arrangement to fix prices.

Example 2　In *X v Y* (1988) the court refused permission to disclose the diagnosis with AIDS of two doctors who were continuing to practice, in the light of the interest in preserving the confidentiality of medical records.

Example 3   The court permitted a campaigning organisation to disclose information concerning the welfare of research laboratory animals to relevant regulatory authorities, but not the press (*Imutran v Uncaged Campaigns*, 2001).

Example 4   In *Lion Laboratories v Evans* (1985) the court was prepared to allow disclosure to the press of confidential documents that showed the claimant's breathalyser product to be faulty, as being justified on the basis of a wide public interest in knowing that convictions based on readings taken from the device might be unsafe.

Public Policy

There are some cases where, as a matter of public policy, agreements for confidence will not be enforced. The most important of these is in relation to skilled employees who leave their firm and propose to enter employment in the same field, perhaps with a rival manufacturer. The court will enforce covenants preventing the ex-employee from working for the competitor, provided that the covenant is not too broad in terms of the geographical area to which it extends and the time for which it operates. The court will also, irrespective of whether there is a covenant in restraint of trade in his contract of employment, prevent an employee or ex-employee from disclosing the industrial or commercial secrets of his employer. However, it will not prevent him from using the general skill and knowledge (as opposed to confidential information) which he has acquired by reason of his employment. Obviously the distinction between general skill and commercial secrets is sometimes hard to draw; but be drawn it must, for otherwise skilled employees would never be able to change their jobs. So important do the courts regard the ability of a skilled person to do his or her job that even an express agreement seeking to bind the employee not to use such general knowledge will be held invalid.

The position of directors deserves special mention: any information obtained by a director by virtue of his office is, in effect, held on trust for the company, and must only be used for the purposes of the company. Since the directors are responsible for the conduct of the business of the company, it is seldom open to them to say that they were not told and did not realise that the information acquired was confidential.

The Duty of Confidence Must be Owed to the Claimant

In *Fraser v Evans* (1969) the claimant sought to restrain by interlocutory injunction publication in a newspaper of parts of a confidential report he had prepared for the Greek government. It was held that although the report was confidential, and although the copyright belonged to the claimant, he could not succeed. He failed as to infringement of copyright since it appeared very likely that, at the trial, a defence of fair dealing (see Chapter 21) would succeed; and he failed as to breach of confidence because the report belonged to the Greek government and not to him. Only the person to whom the duty of confidence is owed can sue to enforce it.

Sales of 'Know-How'

It is not uncommon, in these days, for know-how to be treated as an article of commerce – to be sold outright, like any other property, or to be handed over on terms like those of a patent licence. Even an actual patent licence may often turn out, in reality, to be largely dealing in know-how – it is often the know-how that is worth the money, rather than the more-or-less dubious monopoly given by any patent. This sort of transaction presents no very great difficulty in the ordinary case where both parties are honest. The agreements governing such transactions deal in detail with the degree of 'confidence' to be attached to the information handed over, and especially with the position after the agreement comes to an end.

The Need for Agreements

It is always better to have questions of confidence properly covered by agreement, than to leave them to implications of the general law. Consider once again the case of a manufacturer trying out an invention. Everything may go well, in which case there will be no difficulty. But suppose the inventor's ideas turn out in the end to be more-or-less unworkable. The manufacturer may then drop the whole scheme; but suppose that in the course of finding out that the invention will not work he finds out what is wrong, and so becomes able to make something that will work. What is to be the position then? The manufacturer, especially if he has paid for the right to have first go at the invention, will feel that he has taken from the inventor nothing he has not paid for, that the new ideas are his own and that he owes the inventor nothing. The inventor will probably feel that the manufacturer is either being difficult, or making undesirable alterations in the original scheme so as to get out of paying a proper royalty. If a fight is to be avoided, there ought to be an agreement which will make it clear exactly what the manufacturer is entitled to keep if he rejects the original invention, and just exactly when a royalty or purchase price is in the end to be payable.

Difficult Cases

Of course, there are difficulties no agreement can anticipate; especially as neither inventors nor manufacturers are always as sensible and co-operative as they might be. For instance, if a manufacturer can be interested at all in an invention presented to him, the reason is likely to be that the problem it sets out to solve is one he knew of and perhaps had even been dabbling in himself. His reaction to seeing an outsider's proposal is likely to be to reject it, while being encouraged to go back to his own ideas and make them work – perhaps with a bit of help from the alternative proposals that the outside inventor has put to him. Inevitably, in most such cases, the inventor will be convinced that the manufacturer has stolen his invention, and the manufacturer will be convinced that he has merely pursued (as he 'really' always meant to) his own previous line of development. They will never agree on the facts, and may have to ask a court to decide between them. If a proper agreement is made between them, before the invention is disclosed, this should serve to limit the range of the dispute, and so will save time, costs and some bitterness, if nothing else; but even so, a dispute may be inevitable. It is worth examining in some detail the factors that make disputes so difficult to avoid in many matters of confidence.

The instance just given suggests one factor: that much information seems very much more valuable to the person giving it than to the person listening. Another factor is well illustrated by the example of a merchant who lets suppliers know the names of his customers. The real trouble here is, that the merchant's position is inherently a risky one; sooner or later, it will pay his suppliers or his customers to cut him out, and what seems to them an ordinary change in business procedure will look to him like dirty work. He will look on a list of customers or suppliers as something of great value, since to him it is; but to others, such a list is worth precisely what it would cost to pay a person to compile it from business directories. So often what really matters is not some trade secret, but just trade habits that nobody bothers to alter. The same thing can happen with industrial know-how: the difference between making something well and making it badly can be a matter of secret knowledge, but is more often a matter of skilled management and skilled labour. If a good person gets a job somewhere else at higher pay, and her new employer's products jump ahead in quality, it is easy to assume that some secret has gone with her; but the odds are that secrets played very little part in the matter. So one gets a sort of typical case, where the defendant has been rather careless over the claimant's confidence, not thinking it mattered much; and the claimant is over-suspicious, not realising that any competent person in the defendant's position could do the job without anybody's secrets. Both parties are sure they are 90 per cent in the right: and the result can easily be litigation, whose outcome will be anyone's guess. There are people who deliberately set out to steal their employer's secrets; but most litigation, in this field as in any other, is between people who just did not think sufficiently.

Of course a lot of litigation about commercial confidentiality is pursued to nip in the bud any potential competition from ex-employees. Thus a lot of claimants have succeeded in doing a great deal of damage to (quite honest) ex-employee defendants by getting things like search orders (see Chapter 2) awarded against them based on misleading or incomplete evidence. For many years, the courts were concerned about dishonest defendants walking off with their ex-employer's secrets. Some judges would hand out the most draconian orders (originally intended to deal with crooked record pirates), almost on the nod. There was increasing concern about over-aggressive claimants using the courts to put these defendants engaged in lawful competition out of business. And so significant rules and safeguards have now been put in place. This is important, since the costs of litigation are such that clearing one's name and getting an unjustified order discharged is often a serious drain on a new business's resources. Nowadays, therefore, the grant of search and seizure orders is very carefully controlled and it is a costly business for a claimant to obtain and enforce one. They are in consequence much less used in cases of this kind than they used to be.

Privacy and the Press

Whilst the courts have long protected personal confidences, in England (in contrast to some other states) there is no general 'right of privacy' as such. This said, the courts have developed remedies for cases where the press reveals or threatens to reveal information about individuals which they would prefer to keep under wraps. In recent years, the Human Rights Act, which incorporates the European Convention on Human Rights (ECHR), has been a spur to this development. Article 8 of the ECHR provides that 'Everyone has the right to respect for his private and family life, his home and his correspondence'. As such, the courts have developed an approach which many claim amounts to a tort of privacy in all but name.

A major distinction between the so-called traditional action for breach of confidence and that more recently developed in the name of privacy lies in the existence, or otherwise, of an obligation of confidence. The traditional action is functionally blind to the nature of the information it protects, and will just as happily restrain publication of a commercial secret as a marital infidelity, provided, that is, that there is an obligation to be enforced. For many years, the courts pulled and stretched at the boundaries of this concept, struggling to construct an artificial relationship of confidence between intruder and victim. In more recent years, however, the need to manufacture an obligation in this way has been eradicated, replaced by a more straightforward enquiry as to whether the claimant has a reasonable expectation of privacy. Once this is established, it is a question of balancing the right to private life under Article 8 ECHR with the right to freedom of expression under Article 10 – as, just with the traditional action, there are some instances in which the public interest in protecting the claimant's affairs will be outweighed by a broader public interest in disseminating the information.

The 'Ordinary Citizen' and the 'Celebrity'

Interesting questions arise over whether English law may be seen to treat the 'ordinary citizen' somewhat differently from the 'celebrity' when it comes to the law of privacy. On the one hand, there are comments in some cases (albeit generally in dissent) that suggest those in the public eye have to expect and accept greater scrutiny. On the other are judgments in which the courts abstain, sometimes explicitly, from making any broad pronouncements, preferring instead to advocate an intense focus on the facts – which some may claim essentially amounts to the same thing. In some of the cases there are also shades of the maxim 'As you live by the press, so shall you die by the press.' In particular, if someone actively presents a false picture to the public about matters which would ordinarily be private, the courts recognise that the press is entitled to expose the truth to the public. This was illustrated in *Campbell v MGN* (2004), in which a tabloid newspaper ran a story about the supermodel Naomi Campbell attending Narcotics Anonymous. She had previous made a point of saying (falsely) that she did not use drugs. Her lawyers therefore did not even try to argue that the press was not allowed to report the fact of her drug dependency and the fact that she was seeking treatment, given that she had specifically given publicity to the very question of whether she took drugs. The case went to the House of Lords which said (by a majority) that the newspaper had gone too far in publishing details including photographs of her at the door of the Narcotics Anonymous meeting. Nevertheless, we might question whether an ordinary citizen who had not sought to reveal details of his or her private life would be entitled to protection in respect of matters of this kind – they probably would, but then, in a classic tale of chicken and egg, the papers would also inevitably be less interested in running such a story in the first place.

How Much can the Story be Fleshed Out?

Newspapers obviously want to print not only the bare facts of an embarrassing story, but to give it added colour or credibility by, for example, adding photographs of the activity in question. Assume that publishing the facts is legitimate, how far can they go in illustrating the story? The answer is, unfortunately, not clear.

On the one hand, there may be some judicial sympathy for the newspaper editor who has to make quick decisions which may not always look so good when pored over in great detail in court. It is claimed, often vociferously, that unless there is reasonable latitude, the freedom of the press would be unduly curtailed.

However, a line of cases stretching from the decision of the House of Lords in the *Campbell* case have adopted a rather stricter approach, involving consideration of whether publication of the ancillary material was necessary and whether it was likely to be harmful. Even so, the line between what is permissible embellishment of a factual story and what goes too far is not easy to draw. In general the courts have tended to disapprove of the publication of photographs where the bare story would suffice to put the information before the public (see e.g. the *Campbell* case and the *Theakston* case, referred to below).

Some examples

Example 1   Michael Douglas and Catharine Zeta Jones successfully sued *Hello!* Magazine, which published photographs of their wedding that had been clandestinely obtained. The couple had entered into an exclusive deal with a rival magazine, *OK!*, giving that magazine exclusive picture rights for a substantial sum. *OK!* were also claimants in the action, and they received the lion's share of the substantial damages awarded against *Hello!* (*Douglas v Hello*, 2003).

Example 2   An action was successfully maintained against a photographic agency (Big Pictures Ltd), which supplied the *Sunday Express* with a picture of David Murray, the infant son of author JK Rowling, being pushed in a pram by one of his parents on a public street in Edinburgh. The Court of Appeal considered that the nature of the claimant (the child) in this case tipped the balance in favour of finding that there was a reasonable expectation of privacy. This was the case despite the nature of the activity being completely anodyne and occurring in a public place (*Murray v Big Pictures*, 2008).

Example 3   A well-known presenter of youth television programmes sued to prevent publication of a story about sexual activity with prostitutes, accompanied by photographs. The court permitted publication of the story but not the photographs, observing that photographs had a particularly intrusive nature and that the courts were generally willing to prevent publication of them (*Theakston v MGN*, 2002).

Note: a Brief Excursion into a Dry Debate

A debate has smouldered in the pages of academic journals for over a hundred years concerning the legal nature of confidential information. It is one thing to say that the law will prevent people from taking the fruits of breaches of confidence; it is quite another to work out (as a matter of legal theory) why such protection should exist in the first place. After all, there must be some basis for creating a liability. There are (essentially) three views.

The first (and probably the most ancient) is property-based. This holds that confidential information is a kind of property just like any other which can be transferred and is protected by an action in essence similar to conversion of goods or trespass. There are numerous problems with this theory, not least the fact that breach of confidence does not provide rights *in rem* (which means enforceable against the world at large – anyone), but rather only rights against those touched with the obligation. Moreover, confidential information does not have at least one important incident of other personal property – you are not guilty of theft if you steal it (see, e.g. *Oxford v Moss*, 1978: a student 'stealing' examination paper).

The second is the contractualist view. This holds that confidential information is protected because of a kind of contract, express or implied. Purely contractualist theories of legal liability are out of favour at present, and in any event this theory does not really make room for the notion of stopping a third party, who has got hold of the information from the impartee, from using or disclosing it.

The third is a rather more nebulous approach based on the enforcement of equitable obligations of confidence. This is the approach which is currently dominant. Thus, there is said to be an obligation of confidence based on 'good faith' – it is said that the conscience of the defendant is touched. Although the courts may not be able to define precisely when the principles will be invoked, they know a case for their application when they see one.

In practice, the inability clearly to articulate a basis or framework for protection is not as serious as it might be in other cases. There are usually so many other uncertainties of fact and law in confidential information cases (such as whether the information has the necessary quality of confidence about it) that adding a little disquiet about the basis for granting relief does not make too much difference.

The important underlying point which this debate highlights is that monopolies protected in virtue of the 'proprietorship' of or control over confidential information are only regulated by the courts (subject to the general principles of the Human Rights Act) – obligations of 'good faith' are rather powerful and flexible legal instruments in the hands of judges. Now and again, senior judges remark that unless something is done by Parliament to provide for a self-standing law of privacy, the courts must step in.

26

Database Right

Introduction

English law has long recognised that copyright exists in collections of information (compilations) including rather mundane information such as timetables (see Chapter 18 above). But the right was restricted to preventing copying of the whole or a substantial part of the compilation, not specifically to preventing use of the data itself. Not all EU countries provided copyright protection to compilations and, in 1996, the European Community decided to harmonise the law in this area. It therefore enacted the Database Directive, which has subsequently been incorporated into UK law.

The result of the Directive was the creation of a new kind of intellectual property right: the '*sui generis*' (continental lawyers love Latin) database right. It provides rights in certain circumstances to prevent the extraction or re-utilisation of data in a qualifying database. The main purpose of the right is to give protection to the large (increasingly online) collections of data where the value resides in having a large amount of information gathered together in an organised way

However, the Database Directive is a good example of how not to legislate since the law on its face covers much more than what one would ordinarily think of as a database. Indeed one thing one notices immediately about the Directive is the vagueness of its drafting. It contains many more recitals (the preambles setting the context) than substantive provisions, many of them the fruit of special interest groups getting some helpful text into the Directive to be used later on in persuading the courts that the substantive provisions should mean one thing rather than another.

What is a Database?

A database is defined as a collection of independent works data or other materials which are arranged in a systematic or methodical way and are individually accessible by electronic or other means. This definition is very wide and covers (potentially) ordinary telephone directories, even collections of journal articles which have been subject to an editorial process to arrange them in some systematic or methodical way. Thus, a database consisting of the live scores from football matches around the country is a 'database' for the purposes of the legislation (*Football Dataco v Stan James*, 2013). The definition is not limited to 'electronic' database, any form will do.

Subsistence of Database Right

For a database right to exist, the maker of the database must be a qualifying person (including a qualifying individual corporation, partnership etc). In broad terms, to qualify the maker must be an individual who is a national of or is habitually resident within an EEA state or a body corporate incorporated under the law of an EEA state, based in the EEA, or having operations linked with an EEA state on an ongoing basis. The result is that makers of databases outside the EEA do not qualify. In particular, US makers of databases will not have database right protection. In the US, there is no similar protection for databases and there is accordingly no possibility of reciprocity.

Substantial Investment in 'Obtaining, Verifying or Presenting the Contents of the Database'

As well as being made by a qualifying individual, there must have been a 'substantial investment in the obtaining, verifying or presenting the contents of the database'. This includes any kind of investment – such as financial, human or technical resources, and is judged both qualitatively and quantitatively. There is one major qualification, however: no matter how much investment or work goes into creating a database, you cannot have a right in it if your work and investment consists solely of *creating* the data – this is the wrong kind of investment. Probably the reason for excluding this kind of investment is that otherwise you would get a monopoly in the data itself. Thus the official lists of runners and riders at race tracks, or football fixture lists (the creation of each of which involves a lot of work and skill), do not get database right (*BHB v William Hill*, 2004; *Fixtures Marketing v OPAP*, 2004). On the other hand, you do get a database right if you record what can fairly be regarded as objective data and put that into a database, as happened for instance in the *Football Dataco* case, mentioned above. There the claimants sent people to every football ground at which there was a match playing and got them to phone in to say what was happening and to provide information about goals, scorers and times. This information all formed part of the protected database.

How Long Does Database Right Last, and How Can it be Traded?

Database right lasts for 15 years from the end of the calendar year in which the database was completed or, if made available to the public, from the end of the calendar year in which it was made available to the public. However, if a database is updated regularly, the 15-year period begins to run again if the new (or revised) database would be considered to be a substantial new investment.

Database rights may be sold (by assignment, for example) and may be licensed. There are certain provisions which enable the terms of general schemes established by database right owners to be subject to the control of the Copyright Tribunal.

What the Database Right Protects

There are two kinds of prohibited act: extraction or re-utilisation of the whole or a substantial part of the contents of the database. Extraction is the temporary or permanent transfer of the contents to another medium. Re-utilisation is defined in the Directive as 'Any form of making available to the public all or a substantial part of the contents of the database by the distribution of copies by renting, by on-line or other forms of transmission.' This depends on the scale of the investment which went into what was taken; see the *BHB* and *Football Dataco* cases.

'Substantial part' is considered both qualitatively and quantitatively. Repeated and systematic extraction of insubstantial parts of the contents of a database may amount to the extraction or reutilisation of a substantial part where they imply acts which conflict with the normal exploitation of the database or unreasonably prejudice the legitimate interests of the maker of the database. In copyright law it is an open question as to whether taking small but regular helpings each of which is insufficient to infringe in itself can constitute infringement in the aggregate. The Database Directive makes it clear that it is possible for this to constitute infringement.

Who Can be Sued for Infringement, and Where?

The CJEU has ruled that an infringer can be sued not only in his home country (if he is within the EU), but also in any EU country where he targets the infringing material. Thus Sportradar in Germany could be sued in the UK, where they had an arrangement with Stan James in the UK whereby the unlawfully extracted live football scores appeared on the Stan James UK website – they were targeting the UK (*Football Dataco v Yahoo! and others*, 2012).

Exceptions to Database Right Protection

There are rather complex exceptions to protection for 'lawful users' and there are some of the same limitations as exist for copyright protection (e.g. Parliamentary and judicial proceedings and the like). There are not, however, the exceptions for criticism or review or for reporting current events and the education and research exceptions are narrower than for copyright protection.

Ordinary Copyright Protection for Databases

Somewhat confusingly, databases are also entitled to copyright protection if they satisfy the requirement of originality. For a database, this is the requirement that the database be such that by reason of the selection or arrangement of its contents constitutes the author's *own intellectual creation*. What this means in practice is beginning to be worked out by the courts. In particular the CJEU has ruled that intellectual effort and skill in creating data does not count (*Football Dataco v Yahoo! and others*, 2012). This does not make much intellectual sense, but one can see the same policy reason for it as for the reason to refuse database right protection.

Actions for Infringement of Database Right

Actions for infringement of database right are very similar to copyright infringement claims. All of the usual remedies are available (such as an injunction, damages, accounts of profits). Additional damages may be claimed in the case of flagrant infringements. Exclusive licensees may sue.

27

The European Union –
Free Movement and Competition

The Influence of European Union Law

European Union (EU) law has had a very significant influence on intellectual property. This influence has been greatest in two aspects. First, much of modern IP law has now been harmonised across the EU Member States, generally leading to a greater degree of protection (e.g. more scope or longer duration), new rights (such as the database right) and more limited exceptions. Secondly (and working in the opposite direction), EU rules on free movement and on competition have had considerable influence in reducing the things that proprietors can do with intellectual property rights – particularly in regard to partitioning Member States from one another. As we have seen elsewhere in this text, the Court of Justice of the EU (as the entity formerly known as the European Court of Justice now likes to be called) takes a central role in the interpretation (or misinterpretation, depending on your perspective) of this EU legislation and the national statutes derived from it. The EU's influence in the area covered by this book is therefore something that simply cannot be ignored.

An Introduction to EU Legislation

In terms of the sheer volume of IP-related legislation, the EU has been enormously active. This is only to be expected. By 1787, copyright and patents were considered sufficiently commercially important to warrant mention in the United States Constitution as matters about which the Federal Congress could legislate (US Constitution: Art 1, section 8(8)). It is perhaps unsurprising, therefore, that, over two and a quarter centuries later, the EU now sees (and indeed has done for some time) intellectual property as more of a 'federal' question than one for the Member States alone. Given the EU's provenance as a 'Common Market', it would seem odd if differences in Member States' IP laws (or indeed the territorial nature of IP – more on this later) could disrupt this regime. Accordingly harmonisation of IP rights has been a mainstay of the EU Commission's legislative agenda in this field.

Whilst there was nothing explicit in the Treaty of Rome that concerned the EU's power to regulate intellectual property, this did not stop the legislative programme. As part of the move to create and develop a single market, the EU (and its forebears) passed a fair amount of legislation in the field of intellectual property which was intended to harmonise laws between Member States or to create pan-European rights. Thus, the whole of UK Trade Mark law is based on a Community Directive (and the Community Trade Mark derives from an EU Regulation). The EU has also passed Directives on patents (such as the Biotech Directive and two Directives granting supplementary protection certificates to compensate for delay in obtaining marketing authorisation). However, it has perhaps been most active in the field of copyright, with piecemeal harmonisation of various aspects of the protection and enforcement of rights falling under this umbrella. Legislation has therefore been passed that deals with everything from copyright's duration, through the creation of rental and lending rights, computer software copyright, and (most generally) copyright in the information society.

Since the Treaty of Lisbon came into effect in late 2009, the regulation of IP within the EU has found specific legislative grounding. Now Article 118 of the Treaty on the Functioning of the European Union (TFEU) contains an explicit mandate for the Council and European Parliament, acting in accordance with the ordinary legislative procedure, to 'establish measures for the creation of European intellectual property rights to provide uniform protection of intellectual property rights throughout the Union and for the setting up of centralised Union-wide authorisation, coordination and supervision arrangements.' The EU's interest in IP is clearly not on the wane.

EU Directives

EU Directives in the field of IP (as elsewhere) are addressed to Member States. They set out in fairly general terms what the Member States have to introduce by way of legislation in order to comply. However, they also give some leeway in precisely how that is to be done. Directives must be transposed into national legislation in order to enter into force. A deadline is set for passing suitable legislation, and Member States are obligated to introduce something which complies within that deadline. If a state fails to introduce conforming legislation by the deadline, there are several consequences, arguably the most important of which is that the Directive has so-called 'direct effect'. Direct effect is intended to protect the rights of individuals by ensuring that they can take advantage of the rights conferred by European law even in the absence of national implementing legislation, once the deadline for the implementation of such has passed. This doctrine was developed by the European Court of Justice (as it then was) in the 1960s (*Van Gend & Loos*, 1963) and recognised as extending to Directives a decade later (*Van Duyn*, 1974). Accordingly, if the provisions of a Directive are precise, clear and unconditional, and do not require the adoption of any further measures by the

EU or the Member State, a person can rely on these provisions against administrative authorities of the state (and certain other organs of the state, but not against other private citizens), even though there is no national legislation implementing the Directive. In certain circumstances, if there is a manifest and grave disregard of EU law obligations, a person injured thereby may also, under specified conditions, be able to claim damages from the state for failure to implement the Directive. Once implemented, the Court of Justice of the EU has jurisdiction to interpret provisions of these Directives via the standard reference system under Article 267 TFEU.

EU Regulations

In the field of IP, the EU has also created a number of pan-European rights. As has been seen, application for a Community Trade Mark or Community Design (if successful) provides one registration that covers the entire EU – whether patents complete their journey down the same path remains to be seen, but at the time of writing all the signs indicate that they will. These pan-European rights are created by way of EU Regulations – the most direct form of EU law. Regulations require no implementing legislation, and have binding force throughout every Member State from the instant that they are passed.

Free Movement of Goods and Competition

Notwithstanding the creation of pan-European intellectual property rights, it is fundamental to understand that all IP is essentially territorial in nature. IP rights do not exist in the abstract, there is no inherent exclusivity in an idea (even if expressed in concrete form) once it has moved outside of the creator's head. Exclusivity (protection from competition) is provided by the application of law, not by the nature of the subject matter: and law has territorial restrictions. Accordingly, a UK patent can only provide its proprietor with the right to prevent competitors committing infringing acts in the United Kingdom. Equally, a UK registered trade mark cannot regulate the use of the mark in foreign states; passing off requires a misrepresentation occurring in the UK; and copyright is similarly bound. So too for the other rights: such is straightforward.

Nevertheless, territoriality works both ways. Even though a domestic right cannot be enforced in foreign states, it can be used to stop foreign-manufactured infringing articles from entering the UK market. To do otherwise would destroy the value of the right – imagine a situation where a UK patent holder, for example, was only able to bring infringement actions against the purveyors of products made in the UK: the market would soon be flooded by knock-offs sourced from abroad.

Considered in light of the EU's commitment to free movement and competition, however, these territorial and 'anti-competitive' characteristics of IP present a fundamental problem. The TFEU is set against national rules that actually or potentially partition the single market formed by the EU states, and it also has policies designed to be pro-competition. It therefore outlaws restrictions on the freedom of movement of goods across national boundaries and contains specific provisions directed against anti-competitive abuses of market power and restrictive agreements. How, then, is a balance to be struck?

At one extreme, the answer is clear. It would make a mockery of the system if the proprietor of an IP right was not able to use it to prevent evidently counterfeit items from entering the domestic market – it should make no difference if these items have been manufactured in Bristol, Berlin or Buenos Aires. But what if goods that are considered knock-offs in state 'A' are produced legitimately in state 'B' – e.g. because there is no patent protection in 'B', or because the trade mark, copyright, etc, is owned by different person there? Or if the goods have originated with the proprietor of the UK IP right, but were put into circulation in a foreign state, perhaps for a lower price: what then? And what of the restrictions on competition that are facilitated by IP rights, when does a legitimate ability to exclude competitors turn into an abuse that deserves to be regulated? These are important questions, and for answers we have to look at two complementary, yet distinct, aspects of EU law.

Free Movement – Articles 34 and 36 TFEU

Articles 34 and 36 of the Treaty on the Functioning of the EU provide for the free movement of goods. (Note: cases decided before 2009 will refer to the earlier numbering of the provisions: until 1999, when the Treaty of Amsterdam entered into force, they were found in Articles 30 and 36 of the Treaty Establishing the European Community (TEC), for the decade post-1999 they were renumbered as Articles 28 and 30 TEC).

Article 34 TFEU says that quantitative restrictions on imports and measures having equivalent effect are to be prohibited. However, Article 36 gives specific dispensation to (otherwise prohibited) restrictions in certain areas and for certain purposes, including the protection of industrial and commercial property, provided that they are not a means of arbitrary discrimination or disguised restriction on trade between Member States.

The European Court of Justice has worked out special principles which aim to reconcile the free movement of goods with the territoriality of intellectual property rights.

The Fundamental Rules

First, although the TFEU (and its forebears) does not affect the existence of an intellectual property right, there are circumstances in which the exercise of that right can be prohibited. In other words, whilst some things may technically be infringements, there may be good reason to restrict a rights-holder's ability to object to them in certain circumstances. Second, the rights-holder's rights are exhausted in respect of specific goods when those goods are put into circulation by her (or with her consent) anywhere within the EU. What this means in practice is that, once consensually sold in an EU (or EEA) state, those goods are in free movement – they can be bought by third parties and re-sold and, provided this is all that is done, there is generally nothing that the rights-holder can do about it. Third, Article 36 permits exceptions to the free movement of goods only to the extent to which those exceptions are necessary to safeguard the rights that constitute the specific subject matter of the type of intellectual property in question – which is simply another way of saying that free movement is very important within the EU and that exceptions will only be entertained in well defined circumstances.

As will be seen, these principles only give guidance at the most abstract level. Their effect is best illustrated by a few examples.

Example 1 (Patents Where First Sale is in the EEA)

Sterling Drug held patents for a urinary infection drug in both the United Kingdom and the Netherlands. They sold the drug cheaply in the UK but it was very expensive in the Netherlands. Centrafarm bought some of the drug in the UK and shipped it to the Netherlands. As might be expected, they sold it there at a handsome profit. Held: there was nothing that Sterling Drug could do about this. The rights were exhausted by putting the drug into circulation for the first time in the United Kingdom. (*Centrafarm v Sterling Drug*, 1974). (Note, the result would be the same if the patentee first sold into a country where there was no patent protection.)

Example 2 (Same with Trade Marks)

Metro bought 'Polydor'-marked records in France (where they were cheap) and sold them in Germany (where they were expensive). Held: there was nothing that the trade mark proprietor could do to stop this. The goods were genuine, i.e. originated with the trade mark proprietor, and had been and put on the market in the EU with their consent (*Deutsche Grammophon v Metro*, 1971). Since the entry into force of the Trade Marks Directive (TMD), free movement has found a specific place within trade marks legislation. Accordingly, a provision embodying the same principles as Articles 34 and 36 TFEU can now be found within Article 7 of the TMD, which itself is embodied in section 12 of the UK Trade Marks Act.

Example 3 (Unconnected Parties)

Terranova, who had the mark TERRANOVA registered in Germany, tried to prevent Terrapin (an unconnected company) from importing building materials into Germany bearing the TERRAPIN mark. Held: Terranova could do so (they would be (arguably) similar marks and identical goods with a likelihood of confusion), provided that the mark did not act as an arbitrary means of discrimination or a disguised restriction on trade between Member States (*Terrapin v Terranova*, 1976).

When Rights are not Exhausted

There are essentially two situations in which a consensual first sale by the rights-holder will not trigger exhaustion in connection with those goods sold (with the consequence that their re-sale by a second party within the EEA may be prohibited).

The first is where goods are put on the market outside of the EEA and it is not demonstrated that there is unequivocal consent to their marketing within the EEA. This position was something that the English courts, in particular, were initially sceptical of. If the goods are original: what is the problem? The rights-holder gets their slice of profits when they are first sold, why should it matter if this was in the EEA or elsewhere? However, a number of decisions of the European Court of Justice confirmed that exhaustion was an EU concept, and that consent could not be inferred from such things as: silence; the absence of appropriate contractual reservations in any agreement transferring ownership of the goods; the lack of a warning notice being affixed to the goods; or the fact that the trade mark owner has not communicated to all subsequent purchasers her opposition to the goods being marketed in the EEA (*Davidoff v AG Imports*, 2001). Usually, therefore, consent will need to be expressly provided.

The second is where the goods have been somehow tampered with or altered by the reseller. Classically this will occur in situations involving trade marks, in cases where goods are repackaged or relabelled in order to better satisfy the market of the Member State of import. The rules on repackaging will only apply where goods have been first marketed in the EEA with the consent of the rights-holder (if they have not then there is not even a prima facie case of exhaustion). In such cases, Article 36 (or the equivalent provision in the TMD, Article 7(2)) may be invoked. This allows derogation from the principle of free movement where it is necessary to protect the subject matter of the right. Essentially, the fact of repackaging is considered to detrimentally affect the functions of the mark – notably its guarantee of origin. Accordingly, repackaging is only allowable if: (1) it is necessary; (2) it does not affect the condition of the goods – i.e. there is no physical impairment; (3) the repackaging is not untidy, of poor quality or likely to injure the reputation of the mark; (4) notice is given to the rights holder that the goods have been repackaged; and (5) the importer indicates on the new packaging that the goods have been repackaged (*BMS v Paranova*, 1996; *Boehringer II*, 2007).

Competition – Articles 101 and 102 TFEU

There are two important provisions of the Treaty dealing with competition: Articles 101 and 102. (These too were renumbered: Article 101 was, prior to the Lisbon Treaty, Article 81 TEC, and before that it was Article 85. Article 102 was formerly Article 82 TEC, prior to which it was Article 86.) Along with the principles of free movement, these provisions are designed to protect the integrity of the internal market. However, although both focused on the same general objective, the competition rules operate slightly differently, concentrating on the impact of a particular trader (or group thereof) on the relevant market. As well as being enforceable via proceedings brought by the EU Commission, the competition rules are also directly effective in the national courts. (The Commission is the administrative institution of the EU. It is split into a number of Directorates General (commonly called 'DGs'), each responsible for a particular area of law or policy. One of the most powerful DGs deals with competition policy.)

Article 101

This prohibits agreements 'which have as their object or effect the prevention, restriction or distortion of competition within the internal market'. It is of general application, although there are some specific examples given in the Article of agreements which would normally be caught. These include price fixing, production control, market sharing agreements, and making the conclusion of contracts subject to supplementary obligations which have no connection with the subject matter of the contract. In the field of intellectual property, this latter category is particularly important, and may include things such as tying clauses (for example, insisting that a licensee of a process purchase all raw materials for operating the process from the patentee), charging royalties on non-patented products, or even obliging a licensee to disclose all the new technical information he learns from the operation of the product/process to the patentee.

Block Exemptions

In order to provide some measure of certainty and predictability, the EU has enacted a series of Regulations which grant clearance to certain kinds of intellectual property agreements. These are very useful. If people tailor their agreements to fit the block exemptions they will normally be safe from challenge under the competition provisions; however, there are no complete guarantees. The most recent Technology Transfer Regulation came into force in 2004 and will expire in April 2014. It has a set of complex rules governing what can and what cannot be done (mainly technical – patents, know-how etc) in intellectual property licensing agreements.

Article 102

Article 102 prohibits abuse of a dominant position within the internal market or any substantial part of it. This is not a simple concept: what, for example, are the hallmarks of dominance? It is clear that being in a dominant position will require possession of significant market power; accordingly, if a firm can behave 'to an appreciable extent independently of its competitors, its customers and, ultimately, consumers', then it risks being seen to occupy such a position (*United Brands v Commission*, 1978). Although the importance of market share will vary from one market to another, as a rule of thumb if an enterprise's share of a market is greater than 40 per cent, with the other competitors having much smaller fractions, it may be considered dominant. Nevertheless, there are other uncertainties, and disputes often arise over the definition of the relevant market in such cases.

Possession of an intellectual property right (such as a patent) can put a person into a dominant position, but it does not necessarily do so. Dominance will depend on a range of factors, such as whether there are competing products and the extent to which the proprietor of the patent can act independently of other competitors and consumers. It must also not be forgotten that Article 102 talks of abuse of this position. Accordingly, dominance in a market, whilst necessary, is not sufficient for the provision to bite. Whether a person is abusing a dominant position must be judged individually in each case. Examples of conduct which may constitute abuse include charging excessive prices for products protected by a patent or refusing to licence except upon restrictive terms.

28

Some Aspects of the International Law of Intellectual Property

Intellectual property is an increasingly global topic. Although in many respects IP remains tied to the territorial boundaries of the state that grants the rights in question (or legislates/adjudicates for their creation), the development of IP policy is now something that is inevitably guided by international concerns. We have already seen how the influence of EU law has redefined the IP landscape in its Member States, through the adoption of Directives that harmonise laws and Regulations that create pan-European rights, but the international law of intellectual property is far broader than this.

Public International Aspects of Intellectual Property Policy

A Little History

The effects of IP have been felt at an inter-state level for hundreds of years. (In the sixteenth century, for example, Queen Elizabeth I famously used the offer of temporary monopolies under letters patent to entice foreign artisans to England to teach native craftsmen their secrets, in order that the realm would be improved (stealing secrets is, after all, a brilliant way to advance). Whereas at the start of her reign there was a frightening need for ordnance, by its end English cannon were so good that apparently even the Spanish attempted to buy them). However, international regulation of the subject is a more recent innovation.

The impetus for tackling intellectual property at an international level came from a seemingly innocuous source: an international exhibition held in Vienna in 1873. Potential exhibitors were concerned that the IP laws of what was then the Austria-Hungarian Empire would provide inadequate protection for their creations; this threatened to have a detrimental impact upon participation. As a consequence, a special law was passed securing temporary protection to foreign exhibitors. However, more critically, an international congress on patent reform was also convened. This, in turn, eventually led to the talks that created the grandfather of international intellectual property instruments: the Paris Convention for the Protection of Industrial Property 1883.

The Paris Convention has at its core the principle of national treatment – i.e. that all Convention countries must treat the nationals of foreign states equally to those of its own in matters to which the Convention pertains. Prior to this agreement, states were perfectly free to discriminate on grounds of nationality – indeed under the Patents Act 1836 in the United States there was a raked fee-scale for US and non-US citizens, which meant that whilst US nationals paid $30 for a patent, all others were asked to pay $300 – unless, that is, you happened to be British, in which case you paid $500: some grudges take a long time to fade. The Convention also introduced various rules that made it simpler to gain protection for industrial property in multiple states; one of the most important of these is the right of priority. This rule gives applicants a specified period of time (six or 12 months) following an initial application in a Convention country in which to make applications in other Member States. If an application is made within this window then it is treated as having been made on the same day as the first application, with all the attendant benefits that this brings.

Following the Paris Convention, international attention focused on ensuring mutual recognition of intellectual property rights/facilitating international registration and setting minimum standards for protection. For example, the Berne Convention 1886, concerning certain types of copyright works, lays down fundamental requirements for the copyright laws of its signatory states: minimum term of protection; no formalities (i.e. protection is not dependent upon registration, it arises upon creation of a qualifying work); national treatment, etc.

This pattern was followed in other areas: the Madrid Agreement 1891 (trade marks); the Rome Convention 1961 (concerning Performers, Record Makers and Broadcasting Organisations); the Geneva Convention 1971 (Phonograms). The list could go on (but would be very boring if it did . . .).

More recently, a series of multilateral (and some bilateral) treaties have focused on the provision of more detailed minimum standards of intellectual property protection and restrictions on the exceptions and controls that governments can exercise over intellectual property rights.

The TRIPS Agreement

The most important modern treaty is the TRIPS agreement (Trade-Related Aspects of Intellectual Property Rights – no one mentions the missing 'A' in the acronym . . .). This was established under the auspices of the World Trade Organisation (WTO) in 1994. The TRIPS agreement requires members of the WTO (a number that now includes most of the countries of the world) to adhere to fairly tight intellectual property standards – in many cases going far beyond those demanded under previous international Conventions. In significant respects, the TRIPS agreement places a straitjacket on its signatories, requiring them to respect certain minimum standards of protection and removing much of the flexibility in setting an internal IP agenda that would have been available in the past – gone for example, are the days where state-sanctioned piracy of the type enjoyed by Elizabeth I would be acceptable on the international playing field.

By bringing intellectual property within the international trading system, the TRIPS agreement also provides something that was missing in all earlier Conventions: an enforcement mechanism. Accordingly, although the agreement is not directly effective in the English courts, it has real teeth. Even the US, which provides for generous protection in many respects, has been held to have violated TRIPS by providing inadequate intellectual property protection. In the WTO that provides a right to financial compensation or its equivalent.

Issues Surrounding the TRIPS Agreement and Developing Countries

In recent years, there have been criticisms of the TRIPS agreement, mainly origi-nating from a perception that the standards it requires of its signatories prevent developing countries from mimicking their more developed brethren and copy-ing themselves into greater prosperity. There is an extensive academic debate among economists and lawyers alike as to whether it makes sense (economic or otherwise) for countries to introduce a high level of intellectual property protec-tion when they do not have the resources to benefit therefrom. For developing countries, therefore, some argue that extensive intellectual property rights are a burden, not a benefit. Others, of course, maintain that such rights actually con-tribute to particular kinds of valuable economic activity, whether this be foreign investment or the development of local creative industries or local scientific research. There is some truth on both sides, and a definitive answer to the ques-tion of whether IP is good or bad in these cases may be impossible to reach. (Indeed, even the most talented minds have, as yet, failed to prove whether intel-lectual property offers a net gain or a net loss to society. But as we have it, we might as well make the best of it.) What can be said with some confidence is that the context in which any given intellectual property regime operates is critical to whether it delivers tangible benefits. So while it may pay Kenya to have a sophis-ticated plant-breeder's rights regime (it has an extensive export industry in hor-ticulture), it may not pay it to have a sophisticated patents regime (it may not have a sufficiently large research base for it to be an advantage and it may not attract foreign investment). The devil is clearly in the detail.

Other criticisms of the TRIPS agreement have focused on the impact of intro-ducing rigid, Western-style, patent laws on the ability of poorer countries to obtain less expensive generic pharmaceuticals, particularly for the treatment of AIDS and other important diseases. Whilst there are mechanisms in place to assist developing countries without manufacturing facilities of their own to obtain generic pharmaceuticals from countries where there is manufacturing capacity, it is not clear that this will provide an adequate answer. There are many who accept that pharmaceutical companies need money for research and development (and to pay their shareholders) but find it much harder to understand why those funds should come from those who can least afford it and who may be unable to benefit from the therapy at all if patent level prices are charged. Some states have taken matters into their own hands and, working within the confines of the TRIPs agreement, have instituted limitations on the ability of pharmaceutical companies to gain protection for improvement drugs, such as new pharmacological forms of old products. The Indian Supreme Court has recently (*Novartis v Union of India*, 2013) endorsed the country's controversial section 3(d) of the Indian Patents Act, which prohibits the patenting of a new 'form, property or use' of a known substance unless it results in enhanced efficacy.

Private International Law

Private international law, or conflict of laws (as it is often known), is a collection of procedural rules that deals with such things as jurisdiction, choice of law and the ability of a court (or legal system) to recognise (and enforce) foreign judgments. It is a vast topic in its own right: much too large for a book of this size to do it justice. Nevertheless, the global importance of intellectual property, as well as the global nature of trade, means that the influence of private international law in this area is difficult to ignore. Accordingly, we now turn to consider a few of the more critical aspects of this topic.

Foreign Intellectual Property Rights

Whilst issues of the subsistence of an intellectual property right can usually only be decided in the courts of the country whose laws confer the right, and the courts of other countries have no right to judge these, some issue may be explored by foreign courts. This is best illustrated by example.

Example 1

A young architect thought that a rather more famous architect had taken his designs for a building in Holland and built a building according to those designs in Rotterdam. Making a copy of a work outside the United Kingdom is not an infringement of UK copyright. But the ambitious young architect wanted to sue in the English courts rather than in the Dutch courts. Could he claim for infringement of Dutch copyright in the English courts? For some years it was thought that foreign copyright claims were 'non-justiciable' in the English courts (see comparative example, below). However, the Netherlands and the UK are both parties to the Brussels Convention, which provides for jurisdiction in the EU countries. The court held that he was able to bring his claim for infringement of Dutch copyright law before the English court under the Brussels Convention (*Pearce v Ove Arup*, 1999).

Example 2

The Supreme Court followed a similar line of argument in respect of US copyright in *Lucasfilm v Ainsworth* (2011) – here holding that there were no issues of policy which militated against the enforcement of foreign copyrights. Indeed, states had an interest in the international recognition and enforcement of their copyrights. Accordingly, where there was a basis for in personam jurisdiction over the defendant, and the substantial dispute was about the ownership of the relevant copyrights and their infringement, rather than about their subsistence, then the issues could be raised in the English courts.

Historical Example 3

For many years an ancient order of clever Carthusian monks brewed a delicious liqueur at the monastery of La Grande Chartreuse in France. The liqueur was brewed according to a secret process, jealously guarded. As well as being enormously devout, the monks were evidently shrewd businessmen, and the head of the order, the procurator, one Abbé Rey, ensured that 'Chartreuse' trade marks were registered in various countries, including France and the United Kingdom. Tragedy befell the order when, in 1901, the French government passed a law which declared illegal all unlicensed religious associations failing to obtain authorisation from the state. The monks applied for authorisation, but the French government (which probably thought the Carthusians had had it too good for too long) refused, and the order was dissolved. The monks were forcibly expelled from France and all their property, including their trade marks, was confiscated and sold. But one thing not even the French government could take away from them was their secret process. That, the monks carried with them into their Spanish exile where, not too far from the French border, they cocked a snook at the French government, and set up in business again. The monks were as devout as ever and the liqueur was as delicious as ever.

The inevitable happened. The liquidator, a Monsieur Lecouturier, purported to grant the right to sell Chartreuse liqueur to another (who did not have the secret). Trade mark war broke out. The monks sought to prevent the liquidator, and those claiming under him, from importing liqueur marked 'Chartreuse' into England, relying on their English trade marks. At first, they succeeded. But then the liquidator 'by a contrivance which it is difficult to reconcile with the actual truth' (as the House of Lords charitably put it) somehow got the English trade marks transferred to him, alleging that he was the assignee of the Abbé Rey. The liquidator then tried the reverse trick and managed to prevent the monks from importing their Chartreuse into England.

The House of Lords was evidently outraged. Lord Shaw said: 'I do not see anything conferring upon the liquidator of the property of the Carthusian Order a right to strip that order of their possessions in all parts of the world.' It was held that the property in question (the English trade mark) was situated in England

and must therefore be regulated according to the laws of England. The French transfer did not confer title to the English marks on the liquidator, and the monks won *(Rey v Lecouturier,* 1910).

Patents Example 4

Under the Brussels Convention (which regulates jurisdiction and judgments in the EU), there are special rules relating to claims for the infringement and validity of registered intellectual property rights. Such claims are subject to the exclusive jurisdiction of the courts of the country of registration or deposition. Thus actions concerning the validity of an English patent must be brought in the English courts.

There is, however, no such express rule in the Convention concerning infringement actions. This gives rise to the prospect of suing a defendant (usually a company) in the courts of the defendants' domicile in respect of infringement of patents in a number of different countries. For example, a claimant may chose to sue a defendant based in France in respect of alleged acts of infringement undertaken in England, France and Germany. But since validity is subject to exclusive jurisdiction of the relevant local courts, what if the defendant says by way of defence that the patents are all invalid?

The English courts have taken the practical view that infringement and validity are so bound up together that, absent special circumstances, they should be tried together. Accordingly, if validity is raised as a defence, the whole case (infringement and validity) has to be tried in the country of registration of the patent (*Coin Controls v Suzo,* 1997, *Fort Dodge v Akzo Nobel,* 1998). The ECJ adopted the same approach in *GAT v LUK* (2006), holding that the exclusive jurisdiction of the national registration should be taken to apply whatever the form of proceedings in which the issue of a patent's validity was raised. To permit a court seized of an action for infringement, or for a declaration that there had been no infringement, to indirectly establish the invalidity of the disputed patent, would undermine the binding nature of the rule of jurisdiction.

Of course one cannot sue in any country for infringement if no acts constituting infringement have been done in the jurisdiction of the country conferring the right. So, for example, one cannot sue for infringement of an English trade mark in respect of any acts done in Ireland.

Foreigners Generally Entitled to Claim United Kingdom Intellectual Property Rights

Most foreigners are entitled to many of the copyrights in the United Kingdom pursuant to various mutual recognition treaties such as the Berne Convention. United Kingdom copyright legislation makes special provision for people who are not British citizens to qualify for United Kingdom copyright protection. The rules governing foreigners' rights to claim particular kinds of copyright (such as copyright in films) can be very complicated, and reference should always be made to more detailed works and the statutory materials.

The position with design right is less generous to foreigners: for example, although United States citizens can claim United Kingdom copyright, they are not (yet) entitled to (unregistered) design right. The United States is a rather special case as regards mutual recognition of intellectual property rights, but it is slowly falling into line.

Any foreigner or foreign company can apply for a United Kingdom trade mark, patent or registered design and can sue for passing-off (if there is a reputation in the United Kingdom). For example, the famous Parisian restaurant, Maxim's, maintained an action for passing-off against a restaurant, in Norwich, decorated in French period style and called 'Maxim's' *(Maxim's v Dye,* 1977).

Foreign claimants are treated in exactly the same way as domestic plaintiffs in litigation, but they sometimes have to provide security for the costs of litigation, where domestic claimants do not.

INDEX